ADMINISTRATION:
unity and diversity

L'ADMINISTRATION:
unité et diversité

Benoît Bazoge
Gilles Paquet

Éditions de l'Université d'Ottawa

ADMINISTRATION:
unity and diversity

L'ADMINISTRATION:
unité et diversité

ADMINISTRATION: unity and diversity

L'ADMINISTRATION: unité et diversité

Edited by
Sous la direction de

Benoît Bazoge
Gilles Paquet

Éditions de l'Université d'Ottawa

1986

Données de catalogage avant publication (Canada)

Vedette principale au titre:
  Administration: unity and diversity =
  L'Administration : unité et diversité

Textes en anglais et en français.
Bibliographie : p.
ISBN 2-7603-0160-5

1. Gestion. 2. Administration publique.
3. Entreprises multinationales. 4. Commerce.
I. Bazoge, Benoît II. Paquet, Gilles, 1936-
III. Titre : L'Administration : unité et diversité.

HD31.A32 1986   650   C87-090013-7F

Canadian Cataloguing in Publication Data

Main entry under title:
  Administration: unity and diversity =
  L'Administration : unité et diversité

Text in English and French.
Bibliography : p.
ISBN 2-7603-0160-5

1. Management. 2. Public administration.
3. International business entreprises. 4. Commerce.
I. Bazoge, Benoît II. Paquet, Gilles, 1936-
III. Title: L'Administration : unité et diversité.

HD31.A32 1986   650   C87-090013-7E

© Éditions de l'Université d'Ottawa
ISBN 2-7603-0160-5
Imprimé au Canada/Printed in Canada

TABLE OF CONTENTS/TABLE DES MATIÈRES

SECTION I

Unity of Approach/Unité d'approche

PRIVATE MANAGEMENT/GESTION DU SECTEUR PRIVÉ

PUBLIC MANAGEMENT/GESTION DU SECTEUR PUBLIC

YBP 6/2/87

INTERNATIONAL MANAGEMENT/
GESTION INTERNATIONALE

SECTION II

DIVERSITY OF FUNCTIONS/DIVERSITÉ DE FONCTIONS

HUMAN RESOURCES/RESSOURCES HUMAINES

ACCOUNTING/COMPTABILITÉ

FINANCE

MARKETING

INFORMATION SYSTEMS/SYSTÈMES D'INFORMATION

Préface

Ce livre veut rejoindre deux publics : ceux pour qui l'administration demeure un mystère, un domaine mal compris et qui veulent en savoir davantage sur cette discipline omniprésente ; mais aussi les spécialistes en administration intéressés par des réflexions nouvelles dans leur domaine. Cet ouvrage veut aussi montrer l'envergure et la qualité des recherches menées à la faculté d'administration de l'Université d'Ottawa.

Ce volume ne présente pas un état de la question dans les divers domaines qui composent le vaste champ de l'administration. S'il se veut global, il ne se veut pas exhaustif. Il présente un tour d'horizon rapide de cette discipline. Le gestionnaire doit être une personne orchestre : à l'écoute des attentes de ses employés, attentif aux actions de ses concurrents, observateur-décodeur des mouvements de l'économie. Son travail demande avant tout des capacités de synthèse : il lui faut maîtriser à la fois la psychologie du travail, l'informatisation des données, la gestion de portefeuilles, la mise en marché, etc., et tirer de ces éléments une ligne de conduite efficace et rentable. Pris isolément, la rigueur de la science et l'art de l'orchestration sont insuffisants ; pris ensemble, ils deviennent les fondements d'une compétence professionnelle multidisciplinaire.On a souvent décrié l'administration, faute de pouvoir la situer. Elle a tiré, il est vrai, de nombreux enseignements des sciences pures et appliquées, des sciences humaines, de la philosophie. Le résultat de cet amalgame de compétences est à l'origine de nos architectures organisationnelles, de la coordination de nos activités entrepreneuriales et de la mise en place des fondements du bien-être qui caractérise nos socio-économies.

Ce choix de textes veut illustrer certains aspects de l'univers de l'administrateur perçus par l'universitaire qui l'observe. Notre seul objectif est que cet échantillon de travaux, issus de réflexions de professeurs de la faculté d'administration de l'Université d'Ottawa, contribue à mieux faire comprendre ce qu'est l'administration et, par là même, à asseoir la crédibilité que cette discipline mérite.

Ce volume se divise en deux sections, la première abordant une dimension uniquement managériale, et la seconde, une dimension fonctionnelle. Le lecteur constatera l'unité d'approche dans des secteurs aussi différents que l'administration privée, l'administration publique ou l'administration internationale ainsi que la grande diversité des disciplines à travers les domaines d'intérêts variés de nos chercheurs.

Dans le premier chapitre, Georges Abonyi développe une problématique générale applicable tant au secteur privé que public et qui pose la question de la réconciliation des impératifs politiques et techniques dans l'entreprise. Pierre Bergeron examine les nouvelles dimensions de la gestion dans cette seconde moitié du XXᵉ siècle. Wilbrod Leclerc déplore le manque d'attention que les universitaires portent à la PME. Christian Navarre, pour sa part, souligne les lacunes de l'analyse de la dégradation des entreprises avant de procéder à une modélisation du processus de faillite.

Dans le chapitre II, Rick Van Loon met en évidence les différences entre l'administration du secteur public et celle du secteur privé. Stylianos Perrakis analyse la politique publique face aux oligopoles ainsi que le comportement des industriels. Pedro Arroja examine de façon critique les fondements politiques et bureaucratiques du déficit du gouvernement fédéral. Pran Manga montre comment le Canada est passé d'impératifs de distribution de services de santé à des impératifs de gestion. Gilles Paquet et John Taylor proposent une problématique pour évaluer les programmes de subventions de recherche. Finalement, David Zussman examine les dimensions psychologiques fondamentales qui sous-tendent l'élaboration des politiques publiques en matière d'environnement.

Les problèmes de gestion internationale sont développés en trois volets. D'abord, Louis Calvet étudie certains aspects du développement des entreprises multinationales. Jean-Émile Denis et Jean Lamothe évaluent ensuite différentes méthodes de sélection de marchés d'exportation destinées aux PME. Jean-Louis Schaan, enfin, développe une approche permettant de faciliter les chances de réussite des coentreprises au plan international.

La deuxième section de l'ouvrage illustre la diversité des fonctions administratives. Dans le chapitre consacré aux ressources humaines, Aramanda Subbarao évalue le rôle de ces ressources dans la chute récente de la productivité au Canada, puis propose un plan d'action pour y remédier. André deCarufel et Jak Jabes présentent un état des connaissances sur la théorie des attributions et son impact sur le comportement organisationnel. Alton Craig examine les caractéristiques du système canadien de négociation collective et en évalue les lacunes.

En comptabilité, Ronald Hoyt analyse l'impact des forces sociales sur les techniques comptables et sur la fixation des objectifs comptables. Teresa Anderson propose un modèle d'analyse de l'environnement organisationnel permettant de mieux appréhender son interaction sur les états comptables. Daniel Zéghal examine l'impact des environnements inflationnistes sur la mesure du profit comptable.

Dans le chapitre consacré à la finance, Jean Lefoll montre les limites d'une théorie financière classique : la règle de l'utilité espérée. Fodil Adjaoud propose une étude empirique montrant quelle politique de dividendes adopter face à une variabilité des revenus.

Dans le domaine du marketing, Georges Hénault retrace l'évolution du marketing et la résurgence récente du troc. Sad Ahmed montre, à l'aide d'exemples canadiens choisis, l'utilité du marketing social.

Côté informatique, David Wright précise comment l'approche qualitative et la prise en compte des besoins des utilisateurs ont conduit à une certaine intégration des sciences de la gestion et de l'informatique. Finalement, Denis Caro dévoile certains dangers d'une utilisation incontrôlée de l'informatique dans le monde de la gestion des services de santé.

Cet ensemble de travaux couvre un éventail assez large mais il ne peut illustrer que de façon incomplète ce vaste chantier qu'est celui de l'administration. Il faut espérer que cet échantillon donnera au lecteur le goût d'explorer plus avant.

Avant de clore cette préface, il nous faut remercier Éric Lande qui a été l'un des architectes de la première heure de ce projet, les évaluateurs et lecteurs critiques des articles, Brigitte Rabéjac et Patricia Logan pour leur travail de révision des textes, et la belle équipe professionnelle de Louise Moreau pour la dactylographie des documents originaux toutes et à tous, nos remerciements.

Benoît Bazoge
Gilles Paquet

Foreword

JOHN J. CARSON*

I was delighted to be asked to contribute a foreword
to this collection of essays under the intriguing rubric, New Frontiers
in Administrative Studies. The title not only conveys the extent of
advances made in administration studies, but aptly captures the
scope and cohesiveness of research conducted by every department.
This proof of maturity is undeniable and it evokes for me the long
evolutionary process that finally led to the establishment of the
faculty at the University of Ottawa.

The roots were first established in a conventional Department
of Commerce in a Faculty of Arts. I suspect it was not a completely
comfortable relationship either for the more traditional departments
in an Arts Faculty or for the commercial hucksters and accountants
that had to coexist with them.

In 1969, following an important study undertaken by the late
John Deutsch, the newly secularized university decided to create a
Faculty of Management Science which would subsume the "inartis-
tic" Department of Commerce. Perhaps the hucksters, accountants
(and by now, organizational behaviorists) could coexist more com-
fortably with management scientists (or operations researchers as
they used to be called). To liven things up even more, a Department
of Public Administration was added and a graduate School of Health
Administration was stirred in as well — all under the heading of
Management Science. This became a bit confusing because most of
the faculty did not have a "management" orientation, and those that
did were more entrepreneurial than scientific! In any event, the
faculty did survive this kind of schizophrenic existence for nearly
ten years. One catalyst that helped hold things together for a while
was a highly touted proposal in the mid-seventies (by the then Dean
of Social Sciences) to merge the faculties of Social Science and
Management Science into one. Possibly, the slight similarity of
names gave some credence to this otherwise incredible idea!

In the course of that debate it became apparent that the faculty
needed to clarify its generic goals and objectives in a way that
everyone, including the university authorities, could understand,
rather than continue as a collection of disparate departments that
could be housed anywhere.

*Dean of the Faculty of Adminis-
tration, 1976-1981

After much agonizing, the faculty's four departments gradually recognized that the common thread that tied them together was a shared concern with the development of a professional approach to administration. Hence the Faculty of Administration, the abolition of sectoral departments, and a growing concern with the professionalization of administration in a generic sense. It has been a long, tortuous path through arts, to science, to profession, but it seems to have been a necessary (and not untypical) evolutionary process.

Today's Faculty of Administration has come a long way from the Commerce Department "trade school" that spawned it. In terms of numbers, diversity, and professional qualifications it has become a first-class faculty that competes successfully with its Canadian peer groups in every aspect of academic life — in both French and English — in the daytime and at night!

The publication record has grown exponentially, as has the range and depth of research. Our international commitment is almost impossible to keep track of on any given day, and our service to the community more often than not embraces all of Canada. Indeed, we are on the way to becoming a truly fine professional and academic faculty. This collection of essays provides the latest evidence.

---

1. John J. Carson is Doctor of Laws at York University (1972), Doctor of the University at University of Ottawa (1975) and Doctor of Letters at University of Sri Jayewardenapura in Sri Lanka (1985). He was Dean of the Faculty of Administration from 1976 to 1981.

Section I
UNITY OF APPROACH
UNITÉ D'APPROCHE

Private Management
Gestion du secteur privé

Technique, Experts, and Planning

GEORGE ABONYI

A Public Authority (PA) is involved in the planning and implementation of a regional development program focusing on the cultivation and processing of forest resources. The planning of this program requires a number of more specific and interrelated ex-ante project decisions, including the design of processing plants and the provision of related infrastructure and services, such as improved transportation facilities, extension services, and others. Acting on behalf of the public interest PA perceives the objectives of development to include generating income and employment and raising the level and mix of available skills, given resource and ecological constraints. In the planning process PA may choose to apply methods such as social benefit/cost analysis or some form of constrained optimization.

The public interest, however, masks a diversity of social groups with differing perceptions, needs, and preferences. They are likely to be affected differently by the program and its component projects. In effect, PA is faced with a problem of collective choice in attempting to incorporate diverse and conflicting preferences into a non-market resource allocation decision. In utilizing benefit/cost analysis or some form of mathematical programming as the basis for analysis and choice, PA is implicitly resolving the collective choice problem inherent in program planning. By virtue of the technique employed, the problem is defined as essentially technical in nature, subject to the logic of economizing, whose application requires bureaucratic expertise. Ultimately, however, the acceptability and stability, or viability, of the outcome depend on the preferences and behavior of various groups with a stake in the problem and its proposed resolution (i.e., the program and its component projects) whether these are included in the expert analysis or not. Therefore the technical solution generated by bureaucratic expertise may lead to a less than satisfactory outcome when groups perceiving adverse impacts of the program begin to make their displeasure known.

The problem facing PA involves in part the blurring of the distinction between purely economic decisions and primarily political decisions. Economic decisions tend to be associated with the logic of economizing and the role of markets (at least in North America). Political decisions are associated at the highest level with the logic of consensus and representative democracy, and at the lower level of nonmarket resource allocation decisions with bureaucratic expertise.

The usual approach to the planning of policy-oriented programs presents the general optimization framework as the appropriate organizing paradigm. This case has been made explicitly and is implicit in the majority of the methods offered by economists and management scientists to decision-makers. Implicit in mainline management science techniques is an approach that views society as a unitary actor. Collective choice is then made equivalent to the search for the best choice in the eyes of society as a whole, the collective optimum. Analytic techniques supporting the planning process may be relatively simple, such as benefit/cost analysis, or more complex, as in mathematical programming, multicriteria decision theory, deterministic or stochastic problems, or complicated in still other ways. The basic equivalency, however, remains. The theoretical basis of this approach lies in neoclassical economic theory. It is in fact an extension of the logic of economizing from the individual (consumer or firm) involved in market exchange to society as a whole in nonmarket (sociopolitical) settings. Its implementation — the planning of policy-oriented programs — relies on bureaucratic expertise.

Collective choice in general, and program planning in particular, may be approached quite differently. Society may be perceived to be characterized more by diversity than uniformity, more by localized and individualized interests than societal consensus on abstract objectives, and as much concerned with the possible negative consequences of proposed decisions as with their promised benefits. The planning of policy-oriented programs is viewed within this context not merely as efficiency-based resource allocation decisions guided by the logic of economizing. It is approached as the design of complex sociotechnical systems within an explicitly sociopolitical setting. The primary concern is with the general viability, as distinct from a narrowly and unilaterally defined optimality, of program planning decisions. The more modest objective of collective choice is then to identify collectively acceptable outcomes for interdependent social groups whose norms of rationality, which may not be fully known, evolve in a process of dynamic interaction. This implies the need for some form of participation by relevant interests in the process of analysis and choice, supported by the utilization of interactive techniques. Implicit is the position that the general logic of collective choice ultimately transcends the logic of economizing, and that some form of participation by relevant interests is ultimately more critical to the viability of program planning decisions than is bureaucratic expertise. Optimization techniques thus can and should be used along with nonoptimizing techniques, but within a more general framework.

THE SOCIETAL DECISION SYSTEM

Conceptually, society may be viewed as having two interdependent control systems, in the cybernetic sense, generating policy and resource allocation decisions. One system, focusing on economic decisions, is associated primarily with the role of markets. The second system, generating primarily political decisions, is associated at one level with representative democracy and at a lower (operational) level with bureaucratic expertise. Both these systems, as well as their interrelationship, seem to be experiencing increasing strains.

The Economic Sphere: Market Choice and Collective Goods

In principle, the role of the economic subsystem is to deal with resource allocation decisions. The basic idea of economic theory is that an economic system should be constructed in such a way that production — the utilization of resources — is adapted to the needs of the individual and society. The basic assumption of neoclassical economic theory is that economic decision-makers are rational utility maximizers, i.e., they have a preference ordering that is complete, and that they solve a conditional extreme value problem: they optimize. It is then asserted that the above two statements are equivalent. That is, that production decisions should serve man is assumed to be equivalent to the requirement that every economic agent find a consumption program which maximizes his utility function. The market then provides the institutional setting for implementing this logic.

In the competitive market system, conflicting interests are impersonally mediated at a highly decentralized level by the price mechanism. This is a monetary and reductionist form of regulation in the production and distribution of material means. The relevant characteristic of a market economy is an information system which is identified with the parametric role of prices in a decentralized decision process. The behavioral postulate underlying the system assumes that man the producer/consumer is egoistic, rational, and a utility maximizer. Resources are then allocated "optimally" according to the preferences of individual social units in an informationally economical fashion without central management or control.

However, the relationship in economic theory between individual preferences and collective decisions is purely formal, i.e., logical and not empirical. It assumes that there are no externalities in production and consumption. The resulting optimality, Pareto Optimality, refers only to efficiency in the absence of waste in resource allocation.

The market in the traditionally private sector of the economy is hampered, however, by market imperfections, leading to divergences between individual and collective valuations. There is a growing awareness of production and consumption externalities, of the fragile relationship of Nature to the production process, of administered price and wage behaviors, of changing values and expectations — all seeming to yield market solutions which are nonoptimal from a social perspective and inherently unstable. This environment is further complicated by the ability of organizations and networks of organizations to produce large-scale socio-technical systems with widespread and uncertain consequences. As a result, there is a growing number of articulate pressure groups concerned with the perceived adverse consequences of resource allocation decisions. The implicit unanimity of economic theory is replaced in practice by an explicit "game" of conflict and cooperation among inter-dependent groups. In practice the market system is often not able to transmit through the price system the conflicting as well as co-operative and participatory desires of interdependent social units. Operationally, these devélopments blur the distinction between economic and political decisions.

The market alone may then fail to coordinate the interests of diverse groups in providing socially desirable development as, for example, in the provision of collective goods. The need for collective goods exists because of a discrepancy between the collective needs of some segment of the public and the goods produced by the market as a response to individual decisions.

A collective good may be provided by private and/or public allocation processes. In practice, the planning and implementation activities for this type of goods have begun to shift from the decision-making sphere of individual commercial firms to that of public bodies. Under this arrangement private firms typically emerge as principal contractors for consciously integrated programs that implement public policy decisions. These programs represent a special type of collective good called a public good, whose provision is publicly induced or managed. Their planning usually involves unilateral search by experts for an optimal program, given predefined goals and constraints — for example, the one with the highest benefit/cost ratio. This approach, still based on the logic of optimizing, then relies on bureaucratic expertise aided by appropriate techniques of analysis that support expert judgment. But once we leave the arena of the self-regulating market and the associated implicit assumption of unanimity in the market exchanges of private goods, the planning and implementation of complex sociotechnical systems require a nonmarket allocation process that mediates conflicting world views and inconsistent preferences. This, however, is a political form of regulation within collective choice.

The Political Sphere: Policy and Program Decisions

A problem requiring "political" regulation exists when there are:

1. conflicting perceptions and/or interests,

2. mutual interdependence,
3. some dispersion of information and/or control, i.e., power, and
4. no unifying incentive scheme for aligning conflicting preferences.

Resolution of a political problem then requires some form of consensing, that is, generating collective decisions as stable compromises on specific issues. At the highest policy level this is pursued through representative democracy, and at the operational level implemented through bureaucratic expertise. There are difficulties at both levels.

Representative democracy, fundamentally, is based on the assumption of a relatively stable and homogeneous society with respect to values and needs. This allows agreement, in principle, on general priorities, i.e., objectives and criteria for choice. If general priorities can be agreed upon, bureaucratic experts can generate the required programs implementing policy decisions. This corresponds to the approach of neoclassical economic theory that sees the formulation of a social welfare function as a political issue, but its implementation via market and nonmarket processes as an economizing one. In this context the optimization framework for policy formulation — involving the identification of the best alternative with respect to a given set of goals — may be a reasonable one. That is, once the dimensions of the problem and its solution have been agreed upon, e.g., as objectives and constraints, and are stable over some relevant time horizon, resolution seems to be primarily a technical issue that can be left, in principle, to experts. The assumption is that decisions by representatives and experts can indeed accurately reflect the perceptions and interests of relevant social groups and that agreement, in principle and practice, is possible.

There may be, however, divergences between the assumptions of experts and the actual needs and preferences of the community. This may occur at a number of levels. We can identify three key characteristics of planning:

1. it is concerned with future states of the world and makes predictions about them;
2. it seeks to secure a preferred future according to an underlying value system, i.e., it seeks certain ends;
3. it believes it has a choice of two or more behavior patterns, or plans, i.e., it chooses means.

But the expert is acting on behalf of society. In this, each of the above items involves basic assumptions by the bureaucratic expert about the planning problem he faces. The assumptions involve concepts and interpretations with respect to a notion of public interest, available technology, socio-political-economic conditions, and so on. The assumptions, representing the world as he sees it, underlie interpretations of data and decisions.

Within a general framework of economizing, methodological efforts intended to support program planning have been directed primarily at finding optimal solutions to planning problems once they have been formulated and defined. The assumptions underlying particular techniques delimit the solution space in terms of already specified values, predictions, alternative means. Mathematical logic then guarantees that the plan is optimal given the assumptions. However, the validity of a plan depeñds as much on the validity of the particular assumptions that experts bring to bear on the problem as it does on the accuracy of the logical process employed.

Society is becoming increasingly heterogeneous, with a diversity of interests along regional, sectoral, ethnic, and sub-cultural lines. It seems to be increasingly difficult to achieve consensus both locally and nationally. There are increasing pressures in the political system from a wide and evolving range of interests. We are moving "beyond the stable state."

At the program level this has led to an increasing instability of optimal plans. Programs involve differentiated impacts for different groups. Although a particular program may be optimal with respect to general objectives such as growth in national income, it may be unacceptable to particular interests. Often these interests are the very ones intended to be beneficiaries of the program. It seems to be increasingly difficult to generate collectively acceptable program-level decisions based on global criteria formulated by experts (political, technical, or bureaucratic).

Generating Adequate Collective Decisions

The general problem may be summarized as follows. The difficulties associated with the market system in coordinating the interests of diverse groups have been touched on earlier. As noted, this inadequacy has increasingly drawn the political system into resource allocation or production decisions. If we consider the political system as a "technology" for generating collective decisions, we may observe that this technology seems increasingly to be generating inappropriate decisions. That is, the political decision process is experiencing difficulties in coping with instability and diversity at both the policy and program levels. There seems to be a widening discrepancy between the decision environment and the decision technology. At the policy level this may involve an overload of the decision-information system. At the program level it may involve the (perhaps inadvertent) screening out of important information — on the interests of particular stakeholders with respect to proposed programs — often by virtue of the techniques of analysis employed.

There seem to be two general ways to respond to the problem. One is to define it as a problem in information processing, and therefore seek to increase the efficiency of the existing system. This involves calling for more expertise — more politicians, more bureaucrats, more experts, more techniques — within the existing framework. Alternatively, the problem may be interpreted as one of inherent instability of the present decision technology. The corresponding response then is to reduce the decision load at the center by sharing it with more groups. This implies some form of participatory decision-making at the program planning level, requiring appropriate techniques to support such participation.

Regarding the first response, focusing on a general optimization framework is questionable on the basis of insights gained from work in systems theory and information systems, and in public choice theory and cybernetics, we concentrate on participatory decision-making.

The second type of response begins with the rejection of a rationality separating means and ends in the political and social context of decision-making. In this context whatever initial formulation of ends may exist in the process of program planning, the means, that is the proposed programs, become directly subject to scrutiny from the perspective of relevant interests. This type of response essentially involves expanding the feedback loop between experts ("doers") — be they politicians, analysts or bureaucrats — and a citizenry composed of differentiated interests (the "done by"). This approach requires methodological support for identifying the key assumptions implicit in programs proposed by experts, for linking information on the preferences and behavior of relevant social groups directly to proposed policy-oriented programs. This alternative approach we call "filtering"; it is related to a "stakeholder" theory of policy making. It proceeds from the assumption that in the planning of complex sociotechnical systems those with a stake in the problem and proposed programs should be linked to the planning process in order to screen out, or filter, the unacceptable dimensions of the proposed program. It also identifies the critical importance of the stability of proposed plans in an environment of differentiated but interdependent interests. A discussion of the filtering approach follows.

AN APPROACH TO PARTICIPATION: FILTERING

Filtering As a Basis for Collective Choice

Neoclassical economic theory, its extensions into policy analysis as the theory of public choice, and the optimization techniques of operations research utilized by bureaucratic experts share a common basis. They assume a kind of existence theorem, implying a unitary view of society.

At the base is some concept of social preference. Any method of social choice should yield the socially most preferred alternative — the 'best' option in the eyes of society as a whole.

Our concern is not with the concept of social preference itself. Rather, it is with the implications of a great number of related concepts, frameworks, and methods. Anything that has a connotation of maximization of anything is operationally equivalent to a concept of social preference and the implied view of society. These approaches to program planning place the expert in a key role in determining the basis for optimal decisions.

Alternatively, society can be viewed as composed of individuals who form coalitions in order to protect their interests. They are involved in a dynamic game of cooperation and conflict wherein each group seeks to protect its interests. Program planning decisions then occur within this sociopolitical context and within a natural environment whose limits on viability are not fully understood.

Instead of searching for the best option in the eyes of society as a whole, another point of departure may posit the elimination of unacceptable alternatives as the initial objective of program planning. In this way approximations to "good programs" can emerge as the outcome of an interactive process. Preference judgments then play the role of constraints with respect to a specific set of alternatives. No prior agreement on a collective definition of a good program is assumed, as in the form of a social preference function, nor is general agreement necessary on what constitutes a good program, as in voting rules based on the social preference axiom.

The Process of Filtering

Filtering as an approach to program planning begins with the recognition that there exists generally a multiplicity of interdependent interests with a stake in the outcome. These stakeholders are dependent to varying degrees on the program for the realization of some of their goals, while the program is dependent to some extent on each of these stakeholders for its successful implementation. Therefore they include all those whom experts should take into account, including the experts themselves.

Availability of Information

One dimension of filtering then involves a recognition that information on the perceptions and preferences of the other stakeholders is generally not fully available to bureaucratic experts. That is, the norms of rationality governing what is a satisfactory and acceptable program to the community of stakeholders are not available a priori, i.e., as complete and consistent design criteria, or as arguments in a social welfare function, but instead emerge in a process of interaction. Yet the planning and successful implementation of programs depend vitally on this information. A program unilaterally formulated by technical experts is likely to include assumptions about the preferences and behaviors of particular groups that may be inaccurate, or at the very least highly uncertain. The identification, assessment, and modification of these assumptions implies the necessity for consultation and interaction with relevant stakeholders. It is not, ultimately, the technical experts' knowledge that is critical in program planning, but the substantive knowledge of those with a stake in the program.

Stability of Expectations

The second dimension of filtering focuses on the issue of stability. Here stability has a precise meaning: a plan or scenario is defined as stable if all relevant stakeholders fully expect it to be implemented. That is, each stakeholder intends to implement his part and expects others to implement theirs. Such stability of expectations is of great importance, since program planning occurs in an environment of interdependency among stakeholders with different perceptions and needs. Only jointly acceptable outcomes are likely to provide viable resolutions to shared problems. Thus the emphasis in this dimension of filtering is not on optimization by one stakeholder — for example the experts — with one set of objectives, but on mutual accommodation by many stakeholders, each pursuing different objectives.

Operationally the process of filtering involves the assessment of particular dimensions of proposed programs from the perspective of specific stakeholders. The purpose is to identify those dimensions that are unacceptable to particular stakeholders and/or embody inaccurate or uncertain assumptions about specific stakeholders. These are the dimensions of the proposed program that are likely to yield disbenefits to particular groups, which may in turn hinder or prevent successful implementation. The identification of these potential conflict points — between the assumptions of experts and the preferences of particular groups — may then be utilized to help reduce the area of disagreement, and therefore to enlarge the set of collectively acceptable and stable program plans.

The information generated in the filtering process may be used in a number of ways. It may lead to technical modifications to the proposed program as a response to questionable assumptions, anticipated conflicts, or newly perceived needs. Dialogue may be initiated focusing on particular program dimensions with the objective of reconciling divergent stakeholders.

In general, the interactive process of filtering reduces the risk of misunderstanding as compared with unilateral optimization by experts. It provides a framework for a joint charting of the future collaboratively, by aiming at the evolution of a reasonable consensus from a base of what may initially appear to be unreasonable vetoes. For the community of social groups this process is likely to lead to a closer fit between needs and program design. For individual social groups it may involve a process of self-discovery, perhaps leading to changes in perceptions and preferences as a consequence of focused dialogue. For the experts it is more likely to result in implementable programs that meet the needs of divergent interests.

The assumptions implicit in the filtering approach should also be made explicit. The process is based on the assumption of some level of knowledge of the likely consequences of proposed programs. A range of analytic methods (both quantitative and qualitative) may be utilized here to generate the required information. Filtering also assumes the ability to absorb and process data. Emerging insights on the communication aspects of information and decision support systems can be utilized here to structure the data. Filtering requires the existence or evolution of a common language for the community of social groups. The role of third party facilitators and insights from process consultation may be of relevance in this dimension. Ultimately it is the institutional framework that determines how the information generated by filtering will be transformed into binding commitments or planning decisions.

Filtering represents a general framework for approaching policy and program planning. Its logic may be implemented by means of an increasing number of emerging methods and techniques. In general, these techniques involve interactive procedures that may utilize man-machine systems, including computer and audio-visual services, to support rather than replace human judgment.

Approaching program planning via filtering formulates the problem from the outset not primarily as a process of unilateral optimization by experts but as a process of mutual adjustment among interdependent social groups. Here, too, the role of the expert is vital but different. He contributes initially technical knowledge, i.e., formulating initial technical designs (alternatives), identifying their consequences in physical, financial, and economic terms. He also contributes procedural knowledge, for example, in the form of interactive techniques that facilitate mutual adjustment (including the identification of critical assumptions). However, substantive knowledge of acceptability and valuations resides with other stakeholders.

Adaptive Behavior

The shift from a framework of optimization to one of filtering involves more than just a shift in technique. The behavioral basis for collective choice changes. Even more fundamental, the very concept of rationality in economic decisions changes. We will deal with each of these in turn.

The behavioral basis of filtering sees man not solely in isolation as a utility maximizing agent. Instead, man is viewed as a complex entity in a living environment with which he interacts. In this process of dynamic interaction involving both resource utilization or production (man-nature interaction) and social exchange (man-man interaction), behavior is primarily adaptive, guided by evolving norms that define what are acceptable outcomes (this formulation of behavior is similar to the concept of "homeostasis" in biological cybernetics). Behaviorally, then, filtering is quite general and can accommodate a diversity of attitudes and behaviors including utility maximization, satisficing, and cautious "adaptation." The last, cautious adaptive behavior, requires further comment.

There exists an inherent uncertainty associated with the multidimensional consequences of proposed plans. Caution in the face of uncertainty and complexity may be a rational attitude on the part of a decision agent. Indeed, it seems that individuals and groups often react more readily to the perceived negative consequences of proposed plans. They may be more sensitive to and therefore more easily mobilized for action and participation by developments that are likely to increase costs or decrease benefits than those that may enhance benefits. They may be, in short, more threat-oriented than opportunity-oriented, with a correspondingly greater homogeneity of interests vis-à-vis perceived threats. This admittedly sweeping generalization nevertheless appears consistent with evidence about group behavior in different contexts.

Program planning becomes in this context a process wherein interdependent social groups with differing perceptions and interests seek to reach stable compromises. Generating a viable program then involves the expert in achieving widespread acceptance of specific alternatives which meet a variety of perhaps conflicting interests. In the process, the concept of rationality in resource allocation decisions has taken on a different meaning. We turn to this next.

Neoclassical economics has adopted a particular definition of its subject matter and rationality. This formal definition of economics is stated by Robbins as "the science that studies human behaviour as a relationship between ends and scarce means that have alternative uses." Economics is reduced to formal rationality that deals with the general relationship between means and ends — that is, economizing. In effect, it is subsumed in a formal theory of purposive action, becoming a branch of decision theory. The subject matters of economics and of operations research are defined to be logically equivalent. Economizing, or optimizing, is assumed to be the basis for all human action. This interprets all human actions and interactions as economic in the formal sense of economizing. This conception of instrumental rationality is then applied equally to individuals and groups in both market and nonmarket settings and to society as a whole. An act is rational independent of its effects on others. The basis of program planning by bureaucratic experts utilizing optimization techniques is then rational and economic in this sense.

Even in its original market setting, however, rationality as economizing is subject to limitations. No less eminent economists than Frisch and Koopmans have observed that the competitive equilibrium, even if Pareto optimal in the traditional sense, may involve consequences that are regarded as undesirable from a social point of view. The implication is that the general logic of collective choice must ultimately transcend the logic of economizing. Filtering then implies a fundamentally different conception of "rational" and "economic." From this perspective economic decisions deal with man-man and man-nature relations that are bound up in production or resource allocation decisions including program planning. This approach to economic decisions may be called substantive, following Polanyi. Norms of rationality are defined interactively in a societal (community) setting. Economic decisions, including program planning, then occur within a wider context that cannot be reduced to the logic of economizing.

CONCLUSION

What of the Public Authority (PA), with which we started, concerned with regional development? Clearly it has choices in approaching the planning and implementation of the required program. But the choice of technique will have a critical influence on the outcome. If it defines program planning as primarily a technical problem for experts governed by the logic of economizing, it runs the risk of generating an optimal program that is not viable in a larger sense.

It is therefore often more appropriate to utilize the framework of filtering for organizing the planning process. Program planning is then structured as fundamentally an interactive process, as distinct from an optimizing one. The concept of participation in some form by relevant social groups then becomes a necessary component of program planning. This is more likely to lead to a program that is responsive to needs and realities and therefore more likely to lead to the desired benefits and less likely to lead to unanticipated conflicts. In the process, optimization techniques such as benefit/ cost analysis and mathematical programming may be used in conjunction with interactive methods, but within a filtering framework that is essentially a nonoptimizing one.

Finally, it should be noted that planning decisions are made and techniques are utilized within an institutional environment. The focus here on the role of technique is part of a larger quest for settings that recognize both the individual and the community, that permit both economic progress and human freedom. The more fundamental issue to be addressed, beyond logic and technique, is on institutional design.

REFERENCES

ABONYI, G., "Filtering: An Approach to Generating the Information Base for Collective Choice," *Management Science*, (forthcoming).

ABONYI, G., "SIAM: Strategic Impact and Assumptions Identification Method for Project Program and Policy Planning," *Technological Forecasting and Social Change*, September 1982.

ABONYI, G., "Strategic Assessment of Development Projects and Programs," Presented at the Joint Meeting of TIMS-ORSA-CORS, Toronto, May, 1981.

ABONYI, G., and HOWARD, N., "A Boolean Approach to Interactive Program Planning," *Management Science*, vol. 26, (7), July, 1980.

ACKOFF, R., *Scientific Method: Optimizing Applied Research Decisions*, New York, John Wiley and Sons, 1962.

ARROW, K., *Social Choice and Individual Values*, 2nd ed., New York, John Wiley and Sons, 1963.

ASHBY, R.W., *Design for a Brain*, 2nd ed., New York, John Wiley and Sons, 1960.

BATOR, F. M., "The Anatomy of Market Failure," *Quarterly Journal of Economics*, vol. LXXII, 1958.

BAUER, R., de SOLA POOL, I., and DEXTER, L.A., *American Business and Public Policy*, Atherton, 1963.

BEER, S., *Decision and Control*, London, John Wiley and Sons, 1966.

BENELLO, C.G., and ROUSSOPOULOS, D., *The Case for Participatory Democracy*, New York, Grossman Publishers, 1971.

BRILL, E.D., "The Use of Optimization Models in Public-Sector Planning," *Management Science*, vol. 25, (5), 1979.

BUCHANAN, J.M., *The Limits of Liberty*, Chicago, University of Chicago Press, 1975.

CHURCHMAN, C.W., *The Systems Approach and Its Enemies*, New York, Basic Books Inc., 1979.

DAY, R.H., "Adaptive Processes and Economic Theory," Madison, Wisc., Social Systems Research Institute, University of Wisconsin, #7514, 1975.

FRIEDMANN, J., *Retracting America: A Theory of Transactive Planning*, New York, Ancho. Press, 1973.

FRIEDMANN, J., and ABONYI, G., "Social Learning: A Model for Policy Research," In H.E. Freeman (ed.), *Policy Studies Review Annual*, vol. 2, Beverly Hills, Calif., Sage Publications, 1978.

FRISCH, R., "Economic Planning and the Growth Problem in Developing Countries," Oslo, University of Oslo, Institute of Economics, 1961.

HOWARD, N., *Paradoxes of Rationality*, Cambridge, Mass., The M.I.T. Press, 1971.

HOWARD, N., "The Analysis of Options in Business Problems," INFOR, Vol. 13, (1), February, 1975.

KOOPMANS, T. C., *Three Essays on the State of Economic Science*, McGraw-Hill, 1957.

KORNAI, J., *Anti-Equilibrium*, Amsterdam, North-Holland, American Elsevier, 1971.

LEWIN, A.Y., and SHAKUN, M.F., *Policy Sciences: Methodologies and Cases*, Pergamon Press, 1976.

LINDBLOM, C.E., *The Intelligence of Democracy*, The Free Press, 1965.

MARGLIN, S.A., *Approaches to Dynamic Investment Planning*, Amsterdam, North-Holland Press, 1963.

MASON, R.O., "A Dialectical Approach to Strategic Planning," *Management Science*, vol. 15, (8), April, 1968.

MASON, R.O., and MITROFF, I.I., "Strategic Assumption-Making at Majestic Metals: Arriving at Strategy Through Dialectics," Study Center in Public Services Management and Policy, University of California at Los Angeles, #9, June, 1978.

MISHAN, E.J., *Cost-Benefit Analysis*, 2nd ed., NewYork, Praeger Publishers, 1976.

MITROFF, I.I., and EMSHOFF, J.R., "On Strategic Assumption-Making: A Dialectical Approach to Policy and Planning," *Academy of Management Review*, vol. 4, (1), 1979.

MOSTELLER, F., and NAGEE, P., "An Experimental Measurement of Utility," *Journal of Political Economy*, vol. 59, October, 1951.

MUELLER, D.C., "Public Choice: A Survey," *Journal of Economic Literature*, vol. 14, (2), 1976.

NAGEL, S., and NEEF, M., "What's New About Policy Analysis Research?" in H.E. Freeman (ed.), *Policy Studies Review Annual*, vol. 2, Beverly Hills, Calif., Sage Publications, 1972.

PASK, G., "Man as a System that Needs to Learn," in D.J. Stewart (ed.), *Automation Theory and Learning Systems*, Washington, D.C., Thompson Book Co., 1967.

PASSET, R., *L'Économique et le vivant*, Paris, Payot, 1979.

PERROUX, F., *Unités actives et mathématiques nouvelles*, Paris, Bordas, 1975.

PLOTT, C., "Axiomatic Social Choice Theory: An Overview and Interpretation," Pasadena, Calif., Social Science Working Paper #16, California Institute of Technology, 1976.

POLANYI, K., *The Great Transformation*, Boston, Beacon Press, 1944.

ROBBINS, L., *The Subject Matter of Economics*, 1932.

RUEFLI, T. W., "A Generalized Goal Decomposition Model," *Management Science*, vol. 17, (8), April, 1967.

SCHON, D., *Beyond the Stable State*, New York, W.W. Norton and Co., 1973.

SCHWARTZ, T., "Rationality and the Myth of the Maximum," Nous, Vol. 7, 1972.

SIMON, H.A., "On the Concept of Organizational Goal," *Administrative Science Quarterly*, vol. 9, 1964.

SPULBER, N., and HOROWITZ, I., *Quantitative Economic Policy and Planning*, New York, W.W. Norton and Co., 1976.

STEINER, P. O., *Public Expenditure Budgeting*, Washington, D.C., The Brookings Institute, 1969.

VICKERS, G., *Freedom in a Rocking Boat*, Penguin Books, 1972.

WICKSELL, K., "A New Principle of Just Taxation," 1896, reprinted in R.T. Musgrave and A.T. Peacock (eds), *Classics in the Theory of Public Finance*, New York, St. Martin's Press, 1967.

"Symposium on Optimizing, Implementing and Evaluating Public Policy," *Policy Studies Journal*, Special Issue #3, 1980.

WILDAWSKY, A., *Knowledge, Power and Culture: Technology Assessment as Policy Analysis*, unpublished manuscript, 1977.

WILSON, J.Q., *Political Organizations*, New York, Basic Books, 1973.

La gestion à l'heure de la cinquième vague

PIERRE G. BERGERON

Pour certains économistes, dirigeants d'entreprise et analystes, la présente décennie marque une étape déterminante dans l'histoire des entreprises canadiennes. La récente récession a perturbé les pays industrialisés et plus particulièrement le continent nord-américain. Cette situation économique a amené avec elle un nombre incalculable de faillites et de mises à pied.

Les dirigeants d'entreprise font face à un nouveau défi depuis la naissance de la gestion moderne. Ils envisagent un « scénario de problèmes » qui, auparavant, n'existaient pas. Il y a, d'une part, les problèmes externes à l'entreprise, tels que les taux d'intérêt fluctuants et élevés, la concurrence croissante des entreprises étrangères, les changements technologiques, l'inflation, les groupes de pression externes (consommateurs, gouvernements, communautés) et, d'autre part, les problèmes internes, tels que les conflits entre employés et employeurs, le manque de motivation au travail, l'absentéisme, la bureaucratie étouffant initiative, créativité et innovation, et la centralisation du pouvoir, qui accélère le processus décisionnel, mais qui ralentit la mise en œuvre des décisions. Il serait facile d'en énumérer davantage. Toutefois, le plus grand malaise organisationnel et celui qui semble paralyser le plus le fonctionnement de nos entreprises est le faible taux de productivité.

Peter Drucker cite ce malaise comme étant le principal problème — avec l'inflation — auquel les entreprises doivent faire face à l'heure actuelle. Au Japon, le taux de productivité a augmenté quatre fois plus qu'en Amérique depuis 1945. Au Canada, près de 350 000 travailleurs ne se présentent pas à leur travail quotidiennement ; cela représente plus de 35 millions de jours-personnes perdus chaque année. En 1981, le résultat d'une recherche effectuée par le European Management Forum indiquait que le Canada se plaçait au quinzième rang (sur 21 pays industrialisés) pour sa compétence sur les marchés internationaux. Plusieurs études sur la bureautique montrent que les employés de bureau travaillent, en moyenne, environ deux heures et demie par jour !

Ce problème de productivité a incité le gouvernement canadien à créer le Centre canadien sur le marché du travail et de la productivité ; en coûtera plus de 27 millions de dollars à Ottawa au cours des quatre prochaines années.

Que doivent faire les dirigeants d'entreprise pour corriger ce problème de productivité ? Doivent-ils modifier leurs structures organisationnelles, embaucher des techniciens plus qualifiés, élaborer des plans stratégiques et opérationnels d'une façon plus scientifique ou constituer des comités d'étude gouvernementaux pour se pencher sur ce problème ?

Avant de répondre à ces questions, il est important d'identifier au préalable l'origine de ce manque de productivité. Il semblerait qu'elle ne se situe ni au niveau de la structure organisationnelle, du processus de planification, du contrôle, de la commercialisation ni à celui de la production, mais plutôt au niveau de la gestion des relations humaines. De plus en plus, des livres tels que *Theory Z*, *The Art of Japanese Management*, *Corporate Cultures*, *Intrapreneuring*, *Le Prix de l'excellence*, *A Passion for Excellence*, *The One Minute Manager*, font remarquer d'une manière évidente que les entreprises performantes possèdent une culture organisationnelle et des valeurs partagées par tous les employés et à tous les niveaux de l'organisation.

LA CINQUIÈME ÉCOLE

Ce n'est pas la première fois que le continent nord-américain souffre d'un problème de productivité. Depuis le début du siècle, en effet, la gestion nord-américaine a connu cinq vagues managériales, dont la dernière a pris naissance au début de cette décennie.

L'école classique

La première vague en matière de gestion est apparue au début du siècle avec l'école classique, basée sur l'approche scientifique et logique. À cette époque, certains chercheurs et gestionnaires affirmaient que l'ordre, la logique et le bon sens représentaient les éléments clés de l'efficacité et de la productivité. Certains principes de gestion émergèrent, tels la répartition du travail, la division scientifique des tâches, les quotas de production, etc.

L'école des relations humaines

La deuxième vague débuta vers les années trente et fut une réaction à la première. Ses partisans soutenaient la thèse que les travailleurs ne devaient pas être considérés comme des agents de production uniquement motivés par des stimulants économiques, mais par une certaine considération humaine dans le travail. Le pendule oscilla alors vers une approche humaniste. Les nouvelles valeurs caractérisant cette deuxième vague se retrouvent dans les théories sur les besoins et la motivation, l'approche organique, etc.

L'école quantitative

La troisième vague se manifesta vers le milieu des années quarante et apparut comme la résurrection de l'école scientifique. Préconisant des modèles mathématiques pour résoudre les problèmes complexes, les entreprises commencèrent à se servir des ordinateurs, de la recherche opérationnelle et des modèles de simulation.

L'école globaliste

La quatrième vague a commencé au début des années soixante, alors que les dirigeants d'entreprises étaient à la recherche de moyens pour gérer les organisations dans leur globalité. Les auteurs et les chercheurs de cette époque arrivèrent aux conclusions que : a) les organisations devaient être considérées comme des systèmes ; b) les gestionnaires devaient être flexibles face à l'environnement et c) la gestion elle-même devait être considérée comme un processus.

L'école culturaliste

La cinquième vague prit forme au début de la présente décennie. Lorsque les gestionnaires nord-américains réalisèrent qu'ils perdaient du terrain au détriment du Japon, de l'Allemagne et même de l'Angleterre, les chercheurs identifièrent les méthodes de gestion comme étant la cause du succès des entreprises étrangères. Que ce soit Ouchi dans sa *Théorie Z* ou Peters et Waterman dans *Le Prix de l'excellence*, la leçon est claire : les organisations performantes ont des valeurs et des normes précises et partagées par tous les employés en matière d'innovation, de qualité et de modes de travail. L'identité corporative ou « culture organisationnelle » semble l'élément clé qui garantit l'efficacité et la productivité d'une entreprise.

Au cours des trente dernières années, nous avons vu apparaître dans la littérature managériale un grand nombre d'idées nouvelles, de techniques, de procédés, de structures, de systèmes et de modes de gestion tendant à améliorer l'efficacité des dirigeants (figure I). Même si plusieurs de ces techniques ont permis de résoudre des problèmes particuliers, les notions de motivation et de délégation semblent avoir été oubliées. Le management d'aujourd'hui est tellement différent que certains auteurs suggèrent même de rayer le terme « gestion » du vocabulaire, car son image exprime l'idée de pouvoir, de manipulation, de dirigisme, de contrôle et de dévalorisation de l'employé. Ils proposent de le remplacer par « leadership », terme exprimant l'animation, l'incitation, la motivation et la canalisation des efforts et de la créativité.

LA CULTURE ORGANISATIONNELLE

L'étude de la gestion comparative montre qu'il existe un lien évident entre les organisations performantes et celles qui affichent

Période	1980	1970	1960	1950
Approche ou techniques	1. théorie Z 2. "intrapreneuring" 3. démassification 4. restructuration 5. culture organisationnelle 6. "one-minute manager" 7. "management by walking about" (MBWA)	1. budget à base zéro 2. courbe d'expérience 3. portefeuille d'activités stratégiques	1. "T-groups" 2. Centralisation, décentralisation 3. structure matricielle 4. grille managériale	1. informatique 2. théorie Y 3. gestion quantitative 4. diversification 5. gestion par objectifs

Figure I — Approches et techniques de gestion à nos jours

Source: Traduction libre de "Business Fads: What's in and out," Business Week, 20 janvier 1986, 20.

une culture organisationnelle. Ouchi a été l'initiateur de la gestion comparative. Plusieurs facultés d'administration offrent maintenant ce type d'enseignement, et de nombreux étudiants, tant au niveau de la maîtrise que du doctorat, en font des sujets de thèse.

La gestion comparative intéresse de plus en plus les gens d'affaires et fait l'objet d'articles dans des revues universitaires et professionnelles ; elle est aussi le thème de nombreux livres. *The Art of Japanese Management*, de Pascale et Athos, expose en détail comment Matsushita Electric, fabricant de produits Panasonic, Quasar, Technics et National, utilise les outils de gestion couramment employés dans les entreprises américaines — stratégie, structure organisationnelle, systèmes, contrôles financiers, évaluation de performance au niveau des centres de responsabilité — tout en conservant l'esprit d'entrepreneur, qui permet aux gestionnaires d'agir librement. Il explique aussi comment des entreprises, telles qu'ITT ou United Airlines, ont introduit plusieurs techniques de gestion japonaises dans leurs organisations.

Les recherches ne s'effectuent pas seulement au niveau de l'analyse comparative entre entreprises de plusieurs pays, mais aussi entre compagnies d'un même pays. La revue *Fortune* publie, depuis deux ans, la cote des entreprises américaines. Cette analyse est basée sur un sondage effectué auprès de 8 000 dirigeants d'entreprise, directeurs et analystes. *America's Most Admired Corporations* évalue les entreprises selon huit critères : qualité de la gestion, qualité des produits et des services, capacité d'innovation, croissance à long terme des investissements, structure financière, capacité d'attirer, de former et de garder des employés compétents, responsabilité communautaire et sociale, et utilisation efficace des immobilisations de l'entreprise. *Le Prix de l'excellence*, de Peters et Waterman, démontre de façon convaincante comment des entreprises, telles IBM, Hewlett-Packard, Procter and Gamble, Disney Production, Delta Airlines, Texas Instruments, Johnson and Johnson, MacDonald's, Levi Strauss ou Digital, ont pu obtenir un taux de rentabilité, une croissance des immobilisations, de la valeur des actions et de la valeur nette particulièrement élevés.

Cette culture organisationnelle, dont tous ces auteurs parlent, est la personnalité même d'une organisation et reflète les valeurs et les croyances de ses employés. Chez IBM par exemple, le service à la clientèle est primordial et il incite tous les employés, du président du conseil d'administration aux ouvriers, à soigner la qualité des services offerts à la clientèle. Le concept de valeur organisationnelle n'est pas nouveau. Dans son ouvrage publié en 1960, *The Human Side of Enterprise*, McGregor présentait déjà la théorie Y, expliquant la manière d'améliorer le comportement et la motivation des employés. Un lien étroit existe entre valeur organisationnelle, amélioration de la performance (financière) et qualité de vie au travail.

Un sondage effectué par William M. Mercer Inc. auprès de 305 présidents montre qu'en majorité ceux-ci croient aux valeurs corporatives dans le succès de leur entreprise. Près des deux cinquièmes de ces présidents avaient déjà amorcé concrètement la mise en œuvre de programmes de culture organisationnelle. Paul V. Croke, vice-président de Boston's Forum Corp., firme spécialisée dans la formation, affirme : « le pendule tend à s'éloigner des stratégies pour s'orienter vers le côté social de l'entreprise ».

John R. Opel, ancien président d'IBM, mentionnait que « tous les employés ont un engagement commun visant l'excellence et le service à la clientèle. Les employés se sont adaptés aux croyances et aux valeurs de l'entreprise ». John A. Young de Hewlett-Packard indique que son entreprise fonctionne avec une série d'objectifs corporatifs vieux de plus de vingt ans et qui servent de guide à l'entreprise. Ce ne sont pas des objectifs théoriques, mais plutôt une recette pratique montrant comment gérer une entreprise championne, et qui comprend sept objectifs pour chacun des domaines clés suivants : profit, clients, champs d'intérêt, croissance, personnel, gestion et citoyenneté. Young déclare que « ces objectifs corporatifs donnent à tous les gestionnaires une liberté d'action et la chance d'être créateurs et innovateurs. Ces objectifs sont considérés comme une sorte de « leitmotiv », une philosophie de base, qui encourage tous les employés à effectuer leurs tâches d'un commun accord ». Selon certains auteurs, l'augmentation constante de 25 % du chiffre d'affaires de Hewlett-Packard est liée à ces principes.Warren H. Phillips, de Dow Jones, déclare que « l'objectif premier n'est pas le profit, mais de servir le public. Le retour sur investissement et le profit sont des moyens pour arriver à une fin et non une fin en soi ».

L'article « The Corporate Culture Vultures » mentionne que les entreprises américaines sont actuellement sous le coup d'une révolution culturelle. Les dirigeants à tendance autocratique sont préoccupés par le manque de valeurs de leurs employés. Plusieurs ont même engagé des conseillers, afin d'harmoniser leur culture organisationnelle avec leur stratégie.

L'étude effectuée par Harvey Poppel, auprès de 200 dirigeants d'entreprise du secteur de l'information, pour déterminer les meilleurs attributs de réussite, indique que la culture organisationnelle est considérée comme l'élément le plus important pour les clients et pour les actionnaires. Le résultat de l'étude est le suivant :

DES GUIDES POUR L'ACTION

Les auteurs spécialisés dans la culture organisationnelle nous offrent certains éléments caractéristiques des entreprises qu'ils ont appelées « championnes », « excellentes » ou « innovatrices », et ils expliquent pourquoi elles excellent dans le domaine de la gestion.

Attributs	Clients	Actionnaires	Moyenne
Personnel/culture	2	1	1
Qualité des produits	1	4	2
Dirigeants de l'entreprise	3	2	3
Vision stratégique	5	3	4
Marketing/ventes	4	5	5

Figure II — Ordre d'importance des principaux attributs

Source: Harvey L. Poppet, « Successful Companies and Contributing Attributes » Insights, 10, 1985, p. 3.

Voici donc quelques attributs de gestion qui contribuent à une plus grande réussite.

L'action

Tout d'abord, elles sont orientées vers l'action. Ces organisations appliquent de nouvelles techniques de gestion, telles que les communications informelles, l'approche VM (Visible Management) chez United Airlines et le MBWA (Management By Walking About) chez Hewlett-Packar : les dirigeants se font un devoir de sortir de leur tour d'ivoire et de se rendre sur les lieux de production.

L'écoute des clients

Ces entreprises restent également à l'écoute du client et se préoccupent constamment du service à la clientèle et de la qualité des produits. Chez Disney Production, par exemple, un programme appelé « contradictory use » oblige tous les dirigeants à quitter, pendant une semaine, bureau et uniforme et à exécuter le travail des placiers, conducteurs de monorail, préposés au stationnement ou aux livraisons. Chez IBM, un programme permet d'évaluer, tous les mois, la satisfaction de la clientèle.

L'autonomie

Les dirigeants favorisent l'autonomie, afin de promouvoir la créativité. Chez IBM, par exemple, les dirigeants encouragent la concurrence entre divisions. L'une des caractéristiques des entreprises innovatrices se manifeste également par le degré de tolérance élevé vis-à-vis des employés qui subissent des échecs.

La motivation

Ces entreprises assoient la productivité sur la motivation du personnel. Cette motivation est non seulement économique, mais elle porte également sur la nature de la tâche et le respect des individus.

Une philosophie de base

Elles se mobilisent autour d'une valeur clé, bien connue et acceptée de tous les employés. Thomas J. Watson, fondateur d'IBM, nous rappelle : « la philosophie de base et le système de valeurs de mon entreprise ont joué un rôle beaucoup plus important pour sa réussite que les ressources économiques et technologiques, les structures organisationnelles et même l'innovation ».

Une structure légère

Ces entreprises conservent une structure simple et légère. Chez Toyota, par exemple, il n'existe que cinq paliers organisationnels ; chez Ford, par contre, il en existe dix-sept. Le nombre d'employés au siège social est maintenu à un strict minimum. Emerson Electric possède un effectif de 54 000 employés et ne dispose que d'une centaine de personnes à son siège social. Chez Dana Corporation, l'une des premières tâches du nouveau président a été de réduire le personnel de son siège de 500 à 100 employés.

Flexibilité

Finalement, elles allient souplesse et vigueur en accordant de l'autonomie aux équipes de développement des produits.

Dans un article intitulé « Fitting New Employees into the Company Culture », Richard Pascale propose un guide pour modifier la culture organisationnelle. Son approche a donné de bons résultats dans plusieurs entreprises, dont IBM et Procter & Gamble :

1. Les candidats doivent être soumis à un processus de sélection particulier, afin que leurs valeurs correspondent à celles de l'organisation.

2. L'humilité du nouvel employé doit être testée après de longues heures de travail.

3. Le nouvel employé doit commencer à travailler dans une fonction particulière de l'entreprise, avant de passer à une autre.

4. À chaque étape de sa carrière, l'employé doit être évalué en fonction de ses réalisations et être récompensé en conséquence.

5. Tout au long de sa carrière, l'organisation doit faire comprendre à l'employé l'importance des valeurs.

6. Les valeurs doivent être appuyées par des événements importants mettant en avant l'entreprise, afin d'améliorer la fierté collective.

7. Les dirigeants doivent servir de modèle de comportement à tous les autres cadres de l'entreprise.

UNE FORMATION INADAPTÉE

D'après certains auteurs, l'un des problèmes les plus inquiétants semble être la formation des gestionnaires, que certains accusent de paralyser l'économie nord-américaine. H. Edward Wrapp, professeur de gestion à l'Université de Chicago, critique les programmes de MBA et soutient : « Nous avons créé une aberration. L'un de mes collègues a remarqué fort justement que les écoles de gestion ont assuré le succès de l'invasion japonaise et ouest-allemande sur le marché américain ». Un banquier affirme que ces écoles « ignorent les sciences humaines, alors qu'elles ont un besoin aigu d'une approche plus large, d'un sens de l'histoire, d'apports littéraires et artistiques. S'il ne tenait qu'à moi, je fermerais toutes les business schools ». Un article de *Fortune* intitulé « Tough Times for MBAs » montre la désillusion qu'ont certains dirigeants d'entreprise face au MBA. Les professeurs Robert Hayes et William Abernathy de la Harvard Business School font le point dans l'article « Managing Our Way to Economic Decline » : « Le système ne produit plus de cadres supérieurs qui détiennent une connaissance pratique des techniques de l'entreprise, de ses clients et de ses fournisseurs. Depuis le milieu des années cinquante, les nouveaux présidents de société sont de plus en plus ceux dont les centres d'intérêt et les compétences relèvent des domaines financiers et juridiques, et non de la production ».

Une recherche effectuée par Lynne Hall de Queen's University auprès de 10 000 dirigeants d'entreprise révèle que les MBA sont presque incapables de résoudre des problèmes de gestion. L'étude nous apprend que :

— Les MBA comprennent la comptabilité, la finance et le marketing, mais pas l'importance de la culture organisationnelle, de la responsabilité corporative et des valeurs d'entreprise.

— Ils savent analyser et compter, mais ne sont pas capables de gérer ni de communiquer.

— Ils peuvent généralement résoudre des problèmes, mais ne savent pas les cerner.

CONCLUSION

La vague de planification stratégique des années soixante-dix a été remplacée, dans les années quatre-vingt, par la culture organisationnelle, mais plusieurs dirigeants se demandent si la culture organisationnelle est vraiment la panacée. Changer la culture d'une organisation est coûteux et demande de nombreuses années. Certains dirigeants d'entreprise estiment que le processus peut prendre de six à quinze ans. Il est difficile pour les dirigeants de modifier leur comportement. Les pratiques culturelles sont beaucoup plus que du « charisme » ; elles doivent se manifester par des 'gestes symboliques ». Chez Walt Disney Production, par exemple, les dirigeants ramassent eux-mêmes papiers et détritus qu'ils peuvent apercevoir. René McPherson, qui a transformé la culture organisationnelle chez Dana Corporation, "jetait au panier» les manuels de politiques d'entreprise, en les remplaçant par une seul « page exposant les valeurs de base de la compagnie. Renn Zaphiropoulos, cofondateur et président de Versatec (filiale de Xerox), invite tous les employés, ayant de cinq à dix ans d'ancienneté, à dîner à son club.

Les valeurs, croyances et règles partagées par tous les employés d'une organisation les incitent à travailler en harmonie et à atteindre de meilleurs résultats. Cette nouvelle approche de gestion, ou cinquième vague, amène les dirigeants d'entreprise à se préoccuper non seulement des ressources physiques et matérielles, mais de plus en plus des ressources humaines et du climat organisationnel.

L'amélioration de la productivité dans nos entreprises ne sera possible que dans la mesure où les gestionnaires y veilleront. Cet engagement doit être accompagné d'un programme d'actions qui visera à augmenter la productivité globale de toutes les ressources, afin que celles-ci puissent réellement faire concurrence aux entreprises étrangères. Ceci se réalisera quand la culture organisationnelle sera harmonisée avec les stratégies corporatives. Le réel défi visant l'augmentation de la productivité est celui de la gestion sociale.

Il est certain que l'approche des gestionnaires de demain sera différente des procédés de gestion traditionnels. Les dirigeants ne seront plus seulement des spécialistes en comptabilité, en ressources humaines, en marketing ou en finance. Même aujourd'hui, ils modifient leur approche et s'adaptent à la nouvelle vague qui demande autodiscipline, recherche de l'excellence et croyance absolue dans les relations entre employés.

Les gestionnaires nord-américains d'aujourd'hui ont appris beaucoup en gestion comparative ; ceux de demain apprendront à reconnaître l'importance de la participation aux objectifs. Ils devront être capables de déléguer, de faire confiance, de gérer efficacement leur temps, de savoir écouter, de travailler « avec » leurs subalternes, d'innover et de motiver.

BIBLIOGRAPHIE

ANDERSON, H., « MBA Schools Don't Teach History — But They Should »,
    Montreal Gazette, 21 juin 1986, 14.
BROSE, M. E., « The Rise of the MBA and the Decline of U.S. Industry »,
    Marketing News, 5 août 1983, 13.
DRUCKER, P. F., *Managing in Turbulent Times*, New York, N.Y., Harper &
    Row Publishers, 1980, 10.
« Don't Blame the System, Blame the Managers », *Dun's Review*, septembre
    1980, 88.
FRAKER, S., « Tough Times for MBAs », *Fortune*, 12 décembre 1983, 64.
HAYES, R. H., ABERNATHY, W. J., « Managing Our Way to Economic
    Decline », *Harvard Business Review*, juillet-août 1980, 78.
McGREGOR, D., *The Human Side of Enterprise*, New York, N.Y., McGraw-
    Hill Book Company, 1960.
OUCHI, W., *Theory Z : How American Business Can Meet the Japanese
    Challenge*, Reading, Mass., Addison-Wesley Publishing Company, 1981,
    4.
PASCALE, R. T., ATHOS, A. G., *The Art of Japanese Management*, New
    York, N.Y., Simon and Schuster, 1981.
PASCALE, R. T., « Fitting New Employees into the Company Culture »,
    Fortune, 28 mai 1984, 28.
PETERS, T., WATERMAN, R., *Le Prix de l'excellence : les secrets des
    meilleures entreprises*, Paris, Inter Éditions, 1983.
PERRY, N. J., « America's Most Admired Corporations », *Fortune*, 9 janvier
    1984, 50.
POPPET, H. L., « Successful Companies and Contributing Attributes », *In-
    sights*, nº 10, 1985, 3.
« La qualité au Canada », *Productivités*, janvier-février 1983, vol. 3, (4), 4.
THOMAS, M. M., « Businessmen's Shortcomings », *New York Times*, 21
    août 1980, D.2.
UTTAL, B., « The Corporate Culture Vultures », *Fortune*, 17 octobre 1983,
    66.

The New World of Business: Small Business

WILBROD LECLERC

Most of the microeconomic theories which are still touted today, such as competition theory, were first espoused in the late eighteenth and early nineteenth centuries in a world of small businesses. Not surprisingly, time changed business conditions and, by the end of the nineteenth century, big business, monopoly and oligopoly theory, and anti-trust laws became the most prominent part of the picture. A hundred years later, at the end of the twentieth century, there are now indications that the wheels of history may have turned full circle and that we may be returning in part to business conditions more similar to the ones prevailing at the beginning of the industrial revolution.

There is little doubt that our Western society, and the entire world for that matter, is entering a period of profound social transformation variously called an information revolution, an electronic revolution, or a service revolution. The first revolution was aptly called industrial because it dealt with power, machines, and production. The present one appears to be centered on information, electronics, and services although it will have widespread effects in all industries.

The realization that revolution is upon us must bring us to reflect upon certain aspects of revolutions. There may be a common element among them. Discontent brings change through the ferment which unites countless small units or individuals. Just as the industrial revolution was made in a world of small business units, so will the present revolution probably be made in a world of small business and by small businesses. This does not mean that the giants will disappear altogether. They may all disappear but will be replaced by others. The Fortune 500 is not doomed.

Change will be brought about by small companies that become giants, like the Apple which challenged IBM. Many giants remain giants by spending enormous sums in research to stay at the head of the pack. Despite these efforts, most of the inventions and new ideas have come from individuals and small companies. This situation will endure, but what produces revolutions is that the atmosphere conducive to such activities becomes so generalized that nearly everyone is caught up in it. The present revolution requires an atmosphere of open competition by a host of small individual units. The winners will become the giants of tomorrow.

In the light of these developments, this paper will explore the new world of small business and the role of the universities, through their business or management schools, in providing students with the education necessary for this new world.

THE WORLD OF SMALL BUSINESS

Small business is by no means a new phenomenon. We may have only rediscovered its importance. Even in the heyday of big business, at the end of the nineteenth century, 99% of businesses were small. In Canada today, for instance, there are probably over one million business firms of all types and sizes. Less then 1% could be described as medium or large. Small firms are active in all sectors of the economy: farming, fishing, mining, manufacturing, distributing, and retailing of goods and services.

Large firms are comfortable where economies of scale are available. But in many areas, such as in retailing and services, where the personal contact with customers is important, there are countless opportunities open to small business. Even the giants depend on large numbers of small suppliers and retailers to support them.

Ownership and operations in small firms are usually in the same hands. These firms are often described as independently owned and owner-operated. There are about 40 of them for every 1,000 people in this country. They employ about one out of every five working citizens and produce between one-quarter and one-third of the Gross National Product. Small businesses are significant, not because of their individual size, but because of their large numbers. This is what John Bullock had going for him in 1971 when he launched the Canadian Federation of Independent Business of which he is now president.

The ferment to start small businesses in our economy is evident in the number of new businesses every year. But the desire to create new businesses is much larger than the actual number of businesses created. For instance, venture capitalists accept only one in ten proposals made to them. Hopefuls who have met with a refusal will try other venture capitalists or go it alone and may yet succeed. However, banks and other financial institutions rarely finance such start-ups unless solid guarantees are available and, when such guarantees are available, few potential businessmen end up with venture capitalists.

For banks or venture capitalists financing small businesses, the fundamental problem is the same. Dollars are bet on individuals, and one of the main considerations in producing the financing is the evaluation put on the individuals making the request for funds. Since few individuals are good at everything or can have the time for everything, the evaluation is preferably based on a management team bringing together the required diversity of expertise rather than on one individual. Investors rarely want to put all their eggs in one basket, especially if the risk is high. When the banks lend to a one-owner business, it is because their loans are very much secured by physical or other assets.

SMALL BUSINESS AND EMPLOYMENT

The renewed interest in small business during the last decade is due largely to the role it has played in employment. Small business has been the cornerstone of the recent recovery in both the U.S. and Canada. In fact, it is the smaller companies in industry which have provided all of the jobs. Between 1977 and 1982, companies too small to make Fortune Magazine's Top 1,000 list in the U.S. provided 8.6 million new job openings. By contrast, companies that made the Fortune 1,000 list, including the giants such as Exxon, General Motors and U.S. Steel, lost 15 million jobs during the same period. Even further, companies on the Fortune 500 list today provide fewer jobs than they did as far back as 1969.

According to statistics from the Canadian Federation of Independent Business, companies in Canada with fewer than 50 employees created more than 70% of the jobs during the period 1975 to 1982. In addition, 18% of this new employment was created by firms less than two years old. It is no wonder that small business spokesmen are being listened to when they insist that an innovative entrepreneurial sector is the key to economic recovery and future full employment. For them, entrepreneurship and new venture formation are the key to the future. To achieve this they propose a number of fiscal incentives. Among the measures proposed are the following:

1. Allowing half the funds invested in self-administered retirement savings plans to be invested in private companies and not only public companies.
2. Exempting investments made in small firms from the tax on capital gains if the investments have been held for more than five years.
3. Allowing capital investments made directly in small firms to be treated as income losses if the business fails.
4. Allowing incorporated partnership elections in order to provide outside investors with some liability protection while giving them the tax treatment of a partnership and the possibility of writing off initial losses against their personal earnings.

Such measures would be added to recent government efforts to improve liaison with small businesses and reduce paperwork, red tape, and the tax load. New organizations have been built on both sides of the liaison equation. The federal government has created a Ministry of State for Small Business and Tourism. Small businesses have grouped together in the Canadian Federation of Independent Business and a few other organizations that have been less success-ful. The CFIB has produced a new hero, its president John Bullock. Its concentration on lobbying has made it the equal of the Canadian Chamber of Commerce, which groups both large and small busi-nesses and, as a result, has become more of a local club than a good lobbyist. The difference is due, perhaps, to the disadvantage of being a staid old democratically-oriented organization like the C.C. of C.

START-UPS

The discovery of the predominant role of small business in providing employment has also given impetus to government en-couragement of business start-ups. Large businesses tend to be capital-intensive, and government help at first was oriented to pro-viding financial funds for capital purchases. But larger businesses tend to use these funds to automate and robotize and thus reduce employment. The replacement of labor by capital is profitable in firms large enough to profit from economies of scale.

On the other hand, small businesses don't have the volumes to justify large-scale automation and robotization. They are generally launched in sectors which are already heavily populated by small businesses, such as the retail sector, or in competition with big business, where one can find a comfortable niche. For instance, in Silicon Valley North, a high-technology company will often be launched by a technical employee from Northern Telecom who has an idea for a specific product which is not yet being manufactured. An individual can design and market the product much more quickly than the large firm because the authorization process in large firms tends to be slow, as in all bureaucracies. The fledgling firm's com-petition is typically made up of the Philips, Panasonics, RCA's, and IBM's of this world. But this does not mean that the small firm can be submerged by these world-wide giants. Again, typically, the competition for each of these large firms is a group of less than a dozen employees engaged in designing and marketing a specialized product with similar functions. So there is place to grow and compete with the giants.

Who are the individuals who are attracted to starting up a business? There is probably no way to make a general profile of such an individual because the numbers are so large and the variety so great. Many of them have a family tradition in small business. While this is often true for older Canadian families, it is especially true of new Canadian families which bring with them the tradition and experience of shopkeepers, importers, and independent trades-men gained in their home countries. Another group of entrepreneurs is made up of people who value independence or being their own boss above everything else and are willing to work very hard to succeed. In the high-technology field, many are highly trained professionals or technicians. Finally, in recent years, many individuals thrown out of work by the recessions have taken advantage of their situation in order to make a break with the past or to realize an old dream.

Most entrepreneurs make their decision for more than one reason. However, very few bring with them any kind of formal training in business, a theme which we will explore in greater depth in a coming section on education for small business. Many researchers have linked this particular lack of competence to the high rate of failure for new businesses. Some 80% usually go bankrupt within the first five years.

Of course, training can be obtained in various ways. Colleges and universities offer diplomas and degrees in business administration. But, for most entrepreneurs, the school of hard knocks is often the best training ground. Those who have become great successes in business often have one or two bankruptcies to their credit in their early years. It seems that the most common way to learn is by making enough mistakes. For instance, many inexperienced businessmen have learned the hard way that to go over a line of credit at the bank even by a small amount without a prior understanding with the bank manager is a sure way to immediate financial difficulties and even bankruptcy. Many have learned only through experience that such a state of affairs is considered a capital sin by the bank and brings out the worst in a bank manager.

On the other hand, those who have learned this in a course often forget it because it is such a small thing compared to supposedly much more important things. Even if they do not forget, they are more likely to never need the information because they will likely become specialists or managers rather than entrepreneurs. As specialists in marketing, finance, or accounting, they will need large firms to hire them at large salaries. They will remember what a line of credit is and what it can be used for. However, unless actually involved with line of credit matters, they will never know the importance to any business of its relationship with its banker and the rules, written and unwritten, that govern this relationship. All small businessmen at some time discover that you do not go over your line of credit, even by a small amount, or else.

SMALL BUSINESS AND UNIVERSITIES

The recent changes in attitudes towards small business caught many schools of business napping, just like the rest of the country. But while many other areas have awakened to the new conditions, most universities are still napping.

Surveys among students entering schools of business in the last few decades have shown consistently that over one-half of them are thinking of owning their own business one day, of being their own boss. By the time that universities have finished brainwashing the students with the methods and procedures of big business administration, sometimes barely 5% of the graduating classes are still thinking of going into business for themselves. Schools of business have been very successful in transforming the most dynamic, inventive, and individualistic segments of our young people into problem-solvers, specialists, managers, or administrators for big business or big governments, but not into entrepreneurs.

Of course, some changes have taken place in the last few decades. Here and there, some courses in small business and entrepreneurship have appeared. Some 160 universities in the U.S. and a few in Canada now offer courses in entrepreneurship. But much more should be done. Important changes are taking place and such changes are seldom brought about by big business. Even with their billions spent in research and development, the giants barely succeed in developing better products. They rarely invent new ones. Most inventions have been produced by individuals as opposed to large research departments. The experience of both Silicon Valleys confirms that development and growth come from technical people with ideas who leave large companies and start on their own. This is just as true of the children and grandchildren of Northern Telecom and the National Research Council in Ottawa as of all the Fair-children in California. It is probably fair to say that many of their products and services would not have seen the light of day if these people had stayed in large companies or government. But one thing that few of these budding entrepreneurs had when going into business for themselves was experience in running a business.

Words have a way of reflecting realities, and the proliferation of schools of "management" or "administration" in our universities today as opposed to the old schools of "business" is a reflection of the change that has taken place in these faculties over the past fifty years. They have been transformed from schools of business into schools of management.

What is the difference between the two types of schools? Is it only a question of words? Is there a big difference between business and management? The basic difference is between being your own boss and working for somebody else. It is between making money and making a salary. The new schools are turning out future employees for big business and big governments. They are not turning out the individualistic risk-takers who will become tomorrow's entrepreneurs. Most young entrepreneurs today fall into two main categories. They have little formal education and enter distribution and retail business or they have technical degrees in science or engineering and enter manufacturing and technological businesses. Few of them have business degrees.

The Faculty of Administration at the University of Ottawa has revised its undergraduate program in the last few years. For the first time, the new program introduced a course in Small Business Management that is really a course in entrepreneurship oriented towards starting up a new business. The response by students to the new offering was absolutely unexpected. Instead of the ten to twenty students who usually sign up for an optional course in third year, nearly one hundred students registered for the course. A very high proportion of these were fourth-year students for whom the course had not been available in prior years. These fell mainly into two groups: sons and daughters of families already involved in small businesses and students from other faculties wishing to set up their own businesses in their own special fields. Most of them were thus highly motivated.

This first experience with the course led to the discovery that these students wanted more hands-on practical learning experiences. The textbook used, which was similar to most of the textbooks on small business, was found to be next to useless for third- and fourth-year undergraduates except as a guideline for the preparation of a business plan. Longer cases added by the professor were more useful. In the future, any textbook will probably be used only as a reference book to prepare a business plan, and emphasis will be laid more on the preparation of a total business plan and its presentation to real venture capitalists. To that will be added discussions of longer cases and meetings with small businessmen engaged in different fields of endeavor.

It is also worth mentioning the results of the presentations by these students to actual venture capitalists. As mentioned earlier, these capitalists usually invest in fewer than 5-10% of the proposals made to them. The students succeeded in selling about one-half of their proposals. This must say something for the value of a business education... or perhaps just the value of an education.

Business schools must realize that there are two great markets for small business courses outside their faculties. The first market is related to all the small businessmen, actual and potential, who could use extra knowledge in setting up and running their businesses. The other market is more academic and more captive. It is made up of all the students in other faculties, especially the professional ones, who are thinking of setting up their own businesses. In the past, most of them have done so without any formal education in business. Most of them would have benefitted from such knowledge. It is up to the schools of business to organize formally such specifically designed offerings to other faculties.

Some 300 to 400 high-technology companies have been launched in Ottawa's Silicon Valley North in the last decade. Most of these were started by engineers or technicians of one kind or another. Those who succeeded did so usually because they linked their technical expertise to market and management expertise in one way or another. Those who didn't usually relied too much on technical expertise alone and tended to fail. Many such failures could have been prevented if the owners had been conscious of their shortcomings and had had the opportunity to overcome them. Schools of business surely can remedy these deficiencies.

IMPLICATIONS FOR CURRICULUM

Trends in the world of business as well as recent experience with small business courses lead to a number of conclusions concerning the evolution of business schools.

To begin with, business schools may do well to consider returning in part to their origin, which was business rather than management. In the process of concentrating on management they have sometimes completely forgotten the world of business and especially the world of small business. Because small business is small, and small businessmen must understand the total business, small business courses in third- or fourth-year undergraduate programs can become good capstone courses. Students are better able to understand the total picture for a business of a few million dollars in sales with ten or twenty employees. Policy cases dealing with automobile companies, multinationals, and multiplant operations in large companies tend to be beyond them. They cannot see themselves as president of General Motors, and really have no feel as to what to do in his shoes. They are better able to discuss the total view of an automobile dealership doing $10 or $20 million in business.

Since they can more easily take the total view of a small business, students can learn to synthesize or integrate their knowledge with more success with a small business case. They get to understand what it is to be a generalist and to have to know something about everything. In addition, once they can master the facts of a case, they can make more specific recommendations and envisage the steps that have to be taken in order to implement those recommendations. With larger companies, students have no other alternative than to make a general analysis of the company and make general recommendations because they cannot really put themselves behind the desk of the decision-maker. They cannot avoid sweeping generalities. On the other hand, with small companies, it is easier for them to concentrate on the action required to solve problems rather than simply look for the learned technique to apply in the situation. It is also easier for them to consult real people in business, small businessmen who can talk to them about concrete problems.

Since students who take small business courses in third or fourth year find little to learn in the average small business textbook, some thought should be given to two alternatives. First, introductory business courses in first year should perhaps be concentrated on small business. Such courses could thus become more practical rather than be loaded with every theory on the market for every function of business and every function of management. A second alternative would be to consider small business courses as a specialization for later years where an effort is made to concentrate on practicality, learning by walking and doing, rather than by handing out more principles.

On the practical side, one of the most important things for a small businessman is to be able to sell his plans both verbally and in writing. Meetings with real bank managers or venture capitalists can be meaningful experiences. They will teach students the importance of appearance, the correct use of language, logic, thinking on your feet, salesmanship, etc.

LINKS WITH THE SMALL BUSINESS COMMUNITY

Professors can teach and do research without having any links with the business community. Schools of business as a whole can have few formal or informal links with the business community. Schools that do maintain such links tend to have them with representatives of big business rather than small business. Advisory Committees are typically recruited from the ranks of presidents of large national companies rather than of local business leaders. It is probably fair to say that such a situation is a good reflection of where the interests lie on both sides. Business schools teach the management of big organizations and big organizations are interested in having the schools produce the human material they want to hire. The schools want the advice of big business and big government; the latter want to give their advice to the schools.

Small businessmen are usually grouped together through local Chambers of Commerce or Boards of Trade. Some of these provide the local dean of the faculty of business with an ex officio membership in the organization and on its board of directors; others don't. Some schools maintain some memberships in the organizations; others don't. In general, it is probably fair to say that the local small business community seldom considers that the local faculty of business has much to contribute to it. The business faculty is seen as being one or more steps higher on the business ladder and having little to do with them. It is not surprising then that a recent CFIB survey on the most useful source of business information or advice shows that only 1% look to universities (including their schools of business) and community colleges as a source of information. Small firms prefer their suppliers, accountants, lawyers, and trade associations.

In some provinces, certain schools of business run small business consulting programs. Students offer all sorts of consulting help to small businesses in their community. Just the knowledge of their existence is usually relatively low, depending on the public relations program developed by the students. In larger cities, such programs barely scratch the surface of the small business community. The help provided is valuable, but reaching a large number of such small business people is an impossible task.

Small business student consultants benefit greatly from their consulting experience. First, they get a chance to meet and discuss with many different individuals, small businessmen, loan officers, venture capitalists, future entrepreneurs, etc. They increase their knowledge, experience, and understanding of business. This gives them a decided advantage over their colleagues when job-hunting. Employers and recruiters put heavy emphasis on this type of practical experience during interviews.

The Federal Business Development Bank, through its Counselling Assistance to Small Enterprises (CASE) program, also reaches out to the small business community. Its clients are usually a bit larger than the clients handled by students and are centered in the manufacturing field. Despite the relatively larger sums spent on this program it does not reach many more clients than the students do in a given year.

In general, it seems that reaching out to the small business community is difficult even for those wishing to do so, such as governments, business associations, schools of business, or students. It is not surprising then that most schools of business do very little in this area. Few professors are interested in small business and, as a result, few students give it any thought, although the response to actual course offerings has been surprising.

Even if schools of business have little to gain directly from links with the small business community, it stands to reason that they should maintain some links strictly out of duty to their local community. Such links can range from simple presence or membership of some faculty members to active participation in the activities of small business associations. The faculties of business must make their existence known in the community if their presence is to be felt and their usefulness as a source of information and education is to be recognized.

REFERENCES

BRANNEN, W.H., and BOND, K., "What students say about small business marketing," *Journal of Small Business Management*, Vol. 17, (4), October 1979, pp. 48-54.

JEWKES, J., SAWERS, D., and STILLERMAN, R., *The sources of invention*, London, Macmillan, 1958.

LUCHSINGER, L.L., and LUCHSINGER, V., "New trends in educational programs criented toward small business," *Journal of Small Business Management*, Vol. 15, (1), January 1977, pp. 43-47.

MACDONALD, H.I., "Shaping the industrial renaissance," *Journal of Small Business Canada*, Vol. 1, (4), Spring 1984, pp. 3-8.

MACDONALD, J.A., "A profile of CFIB membership 1983," *Journal of Small Business Canada*, Vol. 1, (3), Fall 1983, pp. 4-13.

MCMULLAN, W.E., and LONG, W., "An approach to educating entrepreneurs," *Journal of Small Business Canada*, Vol. 1, (2), Fall 1983, pp. 32-37.

The Financial Post, Section on Small Business, April 28, 1984, pp. S1-S10.

WIETFELDT, R.A., "A study of job creation in Canada," *Journal of Small Business Canada*, Vol. 1, (4), Spring 1984, pp. 8-14.

Dégradation dans les entreprises : une perspective théorique et des guides pour l'action

CHRISTIAN NAVARRE

En matière de management, l'étude de la faillite n'est pas objet d'intérêt de la part de la communauté scientifique. Des publications récentes (Lalonde, 1983) soulignent les lacunes de la littérature. Les financiers figurent parmi les plus productifs en ce domaine, car confrontés concrètement à la faillite et à ses conséquences, ils développèrent pour en réduire les risques des techniques de repérage et d'identification précoces. Ces techniques furent initialement conçues, en effet, par des analystes des institutions bancaires. Avec la diffusion des techniques d'analyse multivariée se multiplièrent des approches plus sophistiquées. Le principe général de tels travaux (Altman, 1983) fut, le plus souvent, l'identification par la technique de l'analyse discriminante de ce qui distinguait deux échantillons, l'un constitué d'entreprises saines et l'autre de firmes en faillite. Quinze ans de recherche aboutissent aux points suivants :

1. La nature même de ces techniques n'a jamais permis de tenir compte convenablement de la dimension du temps, autrement que par des artifices. Ces modèles sont de type « coupe transversale instantanée», alors que l'étude du processus de dégradation qui conduit à la faillite implique nécessairement une approche diachronique et historique.

2. les techniques d'analyse de données produisent de façon quasi-mécanique un résultat souvent ambigu dont l'élucidation dépend, en dernier ressort, des préférences de l'interprète. Derrière l'aspect scientifique, voire scientiste, apparaît le subjectivisme. La multiplication de critères de discrimination non concordants en témoigne (Castagna, 1981).

3. l'étude du comportement de groupes d'analystes financiers a montré qu'ils se trompaient plutôt moins que les modèles de prévisions et d'identification, et surtout qu'ils s'ajustaient en permanence aux nouvelles données (Zimmer, 1980 ; Casey, 1980).

À un moindre degré, les spécialistes de l'arrêt des produits proposent quelques modèles utiles. La notion de courbe de vie du produit nous vient du marketing. Et pourtant, peu de travaux traitent de la disparition et de l'élimination des produits. Leur apport se situe pour l'essentiel dans le domaine des recommandations techniques de l'arrêt de commercialisation (Salerno, 1981, 1983). Une analyse en profondeur des mécanismes de la dégradation aurait permis d'aller plus loin.

Pour résumer, tout se passe comme si la disparition des entreprises ne présentait aucun intérêt pour l'analyse des ressorts fondamentaux du fonctionnement des firmes ; comme si seuls comptaient excellence et performance. En adoptant une telle démarche, les médecins auraient limité, pour notre malheur, leur domaine de recherche à l'étude des individus en bonne santé avec un intérêt vif et soutenu pour les athlètes. Pourtant l'impact socio-économique des faillites d'entreprises de plus en plus grandes a contraint les hommes politiques dans la plupart des grands pays occidentaux à promouvoir des réformes importantes du droit de la faillite. Entre 1970 et 1980, près de 40 000 faillites d'entreprises ont été enregistrées au Canada, soit une augmentation de 125 % par rapport à la décennie précédente. Des insuffisances d'actif ont été globalement évaluées à 2,5 milliards de dollars. Il est de notoriété publique que les directions d'importantes affaires tombées en faillite (Penn, Massey-Fergusson, par exemple) ont ignoré jusqu'aux derniers moments les signes évidents de catastrophe imminente. Certains groupes d'hommes d'affaires ont exploité cette nouvelle situation. Ils ont fait preuve d'une technicité et de compétences particulières dans le redressement d'entreprises en faillite, au point de l'intégrer comme dimension essentielle de leur stratégie de développement (Cascades au Québec, Tapie en France). Des sociétés financières spécialisées dans le redressement de firmes en difficulté se créent et attirent des capitaux importants dans des activités jugées par les investisseurs au moins aussi profitables et moins dangereuses que les sociétés de capital-risque ou le financement de l'innovation.

Ce décalage entre la réalité brutale des effets du phénomène et son statut scientifique et académique nous interpelle sur le fonctionnement même des sciences de gestion. Le but de cette analyse est de montrer comment la structure de certains paradigmes usuels des sciences de gestion interdit l'émergence de la dégradation et de la disparition des firmes en tant que champ conceptuel autonome et, ce qui est plus important dans le contexte actuel de sous-emploi, de leur redressement. Un modèle conceptuel sera proposé afin de justifier la formulation de quelques dimensions essentielles des techniques et méthodes de redressement des entreprises.

LA PLACE DE LA FAILLITE EN SCIENCES DE GESTION

H. Simon (1974) a montré qu'il était vain de transposer aux sciences de gestion les protocoles des sciences physiques. En effet, l'entreprise, la fabrication d'objets manufacturés, le droit sont des artefacts et n'ont pas d'existence en dehors du projet qui fut à l'origine de leur conception et de leur réalisation. Ce qui importe donc est la façon dont on peut améliorer et contrôler le processus qui de la conception (et en quelque sorte du « délire initial ») aboutit à des artefacts utiles et adaptés aux buts qu'ils étaient censés initialement servir. Les hommes d'affaires ne seraient-ils pas avant tout « des rêveurs pragmatiques » ? Rempli de modèles, de concepts et d'images, le manager est conduit, dans ses tâches opérationnelles, à une certaine « réalité », à l'inverse du physicien qui, partant de l'observation (le protocole expérimental), aboutit aux concepts, aux modèles et aux images de la nature. Dans ces conditions, la seule science possible en gestion serait celle qui rationaliserait les processus de production d'artefacts. Ce serait une science de l'artificiel. Cette thèse est celle de Simon.

Tout cet ensemble d'artefacts ne constituerait-il pas alors un univers duquel surgiraient des invariants de même nature que ceux des sciences physiques ? Il revient à Russel d'avoir montré que la caractéristique d'une classe d'éléments partageant des propriétes communes n'est pas du même type logique que les éléments constitutifs de la classe. C'est ainsi que si l'humanité est constituée de tous les hommes et de toutes les femmes ayant vécu, vivants et à venir, elle-même n'est ni un homme, ni une femme (pas plus que la fameuse pipe de Magritte n'est une pipe, mais l'image d'une pipe) ; elle appartient à un autre ordre logique. Les modèles théoriques de l'entreprise ne sont pas des modèles d'entreprises réelles. Ils ne sont que des artefacts, images et modèles proposés par les chercheurs. À ce niveau se situe l'arbitraire du découpage du « réel » par les chercheurs, ce qui revient à identifier leurs hypothèses non pas pour les déclarer idéologiques ou contraires à la démarche scientifique, mais pour les traiter comme éléments moteurs de l'élaboration du modèle.

Dans cette double perspective (celle d'une science de l'artificiel et de l'arbitraire des chercheurs), les modèles théoriques de l'entreprise s'articulent autour de deux notions essentielles et implicites :

1. La vision de l'homme: soit on lui attribue une rationalité intrinsèque qui se formulera différemment de chercheur à chercheur, soit, au contraire, on lui reconnaît une rationalité limitée et/ou des rationalités multiples.

2. La vision de l'organisation comme système : soit fermé, c'est-à-dire indépendant des effets de l'environnement, soit ouvert, c'est-à-dire procédant de l'environnement, ou soit encore adaptatif, c'est-à-dire dont le fonctionnement est le résultat simultané des effets de l'environnement et de la capacité de

morphogénèse du système pour échapper précisément à ces effets externes.

La combinaison de ces deux critères (l'homme et l'organisation) débouche sur l'identification de six catégories principales, dont chacune respectera les deux éléments essentiels du protocole du chercheur :

1. Certaines théories sont construites dans une perspective déductive et normative. Il s'agit de définir des formes optimales, rationnelles et universelles de fonctionnement. Peu importe la réalité pourvu qu'elle soit conforme au modèle théorique ; tout écart au modèle est jugé pénalisant. Les autres théories sont construites dans une perspective inductive et empirique dont le but est l'identification et l'observation des formes concrètes adoptées par le système observé. Historiquement, en matière de sciences de gestion, ces deux courants contradictoires, l'inductif et le normatif, coexistent.

2. Comme l'a montré Weick (1979), il est impossible qu'un modèle théorique satisfasse simultanément les trois objectifs contradictoires que sont la généralité, la simplicité et la précision. Ils peuvent, par contre, être atteints individuellement ou par paire. Le contenu théorique diffère considérablement selon la combinaison retenue.

Il s'ensuit que ce qui est reconnu comme scientifique présente de nombreuses facettes. Selon la vision du monde et les choix initiaux des chercheurs, chaque catégorie de théories est potentiellement hétérogène. Néanmoins, quant à l'évaluation des apports théoriques relatifs à la question de la faillite, quelques lignes directrices se dégagent.

L'entreprise système fermé, l'homme rationnel

Ces approches sont généralement déductives, globales et découlent de principes de rationalité posés comme universels. Le taylorisme, le modèle bureaucratique, les principes de gestion scientifique, mais aussi l'école des relations humaines se partagent ce terrain. La question de la faillite y est exclue : au mieux, les firmes inefficaces qu'il faut éliminer sont signalées. Leur disparition est bénéfique parce qu'elle libère des ressources qui seront combinées par des firmes plus performantes adonnées aux principes de rationalité. Aux yeux du chercheur, il n'existe qu'une solution optimale, et une seule, autour de laquelle il ordonne la totalité des formes de fonctionnement concrètes des firmes. La question de la dégradation et de la faillite sont donc sans objet. 'Soyons rationnels et tout ira pour le mieux dans le meilleur des mondes possibles ! »

L'entreprise système fermé, l'homme peu rationnel

On y trouve surtout des modèles conçus selon des approches inductives et par réaction aux excès des approches rationalisatrices et simplificatrices décrites dans le modèle précédent. Il est constaté, sur la base d'observations empiriques, que les individus choisissent et décident en situation d'informations rares et ambiguës, selon des critères plus ou moins précis et souvent contradictoires. Les modèles nés de ce constat sont beaucoup plus élaborés et centrés sur la rationalisation non plus de la décision, mais du processus de décision lui-même. La question est moins celle de la formulation de la décision optimale que de la manière de la produire optimale. Des travaux comme ceux de Cyert, de Raiffa illustrent bien ce courant. Les entreprises sont donc dirigées sur la base d'objectifs de satisfaction plutôt que d'optimums. Les coalitions qui se partagent le pouvoir et contrôlent l'allocation des ressources à l'intérieur des organisations ne réagissent que si les surplus de l'organisation s'amenuisent. La disparition de l'organisation est inéluctable, sa situation est celle d'un sursis permanent, son objectif est la survie. La seule manière de retarder l'issue fatale est de rationaliser et de programmer non pas la décision, mais des processus de choix à rationalités multiples et approximatives. La disparition de l'entreprise, banalisée parce qu'inéluctable, est hors des préoccupations des chercheurs. Il n'y a pas de place pour l'étude de la faillite puisque tout le processus de management n'est qu'un effort désespéré pour en retarder la fatale et inéluctable issue.

L'entreprise système ouvert, l'homme rationnel

En adoptant ces deux postulats, le chercheur ouvre son protocole expérimental à la fois aux variables internes à l'entreprise et à celles relatives à la description de l'environnement et à leurs interactions. La question n'est plus d'identifier les formes optimales ou simplement « satisfaisantes » de fonctionnement interne, mais de savoir comment celui-ci est strictement déterminé par les variations de l'environnement ou du contexte. Des travaux comme ceux de Aston College, Lawrence et Lorsch ou Chandler, concluent à la contingence des formes d'adaptation face aux caractéristiques de l'environnement. La variété expérimentale peut être réduite à quelques formes essentielles, résumant et réduisant la réalité observée, qui diffèrent selon les chercheurs. Plusieurs réponses possibles coexistent globalement, mais pour un environnement donné, une seule est adaptée. Ce résultat établi, la question qui se pose est alors d'identifier comment et pourquoi seules quelques entreprises d'un secteur découvrent la « bonne solution ». Plus précisément, pourquoi tous les dirigeants ne découvrent-ils pas la forme optimale d'adaptation ? Cette question pertinente, dont l'analyse exigerait une étude des firmes en difficulté, est restée sans réponse.

L'entreprise système ouvert, l'homme peu rationnel

Comme pour la deuxième catégorie, ce genre d'approche est centré essentiellement sur les processus de fonctionnement interne dans leurs relations avec les effets de l'environnement. L'entreprise est décrite comme un système politique où s'expriment de multiples acteurs, aux objectifs mals définis et souvent contradictoires, soumis et contraints à l'adaptation. La formulation d'une politique rationnelle et rigoureuse est impensable. Les managers rationalisent les processus de planification des décisions selon les mêmes modalités et avec la même approximation que celles des processus politiques. L'entreprise est pour les managers un projet toujours renouvelé et en perpétuelle transformation sous la pression de l'environnement. Le but du processus de gestion ne pouvant être la disparition de la firme, la question de la faillite prend du relief. Faute d'un modèle de référence, celui d'une rationalité extérieure qui guiderait les managers, comment réduire leurs probabilités d'erreurs ? La seule dimension qui subsiste dans le champ du chercheur est le processus d'élaboration stratégique, et son seul apport, sa rationalisation prudente.On trouve dans cette catégorie les travaux sur les processus de décisions stratégiques et leur description en termes incrémentalistes. La faillite sera le résultat de dysfonctionnements du processus de décision stratégique (activités nouvelles, désinvestissement) et d'une incapacité à internaliser et à répondre aux processus de détermination de l'environnement.

L'entreprise système adaptatif, l'homme rationnel

Ce genre d'approche est trés récent et découle directement des limites de l'approche des systèmes ouverts. Pour les chercheurs de cette catégorie, la rationalité est de trouver les voies de l'adaptation à des contextes différents. Les stratégies d'adaptation et les structures concrètes varieront, mais toutes seront isomorphes à des principes généraux supérieurs exprimant une rationalité plus large, celle qui rythme la vie du produit et de l'industrie. Ce projet à été celui de Michael Porter et de son équipe. Empruntant largement aux résultats de l'économie industrielle, la notion de groupe stratégique lie les stratégies concrètes des firmes à des contextes industriels classés essentiellement selon leur position dans la courbe de vie de l'industrie. La faillite traduit une incapacité soit à trouver la forme d'adaptation optimale pour le contexte industriel ambiant, soit à s'adapter d'un contexte à un autre. Pour cause de rationalité supérieure, le problème de la faillite est néanmoins de nouveau évacué. La dégradation est comme le négatif de la réussite, qui seule compte.

L'entreprise système adaptatif, l'homme peu rationnel

La caractéristique principale des managers, en raison des limites qui les affectent, est qu'ils se trompent. L'entreprise se conçoit comme le lieu géométrique de crises potentielles inéluctables. Il revient à Miller et Friesen (1984) d'avoir montré, en développant la notion d'archétype, que plusieurs manières d'être performant (6) ou non performant (4) coexistaient. Par conséquent, pour une entreprise soumise à l'évolution de son secteur, la morphogénèse des structures et des stratégies est essentielle. La question du passage d'une configuration à une autre est explicitement posée. Les auteurs montrent clairement que cette transformation s'observe tout autant dans le sens de la performance vers la performance, que dans toutes les autres directions possibles (performance vers non performance, non performance vers performance, non performance vers non performance). La question de la faillite est au cœur du dispositif théorique en tant que modalité possible d'aboutissement des processus de transformations structurelles.

Les dysfonctionnements menant à la faillite ne seront donc dans le champ de la recherche qu'au prix de postulats fondamentaux :

1. L'entreprise est un système morphogénique dont le sens de l'adaptation est, dans certaines circonstances, celui d'une dégradation permanente et non corrigée du fonctionnement.

2. Les managers ne sont pas toujours en mesure d'identifier la rationalité et la logique profonde qui organisent et structurent une insertion réussie dans l'environnement. Pire, ils peuvent se tromper pendant longtemps.

3. Dans un univers où la rationalité des acteurs est limitée, les processus comptent plus que leurs résultats lesquels découlent directement des premiers.

4. Il faut choisir un niveau logique d'analyse et s'y tenir, c'est-à-dire :
— soit traiter les entreprises comme une catégorie logique et s'interdire d'observer (ou plutôt d'exclure de l'observation) les équipes de direction autrement que dans la boîte noire déterminée par l'environnement qu'est l'entreprise fiction,
— soit traiter l'entreprise comme le résultat plus ou moins réussi de ce qui fut un temps le projet stratégique des dirigeants et se centrer sur les processus d'élaboration des décisions et les équipes de direction.

La théorie a longtemps été dominée par les modèles des catégories 1 et 2. La formulation des modèles de types 3 et 4 date des années cinquante, celle des modèles de types 5 et 6 est toute récente. Avec leur développement s'amorce une théorie plus large de l'entreprise incluant les processus de dégradation qui affectent son fonctionnement.

UN MODÈLE CONCEPTUEL DU PROCESSUS QUI CONDUIT À LA FAILLITE

L'entreprise en faillite est d'abord une entreprise qui n'est plus en mesure de faire face à ses obligations financières, conférant à la dimension financière un rôle moteur dans la compréhension des mécanismes de la dégradation. Toutefois les états financiers ne retracent que des processus plus subtils, se situant en amont et qui se développent au sein du système de décision de l'entreprise (Auger, 1982). Le fonctionnement de ce dernier est lui-même induit par le fonctionnement des structures organisationnelles mises en place par les directions pour l'exécution de leur stratégie. Autrement dit :

1. pour comprendre et expliquer les évolutions financières, il faut comprendre le fonctionnement du système de décision ;
2. pour comprendre comment sont prises les décisions, il faut comprendre de quoi sont faites les structures organisationnelles ;
3. pour comprendre les choix organisationnels, il faut comprendre quels furent ou quels sont les projets stratégiques des directions.

La dimension financière

L'évolution financière d'une entreprise se lit et se mesure à travers les états financiers que sont le compte d'exploitation générale, le tableau des flux de fonds, le bilan. Ils sont établis selon un ensemble de règles et de conventions d'évaluation des ressources mises en œuvre par l'entreprise. On y découvre des images, des modèles, plus ou moins fidèles de la réalite de la firme. Mais ils ne sont pas la réalité. De nombreuses manières de les lire et de les interpréter ont d'ailleurs été proposées. Nous adopterons celle de Donalson selon laquelle les managers engagent et allouent les ressources de telle manière qu'ils puissent, en toutes circonstances, faire face à toutes les obligations financières acceptées. La liquidité financière et la capacité de recombiner les ressources allouées lorsqu'un revers se produit sont essentielles. La mobilité financière permet une réponse flexible à des événements non prévus (Declerck, 1984). Elle se mesure en dressant à un moment donné l'inventaire des ressources financières existantes et/ou potentielles classées comme suit :

1. réserves liquides non engagées (tels les excédents de liquidités ou les lignes de crédit inutilisées) ou négociables (prêts supplémentaires ou émissions d'actions) ;
2. liquidités potentielles qui résulteraient d'une accélération des encaissements (réduction de la durée des crédits accordés aux clients) ;
3. liquidités potentielles qui résulteraient d'un ralentissement des décaissements (augmentation des crédits des fournisseurs) ou d'un report des dépenses courantes (annulation des investissements, licenciements) ;
4. liquidation d'actifs (revente de filiales, d'usines, de marques).

L'insolvabilité n'intervient que lorsque toutes les réserves constitutives de la mobilité financière ont été consommées ou détruites.

Une entreprise sera en difficulté chaque fois que sa mobilité financière sera menacée de diminution. Le dépôt de bilan traduit l'incapacité momentanée des dirigeants à dégager ou à recombiner des ressources. Le dépôt de bilan signale le terme d'un processus qui mène à l'incapacité d'agir. Si l'entreprise dispose de réserves importantes, le processus de dégradation peut être très lent, ce qui est vérifié empiriquement. De plus, même si la mobilité financière devient nulle, le moment de la crise finale sera éventuellement retardé par des manœuvres, parfois frauduleuses, visant à prolonger artificiellement ou à masquer la solvabilité. Par contraste, le processus de relance d'une entreprise en faillite, lorsqu'il est possible, résulte de la reconstitution de cette mobilité financière. De tous les documents financiers, le tableau des sources et emplois de fonds retrace le mieux comment le processus de dégradation se développe. Il permet à l'observateur de découvrir comment les décisions d'engagement des fonds ont affecté les équilibres financiers fondamentaux au cours des périodes. Il est le modèle qui enregistre le plus fidèlement les décisions qui affectent la mobilité financière. Mais il n'est que l'image homomorphe du système décisionnel qui le détermine et le structure.

La dimension décisionnelle de la faillite

Il est devenu courant de distinguer les décisions programmées des décisions discrétionnaires. Dans la perspective de Donalson, les managers construisent des plans d'allocation des ressources pour atteindre les objectifs choisis en fonction de leurs anticipations. Ces choix effectués, l'exécution des plans relève de systèmes plus ou moins sophistiqués dont la finalité est d'obtenir la réalisation des objectifs des groupes organisationnels. Les écarts enregistrés entre les objectifs et les réalisations seront à imputer soit à la médiocrité des systèmes d'exécution, soit à des anticipations incomplètes. Les corrections seront obtenues par le recours à des décisions discrétionnaires et, s'agissant de la mobilité financière, par l'exécution des différentes tactiques décrites plus haut. La dégradation dépendra moins des incertitudes relatives aux anticipations jugées naturelles que de corrections qui ne sont pas effectuées, c'est-à-dire lorsque la part des décisions discrétionnaires aura été réduite à trop peu pour obtenir les effets correcteurs.

La dimension organisationnelle de la faillite

La répartition entre les deux catégories de décisions relève de la nature des structures organisationnelles. Bien que la question soit en général traitée de façon très abstraite, nous supposerons que toute structure organisationnelle donnera des réponses plus ou moins appropriées, pertinentes et partielles aux questions suivantes :
1. Qui dépend de qui ? (répartition de l'autorité) ;

2. Qui fait quoi ? (division, standardisation des tâches) ;
3. Qui informe qui ? de quoi ? (systèmes d'information) ;
4. Qui influence qui ? (effets des interactions entre les personnes).

Les réponses dépendent à la fois de conditions internes à l'entreprise et de la nécessité de l'adaptation. Le choix essentiel est celui des formes de différenciation interne (en particulier le nombre de distinctions fonctionnelles et/ou divisionnelles) et corrélativement celles de l'intégration (plans, hiérarchie, stocks, systèmes de liaison). La structure organisationnelle est conditionnée par tous ces choix, rarement examinés simultanément, qui déterminent la répartition entre les décisions programmées et discrétionnaires. Le fonctionnement variera dans le temps sous l'effet d'un déterminisme interne de renforcement et d'autovalidation produisant une rigidité au changement et l'élimination progressive des décisions discrétionnaires au profit des décisions programmées. La structure fonctionnant pour elle-même et les individus qui en font partie ayant perdu de vue la raison d'être initiale qui justifie leur statut, le coût du changement devient exhorbitant. Alors le système dérive lentement en se déconnectant des exigences de la concurrence et plus généralement de l'environnement. Capacités de décision et de réaction ne peuvent être retrouvées qu'au prix d'un changement de la structure elle même, d'un réajustement général des processus de décision. Le changement des structures, celui de la reconquête de la capacité de décider, ne peut se conduire que de « l'extérieur ». C'est l'œuvre des directions.

La dimension stratégique

La conception des structures organisationnelles est elle-même dépendante des décisions de la direction. Pour ses dirigeants, l'entreprise est l'œuvre qu'ils coproduisent nécessairement avec d'autres. Ils y investissent leur ego, à tel point que certaines situations psychotiques sont manifestes dans quelques entreprises peu performantes. Les politiques conçues par les directions sont concrètement exécutées par tous les membres appartenant à l'entreprise dans le cadre de comportements tolérés et canalisés par la fixation des règles du jeu social interne. On retrouve l'idée de Chandler selon laquelle les structures sont au service des stratégies. Les fonctions de la direction générale seront donc :

1. À un moment donné et pour un couplage donné de la firme avec son environnement, de déterminer les formes organisationnelles les plus adaptées à la réalisation des objectifs d'allocation des ressources. Ce plan tient compte des capacités d'adaptation interne aux événements prévus et d'une certaine flexibilité caractérisée par le niveau de mobilité financière. Ce sont des changements et des variations (de type

1 au sens de Watzlawick,1975) qui ne peuvent intervenir qu'à l'intérieur des règles de fonctionnement existantes.
2. Pour une période donnée, de surveiller l'allocation des ressources et son adaptation à l'évolution de l'environnement.

En pratique, il s'agit du repérage des dysfonctionnements internes (diagnostic), de l'identification, de l'évaluation, et de la mise en œuvre d'activités nouvelles (gestion de projets) et de désinvestissement des activités non rentables. Les changements décidés dans ce cadre (de type 2 au sens de Watzlawick) concernent la modification des règles du jeu elles-mêmes. Ils sont d'un niveau logique supérieur à ceux qui s'opèrent à l'intérieur des règles du jeu.

Sur ces bases, les processus qui conduisent à la faillite relèvent d'abord des décisions ou des non-décisions des directions générales qui sont de créer et mener — et non pas seulement de déjouer — les règles de fonctionnement. Dans cette perspective, leur rôle n'est essentiel que pour des raisons logiques, même si, pour des raisons éthiques, il est satisfaisant de reconnaître la responsabilité ultime à celui qui détient la décision suprême de modifier les règles du jeu. Une première source (et non pas cause) d'erreur résulte du niveau de réalisme qui commande à la fois l'évaluation du fonctionnement quotidien et les conceptions stratégiques. Par exemple, des profits qui se dégradent constamment, des pertes qui s'accumulent, des investissements lourds qui ne seront jamais rentabilisés sont des indices de dysfonctionnements stratégiques. Une seconde source d'erreur résultera du niveau logique choisi lors de la réponse de la direction à une dégradation perçue. On retrouve les catégories de Watzlavick :

1. *Application à des dysfonctionnements de type 1 des solutions de type 2*. Par exemple, compenser les pertes résultant d'une mauvaise productivité (changement de type 1) en lançant un nouveau produit (changement de type 2) dont le premier effet sera d'augmenter les besoins de liquidités et, par conséquent, d'aggraver la situation.
2. *Application à des dysfonctionnements de type 2 des solutions de type 1*. Par exemple, développer la capacité de production à des fins d'économie d'échelle dans un marché en régression constante.

Certaines maximes résument bien la situation : « plus ça change, plus c'est pareil » ; « le problème, c'est la solution ». Les années qui précèdent un dépôt de bilan sont marquées par de nombreuses tentatives des directions pour sortir des cercles vicieux qui étouffent toutes leurs décisions et tous leurs plans. Faute de se situer au niveau logique approprié, les solutions mises en œuvre ne font que renforcer les dysfonctionnements qu'elles sont supposées éliminer. La mobilité financière se dégradera un peu plus à chaque fois qu'un plan aura échoué jusqu'au moment des expédients et de la « comptabilité créative » qui précèdent l'inéluctable dépôt du bilan. Autrement dit, ce qui importe est moins le contenu et la nature de la solution aux dysfonctionnements perçus que le choix du niveau logique auquel se situe la réponse (changement de type 1 ou 2). Évidemment, lorsque les directions sont assumées par des coalitions, leur réforme interne se pose d'autant plus. Pour préserver la coalition, l'engagement du processus de réforme sera d'autant plus tardif que la mobilité financière initiale sera élevée.

Lorsque les fonctions de surveillance (diagnostic et contrôle des processus de contrôle, analyse de la position stratégique) du système d'allocation des ressources en longue période sont mal exercées, les structures organisationnelles déterminent, sans limites réelles, le fonctionnement de la firme. Le volume de décisions discrétionnaires tend à décroître, réduisant progressivement la capacité d'adaptation de la firme. Selon la vitesse d'évolution de l'environnement et le niveau de mobilité initiale, la dégradation se produira plus ou moins lentement. Si une prise de conscience se développe, il n'est pas certain qu'elle puisse déboucher à tout coup sur l'engagement de la firme dans le processus de réforme approprié. Il se peut même que les solutions et mises en œuvre retenues renforcent et accélèrent la dégradation lorsque leur niveau logique est mal jugé. On déduit d'une telle perspective que le rétablissement financier d'une firme en difficulté, à savoir le rétablissement progressif de sa mobilité financière, dépendra de la capacité des directions à retrouver une vision stratégique et de l'imposer à travers les structures appopriées.

LE REDRESSEMENT DES FIRMES EN DIFFICULTÉ

La réussite dans le redressement de certaines firmes est parfois si spectaculaire que l'opinion publique n'est pas très loin de croire à quelques recettes magiques d'hommes providentiels. Pour quelques groupes industriels, la reprise d'affaires en difficulté est devenue la base même de leur expansion et de leurs stratégies. Lorsque la communauté financière dégage des fonds pour la constitution de firmes spécialisées dans le redressement d'affaires, arguant que les profits y sont rapides et moins risqués que pour les sociétés exploitant de hautes technologies, on peut penser qu'une certaine prévisibilité du résultat est devenue possible et calculable. Le modèle conceptuel développé représente le cadre des principales techniques de redressement.

Utiliser le répit offert par les procédures légales

La plupart des codes commerciaux prévoient que le dépôt du bilan d'une entreprise ouvre une période d'exploration de solutions moins radicales que la liquidation des actifs pour effacer la dette. Cette décision est en général soumise à l'appréciation des juges. Durant cette phase, les obligations financières antérieurement acceptées sont momentanément suspendues. Lorsque le moment de déposer le bilan est habilement choisi, la situation financière se trouve de ce fait considérablement améliorée. Si la direction est capable simultanément de limiter les pertes d'exploitation pour atteindre au moins le point de 'cash-flow zéro» et de déstocker et réaliser certains actifs, la trésorerie de l'entreprise peut s'améliorer rapidement, se créant ainsi les conditions d'un redressement par une mobilité financière momentanément retrouvée.

Introduire un nouveau management

Si l'entreprise n'interrompt pas ses livraisons et sert régulièrement ses clients, ceux-ci lui accorderont de nouveau et rapidement leur confiance. En effet, à court terme, la liberté de choix des clients est limitée, voire nulle, pour des considérations immédiates comme des emballages à changer, des stocks de matériels à entretenir, des pièces détachées à remplacer.

Les banques ont souvent avantage à promouvoir toute solution valable qui assure la survie de l'entreprise à court terme et, à long terme, leur procure un client reconnaissant. De plus, les procédures légales offrent toutes sortes de garanties qui protègent les « créanciers des créanciers ». C'est le rôle des services de contentieux des banques.

Si les fournisseurs sont payés comptant, ils continuent généralement d'assurer leurs livraisons. L'usage de l'assurance-crédit atténue les effets des faillites et assouplit les relations entre débiteurs et créanciers. La principale difficulté résulte du fractionnement des approvisionnements en petites quantités, du fait de l'étroitesse de la trésorerie, ce qui augmente le coût global des achats. Cet effet est amoindri lorsque le dépôt de bilan a été correctement géré et calculé.

La confiance du personnel est totalement subordonnée à la mise en place d'un nouveau management incarné, en général, par une nouvelle direction. Il est exceptionnel que la direction d'une affaire en dépôt de bilan conserve la confiance du personnel. Par contre, l'expérience montre que les cadres supérieurs sont peu affectés par la situation et qu'ils maintiennent et, parfois, améliorent leur position.

Mise en place temporaire

Le dépôt de bilan modifie fondamentalement la nature des activités de management. Le rôle des variables externes croît considérablement et certaines activités deviennent même totalement dépendantes de décisions extérieures à la firme. Les décisions sont totalement irréversibles et le management s'inscrit dans un processus « historique » déterminé par les procédures légales. L'instabilité s'installe là où régnait la stabilité : approvisionnements aléatoires, amplitude de l'effectif de présents, productivité en dents de scie,

etc. Les licenciements, plus lourds pour les services fonctionnels que pour les services d'exécution, provoquent la suppression d'activités de gestion jugées inutiles. Il est plus difficile qu'on ne le croit généralement de transférer aux échelons supérieurs des activités fonctionnnelles auxquelles elles ne sont nullement préparées. Pour répondre à tant d'aléas et d'incertitude, les caractéristiques des systèmes de management seront celles de la gestion des projets :
1. objectifs clairs et peu nombreux,
2. procédures de contrôle très simples dont le cycle d'application est court,
3. équipes temporaires et spécialistes de l'extérieur,
4. importance des liaisons entre décideurs et analystes,
5. nécessité de penser quantitatif et qualitatif,
6. planification récurrente,
7. traitement explicite de l'incertitude et de l'instabilité.

Au fur et à mesure que la situation s'améliorera, les procédures se complexifieront, leur cycle d'application s'allongera, les spécialistes de l'extérieur seront remplacés par des ressources internes. L'objectif est de retourner progressivement à la stabilité, à la réversibilité partielle des décisions, à la réduction des effets des variables exogènes, à la liberté d'action. Il est donc naturel de découvrir que les « redresseurs à succès » déclarent qu'ils utilisent des méthodes spécifiques mises en œuvre par des équipes spécialisées, que le nombre d'acquisition d'entreprises à redresser sera en pratique directement fonction de la disponibilité de ces équipes. On retrouve au sein de telles formes d'organisation la mentalité et l'esprit des sociétés d'ingénierie, dont l'activité est fonction elle aussi de la disponibilité des équipes de spécialistes.

Reconstituer sa mobilité financière

Seule la perspective réaliste d'un cash-flow substantiel sera de nature à décider les créanciers au vote d'un concordat qui, somme toute, s'analyse comme un arbitrage entre un sinistre immédiat et un sinistre potentiel. Le degré de confiance inspiré par le nouveau management et les garanties proposées aux créanciers pèseront dans leur décision plus que le détail des calculs prévisionnels.

La mobilité financière dépendra de la nature des remises de dettes accordées, de leurs montants et de reports d'impôts liés au cumul des pertes antérieures au dépôt de bilan. Pour la partie de la dette constituée de prêts, les remises de dettes se transformeront en un rééchelonnement qui n'aura aucun effet fiscal. La solution idéale est de convertir les prêts en capital. Pour la partie de la dette auprès des fournisseurs, toute remise de dette s'apparentera à un profit exceptionnel qui réduira d'autant le cumul des pertes et avancera la date de paiement des impôts, lesquels réduiront naturellement le cash-flow après impôt et la mobilité financière. Pour ces raisons, le calcul montre que, pour obtenir le cash-flow après impôt le plus élevé possible, il est avantageux de rembourser la totalité de la dette sur la plus longue période possible et non pas d'obtenir la remise de dette la plus grande et un échéancier de remboursement rapide.

En définitive, le concordat dépendra de la capacité de négociation des dirigeants, de la crédibilité de leur plan, des garanties offertes. En raison de leur impact sur l'emploi, la situation des grandes entreprises est de fait examinée avec bienveillance par rapport aux petites et moyennes entreprises. Une fois le concordat acquis, la survie sera liée à la maîtrise du processus de management qui replacera la firme sur une trajectoire stabilisée. L'expérience enseigne clairement que la qualité des hommes, notamment de la haute direction, domine toutes les autres dimensions (commerciale, financière, technique). L'histoire de Iaccoca et de Chrysler en témoigne.

Comme l'arbre cache la forêt, la recherche des ressorts de l'excellence — à la mode ces dernières années — masque au chercheur la réalité du tissu socio-économique faite d'un petit nombre d'organisations qui se sont distinguées par leur compétence au milieu d'une masse d'autres dont les résultats les situent dans « une honnête moyenne ». S'il est nécessaire de s'intéresser aux critères de l'excellence, il l'est tout autant de faire fonctionner les organisations avec les gens tels qu'ils sont. Paradoxalement, les qualités demandées aux chercheurs sont plus exigeantes pour effectuer ce travail que celles nécessaires à la compréhension des facteurs rationalisateurs d'un nombre très réduit de firmes ayant réussi. Autrement dit, il est plus difficile de comprendre pourquoi « ça ne marche pas » que « pourquoi ça marche », car le nombre de dimensions à prendre en considération augmente très rapidement. Quelques frontières restent encore à franchir.

BIBLIOGRAPHIE

AUGER, R., LALONDE, C., « Le redressement de la gestion ou la gestion du redressement : un processus possible », *Revue de gestion des petites et moyennes organisations*, vol. 1, (1), 1982.

ALTMAN, E. I., *Corporate Financial Distress*, Wiley and Sons, 1983.

CASTAGNA, A. D., MATLOCSY, « The Prediction of Corporate Failure : Testing the Australian Experience », *Australian Journal of Management*, Australia, vol. 6, (1), juin 1981, 23-50.

CASEY, C. J. Jr, « The Usefulness of Accounting Ratios for Subjects' Prediction of Corporate Failure : Replication and Extension », *Journal of Accounting Research*, vol. 18, (2), automne 1980, 603-613

DECLERCK, R., DEBOURSE, J.-P., NAVARRE, C., *Méthode de direction générale*, Éditions Hommes et Techniques, 1984.

LALONDE, C., « Modèle de recherche sur le comportement du propriétaire dirigeant failli », *Revue de gestion des petites et moyennes organisations*, vol. 1, (2), 1983.

MILLER, D., FRIESEN P. H., *Organizations : A Quantum View*, Prentice-Hall, 1984.

NAVARRE, C., « Propositions pour une méthodologie du diagnostic », *Cahiers de l'ISMEA*, Série Sciences de Gestion, n° 4, 1984.

SALERNO, F., « L'élimination des produits nonperformants », *Revue française de gestion*, novembre-décembre 1983.

SALERNO, F., « L'élimination des produits non performants », *Revue française de gestion*, novembre-décembre 1983.

SALERNO, F., « Comment gérer la mort d'un produit ? », *Revue française de gestion*, mars-avril 1981.

SIMON, H. A., *La Science des systèmes*, EPI, 1974.

ZIMMER, I. A,. « Lens Study of the Prediction of Corporate Failure by Bank Loan Officers », *Journal of Accounting Research*, vol.18, (2), automne 1980, 629-636.

WATZLAWICK, P., WEAKLAND, J., FISCH, R., *Changements, paradoxes et psychothérapie*, Paris, Éditions du Seuil, « Points », 1975.

WEICK, K. E., *The Social Psychology of Organizing*, 2 éd., Addison Wesley, 1979.

Public Management
Gestion du secteur public

The Twins Are Not Identical: Management and Management Education in the Public and Private Sectors

RICK VAN LOON

The public sector, no less than the private, is engaged in a never-ending quest for self-improvement. This preoccupation leads to a steady parade of management consultants, often trained in the private sector and imbued with its values, techniques and mythology, as well as to a large in-house collection of reformers. Periodically in most large public sector organizations, and certainly in the federal government, it also leads to a major review of procedures and systems. The most recent instance in Ottawa was the 1979 Royal Commission on Financial Management and Accountability chaired by Alan Lambert, a former president of the Toronto-Dominion Bank. Its predecessor 15 years before was the Royal Commission on Government Organization, chaired by Grant Glassco, an eminent private sector accountant. Either commission could have used as its motto the words of the Glassco Commission:

> The immediate aim of the techniques of management developed for industry is to attain the organization's goals with the greatest possible economy of effort. Consequently most of the techniques of management developed for business can be adapted to governments, due allowance being made for the different tests by which economy and productivity must ultimately be judged.

The attempt to import private sector techniques into the public sector has roots stretching back to the pre-World-War I Scientific Management movement and continues today with the attempt to apply techniques such as MBO, zero-base budgeting and assorted computer-based management models to the public sector. A parallel subindustry has sprouted in the academic world devoted to comparing the management processes and environment in the public and private sectors with a view to determining the extent of comparability and its implications both for management theory and for management education. This article is situated in that tradition. In it I will turn over a previously plowed field in the light of more recent literature and experience in order to draw some conclusions pertinent to the teaching of public policy and management in Canadian schools and faculties of administration.[1]

My conclusions with respect to comparability should not be surprising to students of the issue. I would like to be able to believe that they would be equally unsurprising to purveyors of private sector management techniques, be they teachers or consultants. On that score, however, I have no illusions. As successive waves of Royal Commission and consultants' reports and academic and journalistic articles only too amply demonstrate, there is no shortage of people willing to apply private sector nostrums to public sector situations in a frequently misguided and sometimes quite deleterious attempt to cure real or imagined problems of public sector management.

The conclusions, quite in line with the contingency school of management studies, will be that "it all depends." It depends on the type of agency and the agency objectives and it depends on the stage we are considering in the management process. But we should also note that there are some overarching features of the public sector environment which suffuse all aspects of public sector management and which will ultimately defeat any intemperate attempt to apply techniques suited to one sector in the other.

We will look first at those overarching features of the public sector management environment. We will then proceed to consider specific differences at the several major stages of the management process before finally drawing conclusions for those of us who seek to give advice either as consultants or, more particularly, as teachers of those who manage.

OVERARCHING DIFFERENCES

In one of his recent writings, the dean of Canadian professors of public administration, J.E. Hodgetts, asks us to confront the question of whether:

> . . .the bureaucratic values of economy, efficiency and effectiveness can be melded with the political values of representation and responsibility, and yet still retain their salutary influence on the work-a-day world of bureaucracy.

Hodgetts thus raises squarely a central dilemma of public administration, for if the values of the public servant and of his "political master" are at odds, a tension is introduced into public administration which has no direct counterpart in the private sector. Paul Pross highlights the difficulty this situation imposes for those who

---

1. The issue of comparability suffuses a great deal of the public administration literature and informs many of the profession's deliberations.

seek to develop a usable body of knowledge about public sector management by noting that:

> ...the tensions inherent in running a democratic state through bureau-cratic structures are so great that any body of scholarship that seeks to understand the phenomena must itself be prone to intense and critical tendencies.

Finally, Hodgetts, in common with many others, notes, "nor is this problem of blending potentially conflicting values rendered more amenable to solution by trends in the sixties that called not so much for a responsible bureaucracy but insisted that it be more directly responsive to its clientele publics, many of which, finding representative institutions wanting, were clamoring for "participatory democracy." Since the clamor of special interests, far from diminishing in the 1980s, has redoubled, this conflict has equally redoubled.

We will consider again at different points in this paper the nature of goals in public sector organizations, but it should be noted here that, as a result of the tensions outlined above, both goals and values in public sector organizations are multiple, potentially conflicting, and potentially quite different at different levels in the organization. The public sector manager, particularly the senior one, may therefore be sent in more directions than his private sector counterpart will ever know.

The public sector manager also manages in a goldfish bowl compared to the privacy in which most private sector management decisions are worked out. While the rubric of ministerial accountability holds that the minister alone is answerable in public for whatever transpires in his or her department, the reality, particularly in those departments such as Indian Affairs or Fisheries or Agriculture which have active clienteles with very specific interests, is that the bureaucrat is very much on the front line and in the public's eye. In addition all aspects of public management are considered fair game for inquiring journalists, and freedom of information legislation makes the bulk of the written material used in public administration available to whoever may demand it. Few private sector managers face such a glare of publicity — and when they do it seems to them anomalous and most unwelcome.

Another fundamental difference between management in the two sectors is the scope of action available to managers. In the private sector the assumption may be safely made that if an action is not precluded by law (and, one might hope, by the dictates of managerial wisdom) then it may be taken. In the public sector the assumption may be made that if an action is not sanctioned by law, it may not be undertaken — and there is almost always a financial officer or a central agency policeman watching to ensure that it is not. Public sector management then sometimes seems like a lifelong version of children's "May I," with the caller having an extraordinary propensity to say, "No, you may not." Again J.E. Hodgetts puts it well by envisaging the dilemma of the private sector manager suddenly dropped into the public sector, where he would find:

> . . .all sorts of measures to protect against the pervasive political context in which he now operates. From taxi tips to building contracts his life would be cluttered by rules and procedures, still pervaded by the Gladstonian ethos of penny wise and pound foolish but all with the perception that these constraints were deemed necessary because the dollar being spent is not the contribution of shareholders but the compulsory levy of Citizens' purses.

The legal authority required of all public sector activities may be viewed as but a subset of the broader notions of accountability. Accountability in the public sector is usually used to refer to the requirement that the public servant answer, through hierarchical authority, to his or her minister, who is in turn accountable to Parliament, which is, in turn, ultimately accountable to the people. Legal authority then assures that accountability. We have already noted that in an era of participatory democracy and special interest clients the notion is stretched in fact to include the accountability of public servants to "their" clients, thus ensuring that the public servant may be stretched at least two ways in his or her real reporting relationships. However, too much should not be made of this difference; after all, the private sector manager is also ultimately responsible both to hierarchical authority and to the client or customer and the difference may be more formal than real.

In both sectors too there may be pathologies of accountability. The private sector manifestation would be an excessive degree of control over expenditures by corporate control functions. The public sector, however, as befits the greater saliency of accountability and legal authority, has developed excess accountability to great heights through the mechanism of the central agency. Different agencies are often spawned in government for each element of managerial accountability with the result that the public sector manager is beset at every step with a different overseer demanding that due process be fulfilled. One senior line manager, speaking on the basis of his experience at both senior levels of government, has remarked:

> The time has clearly come, indeed it is overdue, for fresh decisions to be made as to where authority is to be exercised in many important sectors of management — either in central agencies or in departments, but certainly not in both.

His suspicion that the answer might well be "both — and more of each" is, alas, all too often well founded. It is a frequent observation that there are multiple and conflicting goals behind every government program and that this diversity will tend to confound the applicability of private sector management functions at virtually every step. Almost all public programs have not only the ostensible goals of the program — serving a clientele — but also such important goals as increasing the visibility of the delivering government (and minister), providing an appropriate regional distribution of benefits, and avoiding discrimination (while also frequently providing affirmative action in redress for past discrimination!). Thus a program such as vocational training under the National Training Act may be required to:

1. train people for employment opportunities,
2. keep people in "holding tank" courses in order to lower measured rates of unemployment,
3. support the community college system,
4. provide regional redistribution of money and opportunities,
5. provide visibility for local MPs,
6. give hope to chronically unemployed citizens,
7. provide a justification for the continued existence of a substantial bureaucracy,
8. maintain general support for and visibility of the government delivering the programs.

In fact, all of these goals and probably several others too do pertain, and the program must be managed so as to accomplish at least some minimum level of satisfaction with respect to each. While it is simplistic in the extreme to assume that all private organizations have only the simple goal defined by "the bottom line," or that all public sector programs have as complex a set as do NTA training programs, there is, on average, certainly a greater diversity in the public sector, making the managerial balancing act arguably considerably more complex.

Another "all-encompassing mythology" overarches the public sector. No matter what the cost, it must be managed as a simple entity. Whether it is in the name of equity, equality, consistency, or protection from the assumed predations of patronage, a common set of rules must apply, administered by the central agencies. Having imposed this albatross upon itself, the public sector in Canada and elsewhere then sets about creating semi-independent organizational forms to try to avoid the rigidities. Naturally the central agencies are challenged thereby into trying to reimpose the control which these flexible formats impose. The analogy often used is that of attempting to manage a very large and diverse conglomerate with a single set of rules.

All of these overarching features of public sector management are but manifestations of the impact of the political environment on public administration. The degree of this impact will depend on where one is within the public sector. The job of the postman or the customs officer is not primarily defined by the political environment. By contrast the deputy minister of a department with major policy concerns must constantly be aware of his or her minister's and the government's needs, both programmatic and political.

The degree of imposition of politics on the senior public administrator's world varies with the point in the electoral cycle, peaking in the year before an election is called and being lowest in the first or second year of a mandate, but it is ever-present and no senior public servant ever forgets that aspect of the working environment.

THE MANAGERIAL FUNCTIONS

In this section we will look more closely at the major managerial functions in an attempt to further define the similarities and differences between the two sectors. Although there is an array of possibilities for describing the functions of management, we will use here five broad categories.

Priority Setting, Planning, and Budgeting

At no stage among managerial functions does the political environment have a greater impact than when priorities are set, overall plans made, and budgets struck. The establishment of public sector priorities is, after all, eminently political in nature, and the subsequent planning and budgeting stages must reflect that situation. The senior public servant, whether he or she is responsible for a federal, provincial, or municipal department, a hospital, or a schoolboard, must work closely with and under the direction of the elected politicians in an attempt to provide the requisite services, advising the politician with a combination of political sensitivity and organizational intelligence. There are broad private sector parallels in the relationships between senior management and boards of directors, but the analogy is far from exact, given the nature of the politicians' exposure to the broader social environment and the much fuller commitment to his or her position which the politician brings compared to the infrequent attentions of most boards of directors.

Another significant difference is the immense inertia which lies behind most public sector programs. It is extremely difficult to make more than marginal changes in the overall priorities of government programs, in large part because the program clientele becomes dependent on the existence of the program and will produce protests of an intensity to terrify elected politicians if the program is threatened. Thus, no matter how committed to change they may be, public administrators often become locked into a program structure which is extremely difficult to change.

At no point in the life of the manager does the impact of this tendency of programs to persist, combined with the extreme accountability requirements of public sector programming, become more acute than during budget preparation. Any large municipal or provincial government will have at least a two-year budgetary cycle, and the federal system encompasses a two-year cycle of specific planning within a broader five-year cycle. Typically in a public sector budget the funds are separated by specific program into "votes" and cannot be transferred from one area to another without approval at least of an executive committee and most often of the legislature or council as well. The rigidities introduced by this situation would be anathema to the private sector manager. Then, as noted earlier, the public sector manager will have to pass through several levels of authority before he can expect to actually disburse the money in accordance with the plans, a point we will return to below.

While this by no means exhausts the nature of the impact of the political environment on priority setting, planning, and budgeting, it may suffice to indicate that in many respects the public sector manager operates in a much more constrained world than does his private sector counterpart.

Organization Building and Personnel Management

The next two managerial functions may be considered together since the process of building an organization is pre-eminently one of gathering people together. In the public sector it is frequently observed that over the last decade of constrained bureaucratic growth no resource has been nearly so scarce as a person-year. The process of building an organization therefore tends to become one of scrounging from central agencies the appropriate (minimal) number of person-years, battling for appropriate job classification levels, and then searching an increasingly meager pool of personnel resources (many of the best and brightest having long since been recruited by the private sector) for bodies to fill the positions. If a mistake is made, the exigencies of strong unions, and a job tenure system that provides that dismissal must be "for cause" proven far beyond any shadow of doubt, will ensure that the manager will have to live with the mistake for a very long time. The requirements of representation of all sorts of categories of individuals in the system will ensure, perhaps quite appropriately, that the manager will have to pay heed to constructing a reasonably representative collection of people. The open competition dictates of the merit system will mean that the manager will have to consider a very large number of people or, more likely, develop tricks to partially subvert the system. All of these processes are slow and complex so that even if all goes perfectly, creating and filling a normal position in the federal public sector will not take less than 12 weeks.

To compound the problems further, there are two agencies with which our manager must deal with respect to personnel matters: the Treasury Board which deals with job classification and the terms and conditions of employment, and the Public Service Commission, which deals with recruitment and staffing and, under direction of Treasury Board, with training. While other jurisdictions have managed to produce somewhat simpler models, there are still complications beyond most private sector manager's wildest nightmares. Nor is the situation made better by the particular application of collective bargaining in the public sector, where all authority belongs to the remote Treasury Board which acts as employer for the whole public service, thus ensuring that the line manager has virtually no control over the terms and conditions of employment of his or her people.

Program Implementation

Much of what has already been said bears upon program implementation. However, it is worth emphasizing in general that the control a public sector manager can exert over employees and other resources is much less than that which the private sector manager can exert. The employee is beholden to the manager for the immediate situation in which he or she works, but the manager lacks almost any overall control over employee salaries or career paths. Since the employer, in departmental situations if not in crown corporations, is the public service rather than a particular department, the employee is constantly encouraged to look around for other opportunities to advance in his or her career. Since competitions are essentially wide open to all public servants under the merit system, anyone may apply and must be at least considered. Career planning by the organization is therefore essentially impossible. For better or for worse the individual employee, at manager's or other levels, is on his or her own.

Of course the personnel function will not be the only aspect of implementation affected by the political environment. Other resources (supplies, facilities, or services), must be acquired in accordance with strict rules and procedures laid down by Treasury Board. While these no doubt serve the interests of rectitude they do not necessarily serve those of flexibility or efficiency. In Canada, due attention will also have to be paid to the appropriate regional distribution of benefits and even of offices. Appropriate visibility for the symbols of whatever government is involved will be important. Care will have to be taken not to offend any potential target groups. In extreme (and relatively rare) cases the partisan identification of beneficiaries will be important.

It is important, however, not to exaggerate the partisan impact for, as noted earlier, the line delivery of many of the largest public sector programs is not unduly influenced by the immediate political environment, particularly where broad national services such as the postal service or unemployment insurance are involved.

Thus, provided that the service itself does not become a political issue (as was the case with Revenue Canada in 1984), the line manager can usually implement programs without great concern about the immediate political environment. But even then, many of the peculiarities introduced by the extreme requirements for accountability and the particular nature of public service personnel management will have an impact.

Evaluation and Feedback

The evaluation of public sector programs normally revolves around the concepts of efficiency and effectiveness. The problems inherent in moving from private sector to public sector measurement of these have been outlined by John Langford. With respect to efficiency, he notes:

> The inappropriateness of simple efficiency measures for public and quasi-public corporations is reflected in the misleading fixation with waste ... and the irrelevance of such measures to corporations delivering more overtly public services (e.g. education, health care). The obvious move is to some recognition of social benefit ...

With respect to the related but not identical concept of effectiveness he notes:

> The discussion and measurement of effectiveness (the relationship between the desired output and the benefits received) or cost-effectiveness, already intrinsically difficult due to uncertainty, the unavailability or high cost of data and high manpower requirements, is further complicated by the problems associated with ranking goals and establishing the rules for making trade-offs in conflict situations in which not only are there multiple goals, but there are also multiple proponents or principles to interpret or set goals.

Langford goes on to suggest reforms but these need not concern us directly here. For us the point is simply that, given all of the peculiarities outlined above, any attempt to evaluate either the efficiency or the effectiveness of public sector organizations by the criteria used for the private sector will lead to misleading results. Again for the manager, an appreciation of the modifications which must be made because of the peculiarities of the public sector are important.

THE IMPLICATION FOR MANAGEMENT EDUCATION

In spite of the deep differences in the management environment in the public and private sectors there are very wide areas of similarity. The basic functions are essentially the same ones even if the two environments make them significant variants. The actual building of a highway, a hospital, or an airport is susceptible to the same techniques as the building of a factory or an office tower. The motivation of employees is still essentially a problem of human relations, and leadership is similar in both sectors. Accounting and the actual details of financial planning are broadly similar. Indeed, the apparent indifference of the public sector in Canada as to whether it recruits MBAs (indeed even a preference for MBAs) suggests that many involved in public sector management see more similarities than differences.

Both the similarities and the differences should be reflected in management training programs. For the most part in Canada they are, since the actual courses followed by MBA and MPA students tend to share a broad core of disciplines and techniques such as economics, accounting, human resource management, managerial statistics, project management, and the like. Where education for employment in the two sectors should and does differ is in the much greater emphasis accorded the political environment and formal government structures in MPA programs or in the options selected by MBA students aiming to become senior public sector managers. Thus courses dealing with strategic management, planning, budgeting, and the environment of the manager tend to differentiate between education for the two sectors. Whether the education takes place in a school or faculty primarily oriented towards the public or private sector is likely not of critical importance provided that the public-sector-oriented student is made aware of the particular impact of managing in the public sector and does not go forth into the world of public administration expecting to apply the techniques of private sector management uncritically to the public sector environment. The awareness of the impact of the environment should also be sufficiently subtle that the manager will be able to recognize the differential impact of the political environment on different types of public sector organizations; running a local school board is not the same as running a national department, and the education of the manager should equip him or her to recognize the differences and to deal with them appropriately.

Somewhere between the conception of public and private sectors as two solitudes and the assumption that managerial techniques developed for the private sector can be applied with little or no amendment to the sometimes bewilderingly complex world of the public sector manager lies reality. The nature of that reality depends on the type of organization as well as on such shifting parameters as the point in the political cycle and even the latest poll results of the party in power. If we can equip public sector managers and those who advise them to recognize that and to make an appropriate marriage between the dictates of efficiency and effectiveness and political reality we will greatly improve the cause of management.

REFERENCES

HODGETTS, J.E., "Values in the Administration of Public Affairs," Canadian Public Administration, Vol. 25, (4), Winter 1982, p. 474.

HODGETTS, J.E., "Managing Money and People in the Private Sector, Similarities and Differences," Canadian Public Administration, Vol. 26, (1), Spring 1983, p. 81.

LANGFORD, J.W., "Public Corporations in the 1980's: Moving from Rhetoric to Analysis," Canadian Public Administration, Vol. 25, (4), Winter 1982, p. 635.

MANSBRIDGE, S.H., "The Lambert Report," Canadian Public Administration, Vol. 22, (4), Winter 1979, pp. 531-540.

PROSS, P., Canadian Public Administration, Vol. 21, (3), Fall 1978, p. 451.

Report of the Royal Commission on Government Organization, V.I., Ottawa, Queen's Printer, 1962, pp. 46-47.

WILSON, V.S., "The Influence of Organization Theory in Canadian Public Administration," Canadian Public Administration, Vol. 25, (4), Winter 1982, p. 555.

Uncertainty, Competition and Public Policy

STYLIANOS PERRAKIS

By the age standards of economic science the problems discussed in this essay are rather old, going back more than a century. Indeed, one can safely say that the general policies that we will deal with — the control of industrial concentration and/or the regulation of the conduct of "large" firms — were initially motivated not by economic efficiency concerns, but by the normal desire of a democratic society to avoid the accumulation of too much power within one economic entity. It was only much later that economic theory gave an analytical superstructure to these policies, and it was only very recently that the sophisticated tools of economic science were used in order to throw new light upon some old but persistent problems associated with the application of the policies. The outcomes of these efforts, most of which happened during the last decade, have received the name of the New Industrial Organization (IO), to distinguish them from the old IO discipline, which was dominated by noneconomists (especially lawyers). It is within this New IO that the research described in this essay is situated.

Compared with the big debates generated within the general public by the major contemporary macroeconomic issues such as monetarism, taxation, and the size of the public deficit, the controversies created by the New IO have remained relatively unknown. Their immediate impact upon the average citizen is relatively small, even though their cumulative effect may be very important, while their impact upon particular groups is crucial. For instance, the airline deregulation movement of the late seventies had relatively modest results for the average consumer by reducing his travel bill, but its effect upon the airline industry was major, while the cumulative effect of deregulation in all sectors is undoubtedly very important for every citizen. Yet the interest aroused by such issues in Canada is minimal, in spite of the existence of a significant fund of experience about their results in the United States. To give but one example, the major report on regulated industries, issued a few years ago by the Economic Council of Canada, was left to be savaged by special interest groups, who felt threatened by its contents, without any defense from spokesmen for the general public, whose interests it was supposed to represent. Yet, it is undeniable that, had its recommendations been implemented, it would have saved the average consumer several hundred dollars a year in the form of lower prices in transportation, telecommunications, travel, and food. But the complexity of the issues, the highly technical nature of the discussion, and the relative lack of understanding of the problems involved even among economists, let alone among the general public, have deprived the report of the crucial political support necessary for the implementation of the reforms.

This essay gives a summary of research work related to these topics, work that has extended over more than ten years and has covered several aspects of public policy within the New IO framework. It has used inputs from several disciplines, from management science and finance, as well as from conventional economic theory, but it has evolved around one consistent theme, that of uncertainty. It has covered methodological contributions, empirical investigations, and policy-related analyses, but the original aspect in all these works has been the effect of uncertainty. That effect can be broadly summarized as the need to take certain more or less irreversible decisions with but an imperfect forecast of the future consequences of these decisions. These imperfections, and the modifications that they impose upon the way problems are perceived and structured, have sometimes unexpected consequences upon the existing wisdom, the conventional way that economic decisions are taken if uncertainty is ignored.

The next section presents the main framework of economic analysis pertaining to the traditional IO themes of regulation and competition policy. The third section discusses the contributions of the New IO methodology to these old but persistent problems, while the fourth section makes special reference to uncertainty and the methodological contributions of this research. This last section also presents a concrete case study where these contributions were applied within the framework of the Canadian economy.

COMPETITION AND REGULATION

As is well known, the basic determinant of industrial structure is the relationship of the minimum efficient firm size, the smallest unit that allows the firm to reach minimum cost production, to total industry demand. At one extreme this demand is sufficiently large to accommodate a very large number of firms, able to exploit fully their economies of scale, i.e., to operate at minimum cost; then the industry has a competitive structure. At the other extreme the minimum cost operation can take place at a level of production that is equal to or larger than the total industry demand; the industry is then a natural monopoly. In between we have the most commonly encountered cases, where there are only a few firms (oligopoly) that are able to operate at minimum cost. Figure I shows this configuration.

Figure I — Industrial Configurations

Once a given industry was situated on the above diagram the policy to be adopted towards it was more or less automatically determined according to the "old" IO rules. Since the obvious objective was to have minimum cost production together with low prices for the consumer, a competitive structure was able to achieve these objectives by itself. By contrast, there was an apparent conflict of the two objectives in the case of a natural monopoly, which was resolved by imposing regulation upon the industry, such that the firm would still produce at minimum cost while its prices would be limited by the regulatory authority. They were to be set in such a way that total cost of production would be covered, including a "normal" rate of profit (or cost of capital).

The major difficulties arose with the intermediate oligopoly cases, those in which the industry size could accommodate only a "small" number of minimum cost firms. These cases presented a crucial indeterminacy, for it was not at all clear how the group of firms in the industry would behave. They could, for instance, compete aggressively against each other, a conduct that would give the consumers the benefit of low prices. Alternatively, they could fix their prices and market shares collusively and thus guarantee the maximum possible profits for their group, together with high prices for consumers.

The basic aims of public policy towards oligopolies[1] under this "old" IO framework were to make sure that the behavior of the firms conformed to the competitive, rather than the collusive mode. A large body of law was developed, proscribing certain types of conduct such as direct price-fixing, and regulating other types such as parallel price-setting behavior. Simultaneously with these actions, there were efforts to discourage more concentrated industrial structures, by regulating mergers or imposing divestitures on dominant firms.

This particular approach to the effects of a given industrial structure remained all-persuasive for several decades, until approximately the end of the 1950s. The main problems with it came from the need to balance the traditional judicial safeguards of the rights of the accused with the necessity to infer unlawful activity in the presence of acts that were detrimental to the public interest, but

---

1. These policy aims were broadly similar in Canada and the U.S., even though they were pursued much more vigorously in the latter country.

without any proofs of criminal actions as such. Other drawbacks came from the necessarily ambiguous definitions of the limits, beyond which monopoly may be inferred as being the cost-minimizing structure, and from the lengthy nature of the court cases, which stretched over several years.

The main effect of the New IO upon this state of things was to change the emphasis of public scrutiny from the static to the dynamic and from the short to the long run. Methodologically it represented a massive application of the analytical tools of modern microeconomics to a detailed examination of firm behavior in the face of external economic conditions, including public policies. On a practical level, it constituted a general re-examination of the perceived doctrines of the previous decades, including an emphasis on the flexibility of public policies and their tailoring to the needs of specific situations. Its main tenets will be briefly outlined below, with special emphasis placed on the role played by uncertainty.

THE NEW INDUSTRIAL ORGANIZATION
AND THE ROLE OF ENTRY

The focus on industrial concentration as the key variable of competition policy glosses over several important aspects of the process. The idealized versions of the firm and the industry that were used in the various versions of the old IO models were found to be clearly unsatisfactory when it came to applying these models to concrete cases. For instance, firms in many industries were found to produce not a single, homogeneous product, but several commodities; products were found to differ with respect to time of production, location or quality; industry demands were interrelated; etc. All these brought important qualifications to the method of application of traditional IO policies. The introduction of more elaborate and sophisticated models to accommodate such difficulties took place gradually and slowly, and formed one part of the developments of the New IO. By far the most important such developments, though, were those dealing with the effects of new entry in the industry, and with the impact that such potential competition has upon existing firms. This impact brings qualitative change in the policy prescriptions, as distinct from less fundamental changes in the way the prescriptions were applied.

Entry is stimulated by the existence of supranormal profits in the industry. It attracts new firms who wish to share in these profits, to the detriment of the firms that are already in the industry. The latter, therefore, will take various actions in order to forestall such entry.

Here lies the fundamental divergence of this school of thought from the older, more traditional IO approaches. Some of the actions that are taken to prevent entry by new competitors may, in fact, bring the industry to a state of conduct that is highly desirable from the public interest point of view. Such actions are, for instance, the voluntary limitation of prices and profits in order to eliminate the incentive for new entry. Thus, according to this theory, the state does not need to worry about cartels, price-fixing, and other anti-competitive actions by firms in oligopolistic industries, since such firms are bound to be forced by new entry either to abandon such actions or to see their positions eroded by new entrants. Given the major expenses and lengthy judicial actions of law enforcement in the area of competition policy, it is easy to see the appeal of this new approach if it is, in fact, justified.

A symmetrical argument has also been made on the other side of public policy, that of regulation. For it should be remembered that regulation is a two-sided contract, in which the public authority has the right to limit the economic freedom of the regulated firm, but also undertakes the obligation to protect it from any would-be competitors. Hence, regulated industries imply almost always exclusive franchises for the regulated firm or group of firms. The effectiveness of public regulation in limiting prices while simultaneously preserving industry efficiency and quality of service has been seriously questioned in recent years. The temptation is therefore strong to abandon simultaneously the attempts to regulate prices and service and the protection granted to the regulated firm from potential competition. It is argued that such a competition, arising from new entrants or from the desire to keep entrants out, will result in a more efficient policing of firm behavior than anything achievable by public action.

The crucial question in this approach is, of course, the anticipatory reaction of the existing firms to potential entrants, and the desirability or not of this reaction from the public interest point of view. It has been pointed out that there are most definitely undesirable actions that a firm or group of firms can take that will result in keeping out any would-be competitors. Such actions are, for instance, the building-up of plants larger than necessary to serve existing demand in order to have the opportunity to "flood the market" with products and drive the price down if a new competitor comes into the picture, thus condemning him to ruin. These actions are essentially investments by the existing firm in the erection of barriers to entry of would-be competitors, barriers that may have ultimately undesirable consequences for consumers.

Hence, the role of economic analysis in this context is to identify cases where barriers to entry of the undesirable type are feasible and profitable from the point of view of the existing firms. From the point of view of public policy this role is invaluable, given that it separates the sectors where public intervention is mandated from those where potential entry will be effective in bringing out desirable firm behavior. Economic analysis has performed its task by modelling the interaction between potential entrants and existing firms by means of management science techniques such as dynamic programming and game theory. For instance, Figure II presents a decision tree, showing the conditions under which firms will invest in barriers to entry.[2]

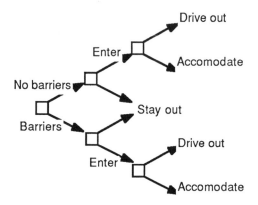

Figure II — Conditions under which firms will invest in barriers to entry

The three decision nodes represent the decisions to build barriers or not, to enter or not given the previous decision and, last, whether to drive the entrant out by imposing losses on him or accommodate him by sharing the market. The optimal decisions depend on the pair of terminal payoffs (profits) in each branch for the existing firm and the entrant. In general, it is thought that in the absence of barriers the existing firm will find it more profitable to accommodate rather than drive out the entrant, and the entrant will find it more profitable to enter rather than stay out. By contrast, it will be more profitable in the presence of barriers for the entrant to stay out, given that it will be more profitable for the existing firm to drive him out if he enters. Hence, there will be entry in the absence of barriers, and no entry when barriers are erected. The final decision whether to build barriers or not depends on a comparison of the profits of the existing firm in the two states: without barriers and with competition, or with barriers and without competition. It should be noted that the erection of barriers to entry is not a costless process, and that the existing firm will have to sink resources in an amount sufficient to convince opponents that it will find it more profitable to fight rather than accommodate entry.

---

2. This figure was adapted from Dixit (1982).

Such barriers take the form of building plants with larger capacity than justified by existing or projected demand, of "excessive" advertising in order to create product differentiation by brand or trade name, of the proliferation of products differentiated by quality, etc. The main difficulty here is to determine the point at which the line is crossed between serving the customers' need for information and product diversity and trying to keep out a competitor. Such a difficulty is compounded by the presence of uncertainty, as detailed in the next section.

THE ROLE OF UNCERTAINTY IN THEORY AND PRACTICE

As mentioned earlier, because of the need to take certain decisions whose consequences are only imperfectly known, uncertainty cannot be ignored in economics. In the context of entry and the role that it plays in the New IO, uncertainty is present at each one of the nodes of the decision tree in Figure II: the payoffs are not known precisely at the time the decisions to enter or to erect barriers to entry must be taken. Such decisions are, on the other hand, irreversible, since they involve the expenditure of funds that cannot be subsequently recovered if things do not turn out as expected.

Uncertainty in the payoffs comes from many sources: variability of sales, due to the business cycle; variability of costs; technological change that introduces new processes or products; changing customer tastes; etc. The task of the business firm is to estimate, on the basis of all available information, the contribution of all these sources to the variability of its net cash flows. The firm ends up with a projected probability, distribution of these cash flows, given a decision to enter or to deter entry by erecting barriers. In practice this analysis takes place by concentrating on one source of variability and assuming that the other sources are not important enough to change the derived results; demand variability was the source considered in this research.

A related issue that arises here is that of the objectives of decision-making where uncertainty is present. Indeed, while under certainty it suffices to compare the cash flows in different situations and to choose the action that brings the largest one, it is not clear how such a comparison will take place under uncertainty. One possible approach is to compare the expected value of these cash flows with the average cash flow on the basis of the available information: this approach ignores the decision-maker's attitudes towards risk. Another possibility is to substitute the cash flow into a given function that represents such attitudes and to take the expectation of that function. Still another method is to subtract a given amount from the expectation, an amount that depends on the cash flows probability distribution and is supposed to represent the penalty that the decision-maker is willing to pay to avoid risk. All these possibilities have been used at various times in the course of this research, and the derived conclusions have turned out to be fairly robust with respect to the approach.

Figure III shows the type of economic modelling that was applied in order to distinguish the important factors in the decisions to erect or not erect barriers to entry. These barriers took the form of investment in plant size large enough to inflict losses on any would-be competitor. The solid lines represent the investment and resulting cash flows when no competitor is going to enter the sector in the foreseeable future, while the broken lines are the same investment and cash flows of the existing firm if a competitor enters one period later. All solid lines are longer than the corresponding broken ones, reflecting the fact that a larger capital commitment is necessary to deter new entry than is justified by demand. Similarly, the cash flows during future periods are not known with certainty at time zero, the time the investment takes place. The existing firm must, therefore, decide whether the increased expectations of future cash inflows balance the extra funds needed to keep the competition out.

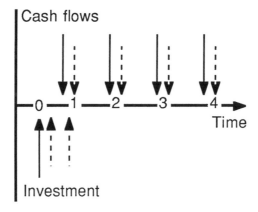

Figure III — Type of economic modelling

The results of the analysis show clearly the effects of uncertainty, even when the decision-maker's attitude towards risk is ignored. To begin with, there are certain circumstances under which the existing firm will find it in its interest to overinvest in order to keep the competitors out, circumstances that do not appear under certainty. Second, the erection of such barriers to entry will not be found profitable if the existing firm does not enjoy any cost advantages over its competitors, unless the firm size corresponding to minimum cost production is "large." The incentive is magnified when this firm size exceeds the "low" tail of the industry demand distribution.

What are the practical implications of this analysis for Canadian economic policy? To begin with, and on a general level, the small size of the Canadian market relative to minimum cost production makes the erection of barriers to entry quite profitable in those industries in which there are "large" fluctuations of demand. These barriers represent both a wasteful use of resources and a source of high prices for consumers. The analysis therefore serves to identify the industries in which public intervention may be necessary, in the form of vigorous enforcement of competition policy or of lower tariffs for competing imports. It separates them from other industries where potential entry may be by itself sufficient to achieve the desired results without the help of public policies.

On a more concrete level, the theoretical analysis was applied to the policy decisions to allow or not allow entry into certain markets for new products in the Canadian telecommunications industry. This industry is dominated by one firm, Bell Canada, which provides several of its services under a monopoly franchise. It also provides other services that use the same technical facilities as the monopolized ones, but that may be opened to competition by decision of the regulatory authority if such a decision is thought to be in the public interest. The case study chosen was the Envoy 100, a new message storage and retrieval system. The options examined were whether to allow competition in the submarket system and if yes, whether to regulate the conduct of the sector's dominant firm.

The first question to be examined was the size of the irrecoverable necessary investment for a firm that wished to compete in the submarket. An analysis of the product's technology showed that this investment was very modest indeed, since most of the equipment used was general-purpose computer terminals that could be adapted to other uses. The irrecoverable investment was mostly in the form of programming and advertising costs.

Second, the ability of the dominant firm to engage in anticompetitive activity that would be detrimental to the public interest was severely limited. The ease of competitor entry and the uncertain nature of the future state of technology in the sector made the erection of entry barriers highly questionable from the point of view of profitability. The only way competition could be deterred was by reducing product price below the level where a competitor could operate profitably, a behavior that had desirable implications for the buyers of the service. The only need for public policy intervention was in order to ensure that the dominant firm would not subsidize the low prices of this and other competitive services by increasing the prices of its regulated services, which it operated under a monopoly franchise.

The recommendation that was therefore given was to allow entry into the subsector and to allow the dominant firm to vary its prices in response to competition. The only restriction was that a portion of the cost of those facilities of the dominant firm that were shared between the regulated and the competitive services had to be charged against these latter services for regulatory purposes. It was argued, on the basis of the theory, that such a policy would result, with a high probability, in a state of industry equilibrium that was the best possible under the circumstances.

CONCLUSIONS

This essay gave a brief summary of several interconnected research efforts within the field of the New IO that covered both theory and practical applications. Its purpose was to situate these efforts within the general realm of public policy, as well as to outline their original features and the way they contributed to the solution of concrete problems. Such problems appear in the twin areas of competition and regulatory policies, areas in which Canadian institutions and practices have been recognized as being in need of a reform.

As outlined above, the original contributions consisted in modelling actual economic situations for policy purposes in a manner that highlighted the effects of one particular factor upon policy design. The factor chosen was uncertainty and the effects that it had upon the decision by firms to enter a particular market. While one may argue that such modelling is by necessity imperfect since it can rarely represent adequately all relevant factors, it does have the merits of impartiality and objectivity. There is currently no substitute method to guide policy in these crucial areas, with the result that the prevailing opinions are, more often than not, those of economic interest groups, at the expense of the general public. This essay is an argument in favor of a different approach to economic policy-making.

REFERENCES

BAIN, J.S., *Barriers to New Competition*, Cambridge, 1956.
BAUMOL, W., PANZAR, J., and WILLIG, R., *Contestable Markets and the Theory of Industries Structure*, San Diego, 1982.
DIXIT, A.K., "Recent Developments in Oligopoly Theory," *American Economic Review Papers and Proceedings*, 72 (2), May 1982, pp. 12-17.
ECONOMIC COUNCIL OF CANADA, *Reforming Regulation*, Ottawa, 1981.
PERRAKIS, S., "Rate-of-Return Regulation of a Monopoly Firm with Random Demand," *International Economic Review*, Vol. 17, (1), February 1976, pp. 149-162.
PERRAKIS, S., "On the Regulated Price-Setting Monopoly Firm with a Random Demand Curve," *American Economic Review*, Vol. 66, (3), June 1976, pp. 410-416.
PERRAKIS, S.,"Factor-Price Uncertainty with Variable Proportions: Note," *American Economic Review*, Vol. 70, (5), December 1980, pp. 1083-1088.
PERRAKIS, S., and SILVA-ECHENIQUE, J., "The Profitability and Risk of CATV Operations in Canada," *Applied Economics*, 1983.
PERRAKIS, S., and WARSKETT, G., "Capacity and Entry Under Demand Uncertainty," *The Review of Economic Studies*, July 1983, pp. 495-511.
PERRAKIS, S., and WARSKETT, G., "Uncertainty, Economies of Scale and Barriers to Entry," Working Paper 82-54, Faculty of Administration, University of Ottawa, 1982.
PERRAKIS, S., and ZERBINIS, J., "An Empirical Analysis of Monopoly Regulation Under Uncertainty," *Applied Economics*, Vol. 13, (1), March 1981, pp. 109-125.
PERRAKIS, S., SILVA-ECHENIQUE, J., WARSKETT, G., and de FONTENAY, A., "Réglementation de l'intégration verticale et de la concurrence dans les nouveaux services," report presented to the Department of Communications, 1982.
PERRAKIS, S., WARSKETT, G., and de FONTENAY, A.,"Réglementation des télécommunicateurs et risque: évaluation de l'impact de la concurrence," report presented to the Department of Communications, Ottawa, 1983.
Report of *The Royal Commission on Corporate Concentration*, Ottawa, 1978.
SCHERER, F.M., *Industrial Market Structure and Economic Performance*, Chicago, Rand McNally College Publishing Company, 1980.

Government Deficits, Political Democracy, and the Welfare State

PEDRO ARROJA

The federal budget deficit recently reached an un-precedented level of $35 billion. Public and professional debate on the size of the deficit has been premised on a disputable view of the world. This view is based on the Keynesian theory of functional finances. It is assumed that the government is run by an unselfish bureaucracy acting in the public interest, whose purpose is to calibrate the levers of fiscal policy to ensure full employment and price stability.

Over a period of slow economic growth and high unemployment, government deficits are warranted because they stimulate aggregate demand and employment. As long as those deficits remain cyclical or automatic, it is argued, they are self-correcting and do not impose a permanent financial burden on the economy.

Thus Bossons and Dungan (1983) claim: "If the economy were at full employment and the government surplus or deficit were correctly measured, the current taxation and expenditure programs of all government combined would yield a surplus of $6 billion. As a result, the current fiscal position of Canadian governments is depressing rather than stimulating the economy." Similar conclusions have been expressed by others (e.g., Bruce and Purvis, 1983; Rousseau, 1983).

In this paper it is argued, first, that deficit financing of government spending is the necessary outcome of the self-centered maximizing behavior of politicians and bureaucrats in a political democracy; second, that existing deficit estimates overstate its automatic component and understate its discretionary component. Taken together, these have been the sine qua non for the growing public sector deficits experienced in Canada over the last ten years.

FUNCTIONAL FINANCES

In the theory of functional finances, the government is assigned the role of stabilizing the economy through a functional utilization of its finances. If the economy is operating below capacity, government expenditures should be increased and/or tax revenues reduced

so as to stimulate aggregate demand; above full employment, the
rule is reversed so as to prevent undesirable inflationary pressures;
at full employment, the impact of fiscal policy on aggregate demand
should be neutral and the budget balanced.

Starting from a position of full employment and budget balance,
if the economy moves into a recession a deficit is generated as
expenditures increase (e.g., unemployment insurance and welfare
benefits) and revenues fall (e.g., income taxes). This deficit is cyclical
or automatic, for it is beyond the control of policy-makers.

In the case of a prolonged recession, some extra fiscal stimulus
might be needed. This calls for discretionary expenditure increases
or tax reductions. Discretionary actions of policy should use instruments that are symmetrically reversible with respect to the employment gap; otherwise, an unwarranted deficit is produced as the
economy returns to full capacity. Symmetrical reversibility ensures
that, as the economy moves above normal levels of capacity utilization in the next stage of the cycle, discretionary levers of policy
can be set so as to mirror their recession image. With the economy
expected to move on average over time along a full employment
growth path, the principle of (full employment) budget balance is
respected.

Implicit in this theory is a government run by a group of
thoughtful bureaucrats seeking the public good, in particular price
stability and full employment, by means of a considered utilization
of fiscal policy instruments.

TOWARDS A POSITIVE THEORY OF DEFICIT FINANCING

A different view of the world holds that bureaucrats (in the
broad sense to include politicians as well) are self-centered utility
maximizers. The arguments for their utility function include income,
job security, prestige, and popularity. These are interrelated. Higher
popularity is the vehicle for more prestigious, better paid jobs. It is
achieved by meeting voters' demands.

Demands for any specific public program are bound by organizational costs. When the community of voters sharing a given interest is small, those costs are small and a special interest group will
emerge. The interest group internalizes the benefits of the program,
but the costs are perceived as largely external and borne by the
general taxpayer. An accepted law of human behavior then applies.
It states that when the perceived price paid for any given good or
service is small, demand will be increased to the level of satiation.

On the supply side, the cost for the bureaucracy of delivering
any specific public program is the reduction in popularity that
results from the higher level of taxation required to finance the
program. As the number of public programs increases, or as existing
programs become wider in scope, such cost will increase at the
margin.

The marginal cost for the bureaucracy of supplying public programs can be reduced by replacing tax-financing by debt financing
provided one condition is met; namely, that the resulting deficits
be perceived by the population (and to a large extent by the bureaucracy itself) as temporary and self-correcting, i.e., that they be regarded as cyclical or automatic deficits. If this is the case, a second
law of human behavior applies. It states that when the perceived
(marginal) cost of producing any given good or service is small,
supply will be increased to meet any level of demand.

Provided deficits are perceived as a cost-free process of delivering public programs, the multiplication of those programs and the
rising levels of government spending follow as a matter of logical
necessity: if demand for any given good or service is large (because
the perceived price is small) and supply is large (because the
perceived marginal cost is small), output will necessarily be large.

The above argument, which stresses on the demand side the
role of special interest groups, seemingly fails to explain the growing
output of the so-called universal social programs where the emergence of special interest groups is less likely. It is unlikely that
upper income classes would incur the organizational costs required
to demand their access to such universal programs as Family Allow-
ances, O.A.S., welfare and unemployment assistance, and public
education and health, and their relatively poorer fellow citizens
would certainly be even less likely to do so on their behalf. The
fact, however, is that upper income classes do also enjoy the benefits
of such programs. Who then expressed on their behalf the corresponding demands? The answer is the bureaucracy itself. By offering
a benefit to the general citizenry without imposing a corresponding
perceived price,[1] the bureaucrats can further their own interests at
no perceived cost. Universality is thus a creation of the bureaucracy.

Increasing government spending is not a new phenomenon.
What is new in the current situation is that it has been increasingly
deficit-financed. The origins of this phenomenon in North America
date back to the early sixties, when an American administration for
the first time embraced the principles of the theory of functional
finances (Buchanan and Wagner, 1977). Since then, U.S. government
deficits have steadily increased, and the same has been the case in
Canada since 1974. Somehow, deficits came to be perceived as a
low-cost process of financing public spending. Although the adoption of Keynesianism per se is a necessary condition for this change
in perceptions to occur, it is not a sufficient one. What is required
is that deficits be regarded as mostly temporary and self-correcting,

---

1. Even when universality is financed by taxes, rather than by debt,
there might be little correspondence in
the minds of most citizens between the
rising tax burden and the fact that the
government is indiscriminately offering
such benefits to persons who would otherwise be ready to pay for or forgo them.

thus irrelevant from a financial point of view. This has been achieved by the distinction between full employment and cyclical deficits.

FULL EMPLOYMENT AND CYCLICAL BUDGET DEFICITS

The partition of actual deficits between a full employment component and a cyclical component draws on the distinction between income-related and non-income-related government revenues and expenditures. Based on this classification, Government Expenditure (E) and Revenue (R) functions can be written as:

$$E(Y) = \begin{cases} E_o + e(Y_p\text{-}Y) \ (e > 0) & \text{when } Y < Y_p \\ E_o & \text{when } Y \geq Y_p \end{cases} \quad \text{... (4.1)}$$

and

$$R(Y) = R_o + tY \qquad (0 < t < 1) \qquad \text{... (4.2)}$$

where E_o and R_o stand for non-income-related expenditures and revenues (e.g., interest on the public debt, general administration and defence spending; some forms of indirect taxation); e and t are the marginal spending and tax propensities, respectively, Y is actual aggregate income and Y_p potential or full employment income. Income-related revenues, tY, are those which change with the level of aggregate income and employment, as most tax revenues. Income-related expenditures, $e(Y_p\text{-}Y)$, include those expenditures designed to assist the unemployed (unemployment insurance and welfare payments, spending on job creation and job training programs, production and employment subsidies, etc.); they are positive when the economy is operating below full employment ($Y < Yp$) and zero otherwise.

For given E_o, R_o, e, t, Y and Y_p — of which e, t and some components of E_o and R_o are within the discretionary control of the authorities — the actual budget deficit is:

$$D(Y) = E(Y)\text{-}R(Y) = \begin{cases} (E_o\text{-}R_o)\text{-}(e+t)Y+eY_p & \text{when } Y < Y_p \\ (E_o\text{-}R_o)\text{-}tY & \text{when } Y \geq Y_p \end{cases} \quad \text{... (4.3)}$$

The Full Employment Budget Deficit (FEBD) is:

$$D_p = D(Y_p) = (E_o\text{-}R_o)\text{-}tY_p \qquad \text{... (4.4)}$$

and the Cyclical Budget Deficit (CBD):

$$D_c(Y) = D(Y) - D_p = \begin{cases} (e + t)(Y_p - Y) & \text{when } Y < Y_p \\ t(Y_p - Y) & \text{when } Y \geq Y_p \end{cases} \quad \dots (4.5)$$

The key normative principles of the Theory of Functional Finances can now be restated in terms of equations (4.4) and (4.5) as follows. Proper fiscal management should involve the manipulation of tax and expenditure instruments so that the FEBD (equation (4.4)) averages zero over the business cycle. As for the CBD, it is believed that it does so automatically.

THE FEBD AND DISCRETIONARY FISCAL POLICY

Flowing from the above principles, the FEBD has come to be used as a measure of the stance of discretionary fiscal policy. Contrary to a cyclical deficit, which is beyond the control of the authorities, a FEBD is the result of voluntary acts of policy. Furthermore, it is argued, a cyclical deficit is transitory as it will be paid for by a cyclical surplus; a FEBD, on the contrary, must be financed by debt issue. In this sense, the FEBD has also been used as a measure of how responsibly the financial affairs of the government are conducted.

Existing estimates of the stance of discretionary fiscal policy using the FEBD are biased due to two sorts of difficulties, one conceptual, the other statistical. As a result, for the year 1983 alone, the FEBD underestimated the discretionary deficit by at least $17.5 billion. This was done at the expense of an over estimation of the automatic deficit by the same amount.

The first difficulty is conceptual. Any proper measure M of the stance of discretionary fiscal policy must satisfy, simultaneously, the two following conditions: first, any change in M must be the result of, and only of, discretionary actions of policy; second, any discretionary action of policy must be reflected in a corresponding change in M.

Although the FEBD meets the first of these conditions (provided it is assumed that potential output can be accurately forecast), it does not meet the second, as a glance at equation (4.4) above shows. Actions of policy affecting income-related expenditure programs (policy instrument e), while discretionary in nature, are not captured by the FEBD; rather, they are included in the CBD (equation (4.5)).

Suppose the economy is running below capacity for a prolonged period and the government decides to increase assistance to the unemployment by increasing spending on job creation and job training programs, by raising marginal benefit rates on unemployment insurance and welfare relief, or by any other action affecting parameter e in equations (4.1) & (4.5) above. That any of these actions represents a discretionary act of policy with a short-run, positive effect on aggregate demand is unquestionable. However, the higher level of spending is credited to the cyclical or automatic deficit, rather than to the full employment deficit.

Thus, in a situation of less than full employment, the FEBD understates the discretionary deficit. Estimates provided in the appendix 1 suggest that over the period 1968-1983 the actual stance of discretionary fiscal policy was, on average per year, $7.5 billion (in 1983 prices) more expansionary than that suggested by conventional FEBD estimates.

Estimates of FEBDs can be used to compare the stance of policy between two full employment positions of the economy. They cannot be used to infer the stance of policy when the economy is below capacity. This is so because there is a class of discretionary acts of policy, namely, that including all those programs designed to assist the unemployed, whose raison d'être is the fact that the economy is below full employment.

From a financial point of view, the inclusion of discretionary, income-related expenditure programs in the cyclical deficit has had the effect of considering as temporary what is a permanent financial burden on the economy for a given tax-expenditure structure. As Figure 1 shows, the cyclical component of the deficit is assymetrical with respect to full employment income, with the factor of assymmetry being income-related expenditures, $e(Y_p-Y)$.

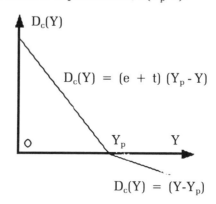

Figure I — The Cyclical Budget Deficit

A cyclical deficit generated when actual income falls short of potential by, say, $10 billion, cannot be pqaid for by the cyclical surplus produced at a level of income $10 billion above potential. Above full employment, cyclical surpluses cannot pay for more than that portion of the deficit that is due to tax revenues forgone during the recession. Given the structure of taxes and expenditures, the difference must necessarily be financed by debt issue.

The second difficulty is statistical. Existing estimates of full employment and cyclical deficits are based on the assumption that the economy fluctuates over time around some normal level of activity, which is currently defined as a level of factor utilization corresponding to a (natural) rate of unemployment of 6%.

According to most estimates, the natural rate of unemployment in Canada rose from 3-3.5% in the early sixties to 6.5-7% in the mid-seventies; since then it has declined steadily to its current level of 5.5-6% (Fortin and Phaneuf, 1979; Dungan and Wilson, 1981; Bossons and Dungan, 1983). On the other hand, the measured rate of unemployment over the last 15 years fell below the natural rate only twice, in 1973 and 1974, and then only marginally so. In the remaining 13 years; it stayed above — and in the last 3 years it was almost twice as much as — the natural rate. Over the next 4 years, even the most optimistic estimates predict a measured unemployment rate well above the current (and declining) 6% natural rate (Department of Finance, 1983).

Accordingly, current estimates of the natural rate understate the true normal, in the sense of substainable or modal, unemployment rate in Canada. The consequences of this for existing full employment and cyclical deficit estimates can be seen from equations (4.4) and (4.5). By understating the true normal rate of unemployment and consequently overstating the level of potential (sustainable or modal) income, those estimates are inappropriately reducing the size of the FEBD and increasing that of the CBD. Such estimates are considering as tax revenues forgone due to the recession tax revenues that can never be realized, as they are treating as recession-induced expenditures. Some expenditures that will persist once the recession is over and the economy returns to sustainable, normal levels of activity.

It is estimated that a one percentage point increase in the measured rate of unemployment relative to the normal rate adds approximately $2.5 billion to the measured deficit (Bruce and Purvis, 1983). On the other hand, current and future prospects for the Canadian economy suggest that the sustainable rate of unemployment in Canada might be in the neighborhood of 10% (Parkin, 1983). Thus, on this account alone, current deficit estimates understate the size of the discretionary deficit and overstate that of the automatic deficit by $10 billion a year.

CONCLUSIONS

Modern political democracies are biased towards spending and against taxation. The increasing levels of spending typical of the welfare state cannot exiswt without a view of the world that portrays deficits as a cost-free process of financing public outlays. These are the Keynesian cyclical or automatic deficits. Somehow, thus, actual budget deficits must be portrayed as being largely cyclical. This has been achieved in two ways. First, by treating as cyclical the discretionary increases in social programs, particularly those to assist the unemployed and needy. Second, by treating as temporary the revenue losses and expenditure levels that are permanent. Taken together, this has led to a systematic underestimation of discretionary deficits and overestimation of automatic ones. For 1983, the bias amounts at least to $17.5 billion, or 76% of the recorded deficit.

Most of what is currently perceived as a cyclical deficit is a discretionary deficit. This will not be paid for by some future automatic budget surpluses. Rather, it must be paid for by very discretionary, future tax increases and/or expenditure reductions. The sooner the Canadian public realizes this, the smaller will be the mortgage on its own future.

APPENDIX 1

The average amount per year, over the period 1968-1983, of discretionary increases in income related expenditure programs not accounted for by the FEBD, but included in the CBD, is estimated as follows:

The equation:

$$E_t - E'_t = a + b \, (UNP)_t \qquad \qquad ... \text{(A-1)}$$

where:

E_t =   total government spending (millions of 1971 dollars);

E'_t =   total government spending that would have occurred in year t had it grown at the same rate as real GNP since 1950 (millions of 1971 dollars);

UNP_t =   number of unemployed persons in year t (thousands);

is fitted separately to the periods 1950-1961 and 1968-1983; the years 1962-1967 of continuously declining unemployment are excluded. The nature of the regression is such that, a priori, a = 0 and b > 0.

Furthermore, if the hypothesis of discretionary improvements in income-related expenditure programs in the last 15 years or so is to hold, the parameter b for the period 1968-1983 must exceed that for 1950-1951.

The regression estimates are as follows (in brackets the standard errors of the estimates)[2]:

$$E_t\text{-}_t' = -531.64 + 10.00 \ (UNP)_t \qquad 1950\text{-}1961$$
$$(401.49) \quad (1.33) \qquad\qquad R^2 = 0.86$$

$$E_t\text{-}E_t' = 1231.32 + 26.12 \ (UNP)_t \qquad 1968\text{-}1983$$
$$(1030.61) \quad (1.30) \qquad\qquad R^2 = 0.97$$

In both cases, parameter a does not pass a significance test, while parameter b over the period 1968-1983 is statistically greater than over the period 1950-1961. Between 1950 and 1961 the government was spending an average of $10.00 thousand at the margin per unemployed person; this amount increased to $26.12 thousand over the period 1968-1983, a difference of $16.12 thousand. From 1968 through 1983, the average number of unemployed persons per year was 695 thousand, compared to the 532 thousand that would have been unemployed had the economy operated on average at full-capacity[3]. The amounts 16.12 (695-532) = $2.6 billion represents the average amount of discretionary spending on income-related programs over the period 1968-1983, relative to that prevailing over the fifties. Evaluated at 1983 prices, it amounts to $7.5 billion.

---

2. The estimations use 3-year moving averages of actual data. The source of data is Department of Finance, Economic Review, 1983.

3. For this purpose, the natural rate of unemployment is assumed to grow linearly from 3.7% in 1968 to 4% in 1972 and from 4% in 1972 to 6.5% in 1976, and to decline from 6.5% in 1976 to 5.8% in 1983.

REFERENCES

BOSSONS, J., and DUNGAN, D.P., "The Government Deficit: Too High or Too Low?", *Canadian Tax Journal*, Vol. 31, (1), 1983, pp. 1-29.

BRUCE, N., and PURVIS, D.D., "Fiscal Policy and Recovery from the Great Recession," *Canadian Public Policy1*, Vol. 9, (1), 1983, pp. 53-67.

BUCHANAN, J.M., and WAGNER, R.E., *Democracy in Deficit - The Political Legacy of Lord Keynes*, London, Academic Press, 1977.

Department of Finance, *The Canadian Economy in Recovery*, Ottawa, February 1983.

DUNGAN, D.P., and WILSON, T.A., "Potential GNP: Performance and Prospects," University of Toronto, *Institute for Policy Analysis Report Series*, 1981.

FORTIN, P., and PHANEUF, L., "Why is the Unemployment Rate so High in Canada?", paper presented at the meetings of the *Canadian Economics Association*, 1979.

PARKIN, M., "What Can Macroeconomic Theory Tell Us About the Way Deficits Should Be Measured," in D.W. Conklin and T.J. Courchene, eds., *Deficits: How Big and How Bad?*, Ontario Economic Council, 1983, pp. 150-188.

ROUSSEAU, H., "The Dome Syndrome: The Debt Overhanging Canadian Government and Business," *Canadian Public Policy*, Vol. 9, (1), 1983, pp. 37-52.

Medicare: Economics, Ethics and Distributive Justice

PRANLAL MANGA

Biomedical ethicists have traditionally concentrated on issues that arose in the context of patient-physician relationships (e.g., euthanasia, informed consent, physicians' obligations to inform patients) or patients' rights (e.g., abortion, commercialization of human tissue and organs, right to refuse medical treatment). Recently, however, they have devoted increasing attention to the allocation of health care resources, with particular regard to questions of distributive justice, or to put it in more pedestrian terms, to equitable access to health care services.

There are numerous theories of distributive justice in the philosophical and ethical literature in medicine. Some are Rawlsian in nature, involving varying formulations of a contractarian theory of justice; others are derivative of utilitarian or egalitarian principles. While there are important differences between them, they all proclaim that society is morally obliged to assure its citizens a right to health care services through its public policies. The theories also differ in the way they define equity and often use the terms "equity" and "equality" interchangeably, but the underlying meaning of the concept invariably involves the elimination of economic, social, geographic, and other "unfair" or "unjust" obstacles to persons' access to services.

MEDICARE PROGRAMS AS SOCIETAL ETHIC SERVICES

Economists, usually of the neoclassical persuasion, have traditionally been concerned with issues of allocative and technical efficiency in health care markets. Allocative issues, as much as they were a concern of governments, were conventionally approached through the examination of various forms of market failure. The conservative ideology that dominated the economists' policy recommendations rested on the view that market failure was a necessary but not necessarily sufficient condition for government interference in private decision-making. Thus government provision or financing of health services that were essentially public goods (e.g., immunization) was acceptable. Services that featured various types or degrees of externalities (e.g., basic medical research) may be justifiably financed by government. Public regulations were legitimate if they were intended to correct for imperfections on the supply side (e.g., price advertising, reforming competition policy to counter the professional regulations or etiquette that inhibits competition) or consumer ignorance or uncertainties on the demand side (e.g., state-sanctioned professional licensing, provision of information, product safety regulations, system of torts and legal liability). Equity and distributional questions were often addressed as an afterthought or as an aside, with preference for solutions involving income transfer mechanisms or voucher systems rather than in-kind transfers. Also, categorical[1] rather than universal schemes were advised. Reality does not conform well with the prescriptions or the proscriptions of economists. It is at least arguable that governments have not done enough to promote effective competition among the suppliers of health care services in the physician, dental, pharmaceutical, and medical devices submarkets. More pertinent for the purposes of this brief paper, Western industrialized countries exist in defiance of many economists' counsel against such publicly financed, uniform, comprehensive, and universal schemes.

However, recently economists and policy planners generally have become far more conscious of the ethical aspects of health policy and allocative decisions in the health care system. One contributing factor is, of course, the very existence of Medicare-like programs which are presumably based on a societal ethic that requires equitable access to health care services. Another factor is undoubtedly the widespread view that rising health care costs have not provided a commensurate increase in benefits in terms of reduction in morbidity or premature mortality or finer measures of health status. Though the dominant health policy concerns have shifted from one of distributive justice to one of efficiency, there is a growing appreciation of the conflicts between the two sets of objectives. It is precisely this underlying conflict that is exemplified by the recent passage of the Canada Health Act. The Act in effect declared that some forms of cost-containment policies, such as physician extra-billing, hospital user fees, and the disenfranchisement of persons through the use of insurance premiums, pose too serious a threat to the distributive justice features of Medicare. Yet another factor is the increasing recognition that equitable distribution of health care services, however defined, has failed to bring about equality in health status across the various socio-economic groups.[2] This paradox obviously begs the question as to just what

---

1. The best-known examples of categorical programs in the USA are Medicare and Medicaid and in Canada, Pharmacare and Denticare.

2. Recent analysis of the Canada Health Survey provides rather clear evidence of this paradoxical result.

our health policy objective is. Is it to equalize health status or merely to equalize access to health care services? If it is the former, is the emphasis on distributive justice focused on health care services justified?

Perhaps the normative question of just what the distributive role of health services ought to be needs to be reexamined. It might be argued that the degree of political consensus which existed around Medicare-type programs was not due to fundamental agreement about the proper end of health policy or belief in distributive justice. Rather, such programs may merely be "the residual beneficiary of economic progress" sustained during the post-war period. In a non-growth economy, the argument goes, there would undoubtedly be sharper controversy about both the level of health expenditures and the distribution of its burdens and benefits. In brief, the underlying political controversies on health policy may have been merely dormant over the past three decades, requiring only the right social and economic circumstances to bring them out in the open.

Incidentally, one could also argue that Medicare is not so much concerned with distributive justice as it is simply an instrument to pool the financial risks of illness. A public insurance plan was chosen over several private insurance plans because of economies of scale and because of the monopolistic power that one insurer commands in regulating provider prices and health care costs generally. While such a view is certainly consistent with our present system, a historical review of Medicare clearly indicates that this was not the central rationale for the development of our public insurance programs.

MEDICAL INNOVATIONS AS A SOURCE OF COST INCREASES

But by far the most important reason why virtually all analysts are increasingly cognizant of the ethical implications of health care costs is related to the truly remarkable growth in medical technology. The consequent expansion in the range of medical services that can be provided inexorably increases health care costs. This fact in and of itself is not particularly meaningful. Some medical innovations have been retrospectively judged to be horrible failures. Most have yet to be evaluated. Many are alleged to be benignly inefficacious, while others have been immensely successful, bordering on the miraculous. The real question to ask about medical technology and devoting even further resources to health care delivery systems is, what are the payoffs in terms of improved health that such investment of resources is expected to yield? The current consensus is that the yield is marginal at best. The concern with unwarranted cost increases is often juxtaposed with the seemingly irresistible promise of life-saving medical technologies, creating obvious tensions between the ethical and economic concerns of public policy.

The dilemma is obviously more serious if a public policy decision to forego the adoption of some technology or therapy may condemn some patients to continued illness and sometimes even to death. A particularly vexing issue is the right of the elderly in relation to their access to scarce biomedical resources. If allocation decisions appear to or are intended to reduce the availability of health care services to targeted or identifiable groups, important questions of distributive justice arise.

It is important to recognize that such tensions exist at both the macro-allocation and micro-allocation levels of decision-making. The cost and limited availability of almost all of the lifesaving or crisis intervention therapies have focused attention on both the economists' classic problem of scarcity and the necessity of making difficult moral choices within hospitals as well as on the bureaucracies of government. That ethical dilemma was frequently encountered in clinical settings has always been acknowledged. But macro-allocation and budgetary decisions are not ethically neutral, though many public officials pretend otherwise. Thus public decisions to permit or prohibit the use of certain medical technologies or fund the activities of clinical researchers all indirectly determine the boundaries of private decision-making confronted by individual patients, doctors, and hospitals. It is important to note that economic and ethical considerations of health policy are not always in conflict. Indeed, they sometimes point to the same public policy option as, for example, in the case of promoting palliative care facilities, the patients' right to refuse medical treatment, and the prohibition against the commercialization of human organs. But more often than not there are conflicts, and despite the greater appreciation of this fact, public policy determination is far from clear or simple.

Neither ethics nor economics can provide clear answers to the question of how many resources society should devote to health care services. While Medicare appears to be too utopian and egalitarian to its critics, governments have always recognized that society cannot and will not satisfy all health care needs. Health care needs appear to be virtually infinite. Also, with the recognition of broader definitions of health, governments have come to realize the importance of determinants of health other than medical and hospital services. The value society places on health care services and, at least in the abstract, on saving lives, is not infinite. The need to trade off health care versus other social goods is both obvious and inescapable. Medicare is perhaps more appropriately thought of as defining a situation in which everyone has an equal risk of having unsatisfied needs or is compensated for having a higher level of risk to health.

Medicare replaced the distributive ethics of libertarianism, where allocation and rationing is achieved through prices, incomes, and wealth, by an egalitarian distributive ethic where rationing is done by other mechanisms such as waiting lists, random selection, queuing, control over capital facilities, and regional scarcities of resources. Medicare does not promise, let alone provide, unconstrained right to health care services, except within available resources. Early opponents of Medicare failed to appreciate that Medicare would prove to be affordable largely because of the government's ability and willingness to limit the budgets and resources devoted to health care services.

Just what constitutes an appropriate level of resources to assure the fulfillment of the principle of distributive justice implicit under Medicare and at the same time allocate resources among society's competing wants is an immensely complex issue. The macro-allocation question is, in the words of a renowned bioethicist, "almost, if not altogether incorrigible to moral reasoning," and the economist might as well add, and to rational economic determination. The question is in practice resolved through political processes that reflect as closely as possible the values, preferences, and priorities of society.

Whether these processes perform this task sufficiently well is an interesting question. There is the obvious difficulty that a majority can coerce a minority into accepting a level or risk of unsatisfied needs that the minority would not have chosen themselves. Also, under our liberal democracies political parties do not offer discrete, single policies to the voters but rather "full-line supply" or policy bundles, thus weakening the extent to which society determines its own policy in specific matters. The best that can be said for our current system of decision-making is that while it is unavoidably a hit-or-miss affair, we have yet to develop practical alternatives.

A CONFLICT BETWEEN PHYSICIANS AND BUREAUCRATS

It is important to distinguish between the different ways ethical and economic considerations impinge upon the various decision-makers. The physician is not a policy maker and should not be expected to make the complex trade-offs between national priorities in the context of his own practice. His responsibility is to his patient, and society has good reasons for insisting that he unstintingly fulfills that responsibility of personal care given the available resources. The accountability and obligations of a physician are not identical to those of a bureaucrat. The intensity of the ethical dilemmas and the nature of the conflict between efficiency and effectiveness versus ethical considerations are different for the two types of decision-makers. In general it is naive and unfair to insist that physicians take into account the economic implications of the difficult choices that they sometimes have to make in treating their patients. This is not to suggest that they should never be required to weigh the costs or benefits of their decisions but that there are serious ethical and practical limits to their ability as physicians to do so. To borrow two concepts from Max Weber, the conduct of a physician cannot be assessed in purely "goal-rational" terms (that is, in terms of the symbolic values, attitudes, and virtues a policy or action expresses). There are many cases in medicine where it is important to preserve society's cherished myth that an individual's life was not sacrificed to save money.

Indeed, it is not just physicians and health care providers but society in general that is willing to devote enormous amounts of resources — and in ways contradicted by cost-benefit, cost-effectiveness or risk analysis — to save identifiable lives as distinct from "statistical lives." Society values symbolic gestures to reaffirm its virtue and character, or what is sometimes called "agent moral-ity." There are, of course, numerous illustrations of this. Much energy and expense are expended in highly publicized cases of life-extending technologies such as organ transplantation. Recent in-stances of mass appeal for organ donations are yet another manifes-tation of the same phenomenon. It might be noted here that both the shortages and the solutions to the shortages of solid human organs raise profound ethical concerns. However, should the prob-lem of shortages be somehow resolved through changes in policy in donating organs, the commercialization of organs, or the rapid de-velopment of artificial implantable organs, the economic implica-tions of such development could be considerable. Vast sums of money are spent in search and rescue missions when an airplane is downed in the North or workers are trapped in mines. The latter example is particularly noteworthy since many mining companies invest very little to prevent mine disasters even though they could save more lives in the long run for the same overall costs. The expenditure on an intensive care neonatal unit would save more babies and reduce more infant morbidity and handicaps were the same amount of funds used in a nutrition program targeted on pregnant teenagers. The value-stratum rational behavior of physi-cians and the agent morality behavior of society are no doubt ethically motivated but are probably unsound economics and ill-advised as a basis for the allocation of resources. If society were to increase its crisis or rescue intervention and life-extending budgets by withdrawing resources from elsewhere such as public health, occupational health and safety, or traffic safety, it would result in the paradoxical situation of society symbolizing its concern for human life by actually doing less than it could to save lives. With the advent of a greater and expanding range of life-saving or life-extending technology and its obvious appeal to the public and health care providers, the prospects of reallocating resources from high technology crisis-oriented medicine to other forms of health care services, even if these are more cost-effective, or to other areas of social policy, are rather meager.

TOWARD THE HARD CHOICE

Medicare in Canada has succeeded in bringing about a degree of equity in access to hospital and medical services probably unmatched by any other country. There is abundant empirical evidence indicating that the distribution of services is primarily and largely determined by health care needs. But there is also no doubt that the poor in Canada enjoy considerably inferior health status in terms of mortality or morbidity relative to the rich, despite the equitable access to and, in fact, greater use of health care services. Some of this is perhaps due to reverse causation, that is, the effect of disability and illness on income. However, the relationship between poverty and higher mortality and morbidity is marked even among children. This is a finding that is also common in other countries. It is difficult to resist the conclusion that equalization of access to health care services does not result in equality in health status. This paradox is likely to worsen, since lifestyle modification first popular in the seventies has been far more effective in the richer and better educated groups. For instance, smoking cessation has occurred primarily among the better-educated and higher-income groups who also apparently pay more attention to nutrition and physical exercise, and probably have better physical and workplace environments. A much greater effort to reach the poor is thus needed if society wishes to close the gap in health status between the different groups. This is not to be construed as an attack on the principles that characterize Medicare. The problem is not with Medicare per se. The essence of Medicare is to assure access to necessary medical services to those in need and it fulfills this objective very well. The paradox raised here only makes us question the wisdom of the way we have allocated our resources and suggests that alternative allocations could be more beneficial in terms of the health of Canadians. What should the balance be between treatment and the prevention and health promotion activities that were so highly recommended in the renowned Lalonde document of a decade ago? Canadians appear to have steadfastly maintained their support for the principle of distributive justice when applied to access to health care services. It would be ironic if the same society wished to see existing inequalities in health continue or become worse over time.

The issues raised here are but a few of the ethical and economic policy dilemmas faced by society. We have yet to consciously decide on how much unmet need we should tolerate, and how much health care and modern medical technology should be provided through our programs. Though such decisions always do get made, they are probably arrived at by a combination of incremental budgeting and response to moral and political pressure. Anchoring allocation decisions on the basis of economic considerations in terms of efficiency and effectiveness in conjunction with ethical considerations is, of course, a difficult matter, not least because it requires the kinds of information and analyses we do not now readily generate. Long range decision-making with a genuine effort to anticipate and plan for the economic effects and ethical aspects of new developments in medical technology is rare. But the march of medical technology and the ever-pressing economic limits compel us to begin to make the hard choices we have not really had to make so far.

REFERENCES

CHILDRESS, J.F., *Priorities in Biomedical Ethics*, Chapter 4, Philadelphia, Westminster Press, 1981.

DANIELS, N., "Am I My Parents' Keeper?", in *Securing Access to Health Care*, Washington, D.C., 1983, Vol. 2, pp. 265-291.

GORDON, T.J., GERJUOY, H., and ANDERSON, M. (eds.), *Life-Extending Technologies: A Technology Assessment*, New York, Pergamon Press, 1977.

GREEN, R., "Health Care and Justice in Contract Theory Perspective," in Veatch, R.M., and Branson, R. (eds.), *Ethics and Health Policy*, Cambridge, Ballinger, 1976, pp. 111-126.

HARRON, F. et al., *Health and Human Values*, Chapter 7, New Haven, Yale University Press, 1983.

HIATT, H., "Protecting the Medical Commons: Who Is Responsible?", *New England Journal of Medicine*, 31 July 1975, pp. 235-241.

KLEIN, R. et al., *Priorities and Inflation*, London, Centre for Studies in Social Policy, 1975, p. 1.

MANGA, P., BROYLES, R., and ANGUS, D., "The Utilization of Medical and Hospital Services under Medicare: An Analysis of the Canada Health Survey."

NEWHOUSE, J.P., and FRIEDLANDER, L.J., "The Relationship between Medical Resources and Measures of Health: Some Additional Evidence," *Journal of Human Resources*, Vol. 15, (2), 1979, pp. 200-218.

President's Commission for the Study of Ethical Problems in Medicine and Biomedical and Behavioural Research, *Securing Access to Health Care, Vol. 2: Appendices, Sociocultural and Philosophical Studies*, Washington, D.C., March 1983.

RAMSEY, P., *The Patient as a Person*, New Haven, Yale University Press, 1970, p. 240.

SADE, R.M., "Medical Care as a Right: A Refutation," *New England Journal of Medicine*, Vol. 285, (23), December 1971, pp. 1288-1290.

STARR, P., "The Politics of Therapeutic Nihilism," in Conrad, P., Kern, R. (ed.), *The Sociology of Health and Illness*, New York, St. Martin's Press, 1981, pp. 434-448.

VEATCH, R.M., *A Theory of Medical Ethics*, New York, Basic Books, 1981.

The Markmanship of Research Grants Programs: An Evaluative Framework

GILLES PAQUET
JOHN H. TAYLOR

The general climate of restraint facing all governments in Canada since the 1970s has heightened the perennial
concern to ensure that the public gets and is seen to get value-for-
money in every sector where public money is spent, including
research activities. Consequently, one has witnessed a growing tendency for governments to monitor and direct the use and allocation
of public funds for research activities.

This increased government oversight and intervention has proceeded, generally speaking, in three phases:

1. Governments have reduced the amounts of money (in real
terms) available for research: funding generally did not keep pace
with inflation for research-funding agencies. In part, at least, governments seemed to feel that all programs, including research funding, would have to carry the burdens of restraint. But there was also
a sense that the long-run objectives that research activities are
purported to serve could more readily be sacrificed than the urgent,
short-run needs in other areas. During this first phase, it has been
argued that little real damage was done to programs: funding agencies eliminated some of their less useful activities, introduced cost-
saving devices and streamlined the administrative apparatus charged
with the disbursement of funds. Despite the views of governments
with respect to the relative value of the different types of research,
agencies were left very much to themselves to make whatever compromises and accommodations they might.

2. Such compromises were bound to become more and more
difficult as finances continued to fail to keep up with inflation: basic
program funding came to feel some financial pinch. A strong reaction from the research community ensued. Governments responded,
not by increasing research funding as they were asked to do, but by
questioning the lack of congruence between the observed pattern of
research funds disbursed and the pattern called for by the explicit
socio-economic objectives of the elected governments. Once again,
compromises were hammered out: additional funding over and beyond the existing baseline funding would be made available but

only to promote research in areas deemed by government to be a priority. This second-round intervention has given rise to strategic grants programs of all sorts in Canadian funding agencies. Government, in some areas, had decided to set the agenda.

3. Such exercises inevitably led to a third round of probing: the line of questioning was extended to the baseline funding. Could it be said with assurance that the basic sum of money allocated to researchers via peer-evaluation review for basic researcher-initiated projects constituted a sound expenditure of public monies? Was it productive or useful, and if not, could this money be re-routed to other uses?

There were two types of responses to those government pressures. The first one came mainly from the academic community. On principle, it went as far as stating that governments had no right to interfere in the affairs of the mind.[1]

3. Such exercises inevitably led to a third round of probing: the line of questioning was extended to the baseline funding. Could it be said with assurance that the basic sum of money allocated to researchers via peer-evaluation review for basic researcher-initiated projects constituted a sound expenditure of public monies? Was it productive or useful, and if not, could this money be re-routed to other uses?

There were two types of responses to those government pressures. The first one came mainly from the academic community. On principle, it went as far as stating that governments had no right to interfere in the affairs of the mind.[1]

A second reaction came largely through reflections of thoughtful bureaucrats. The most articulate of the members of this group may be Frank Milligan. For Milligan and those who thought like him, while it might be nice to be able to effect such calculations of costs and benefits that would ensure a maximum utility from the disbursement of research funds by governments, it is simply not feasible. In Milligan's words, "the economist's concept of marginal utility ... is more a metaphor than a model" in the realm of research grants programs evaluation. Such matters, according to him, belong to the world of the incalculable.

It is our view that both these academic and bureaucratic reactions (that evaluative procedures should not or could not be applied to research grants programs) are misguided, self-serving and indefensible. The nonevaluability of the programs serves as a basis to declare, almost per se, that the marksmanship of the programs, as they are, is of necessity quite good, i.e., effective, efficient and economic.

---

1. This is an argument which many academics have pronounced ill-founded. Joseph Tussman, for instance, argues that there is reason for government to concern itself with the affairs of the mind.

Research grants programs are evaluable and should be evaluated. Indeed, the only way for the scholarly community to ensure appropriate levels of both government money and government intervention — presumably a maximum of the former and a minimum of the latter — is to demonstrate both the value of funded researcher-initiated research and the productivity in cultural, educational and economic terms of such a process of allocation of public monies.

A FRAMEWORK

Our conviction on such questions rests on a wide ranging review of the experiences of many research-funding agencies and on a series of experimental studies we have conducted on the evaluability of the Research Grants Program (RGP) of the Social Sciences & Humanities Research Council (SSHRC). These experiments were designed to develop a framework likely to be of use in evaluating such a program.

The Basic Premises

The evaluation framework we propose is constructed on the basic premise that research is an activity geared to the production of new knowledge, new information. To that extent, research poses a problem to any private enterprise system. The production of knowledge is costly and requires the investment of resources. It is also an activity with a high coefficient of risk and sometimes only a long-run pay-off.

Private citizens are not likely to invest resources in large quantities in such undertakings unless the financial benefits from new knowledge (if and when they accrue) are channelled to them. But new knowledge, once produced, is in the nature of public good: it can be used by one without precluding use by others. Consequently, it would appear to be socially beneficial to make it widely available to all interested, at a nominal cost. Yet, if this is done, there will be little financial incentive for anyone to invest in the production of new knowledge.

In order to resolve this problem, many techniques have been developed, from temporary monopoly on the new knowledge by its private producer (patent), to public subsidy to the private production of new knowledge (research grants), to tax breaks for corporate research, or to government-managed research as in Agriculture Canada or Parks Canada. All are efforts to alleviate the chronic problem of underinvestment in the production of new knowledge in a market economy.

In a world of perfect information, one would know how far to carry the investment in the production of new knowledge and what subsidies or potential rules would be most likely to ensure the appropriate level of research activities. One might expect that investment in research should proceed until the marginal social rate of return of such investment would equal the marginal social rate of return on other types of investment. In the same way, the allocation of resources to the production of new knowledge in different fields, in different institutions, and according to different paradigms and techniques would be pursued to the point where the prospective social rates of return on the last dollar spent in each direction were equalized.

However, the information required to arrive at those solutions is simply not available. Consequently, there is a continuous debate as to whether the resources allocated to the production of new knowledge are sufficient and whether they are allocated in the best way.

If and when a national government or a provincial government makes available public funds as a subsidy to promote the production of new knowledge, it can be presumed that it is in the spirit of alleviating the problem of chronic under-investment in this sector with the ultimate purpose that more new knowledge useable in the national or provincial territory will ensue directly or indirectly. Anything else would entail a misuse of public funds extracted from the national or provincial taxpayers.

The Research Cycle

The question remains as to the best way to interfere with the research process to energize it by allocating additional resources to it and to make the highest and best use of the always limited funds available for the purpose of research. To fix ideas, one might suggest that the research process can be stylized as a research cycle. Any government, we claim, faces such a research cycle and has to decide to what extent it wishes to interfere with the on-going cycle (if at all), and in what ways.

The research cycle, in broad terms, is our label for the set of stylized activities through which a trained scholar/scientist produces new knowledge.

The traditional view of the scholar/scientist depicts him/her as the manager of the research cycle but also as an artisan: he produces a commodity, is attentive to the quality of the product, trains protégés in the techniques of the craft and in the values of the guild. The scholar/scientist also tries to control the work-place through admission of new members and by keeping those who pay salaries and grants at arm's length. Control of the work-place and assurance of quality in this context are effected generally by peer-evaluation at all stages from training to final output. The research cycle can best be appreciated by referring to Figure I.

For the scholar/scientist, the chief recipient of agency funding, the central task is to ask a number of questions triggered by the

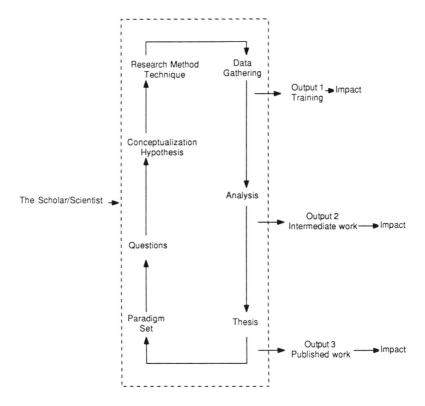

Figure I — A Schematic Representation of the Research Process

paradigm-set in his/her area of study. In many ways the paradigm is the cumulative result of the free-search process and yet it is, like fashion, often less the result of the free market of ideas finding its own equilibrium than the result of a cumulative process the direction of which may or may not result in some superior search process or outcome.

Researchers define their questions and conceptual frameworks within the ambit of one of these paradigms. Some say that they need nothing more than time as input into the process of production of new knowledge. In fact all researchers need at least some overhead capital in the form of library resources, office space, inter-library loan arrangements, facilities, etc. Other scholars/scientists require, in addition to this overhead capital, some direct financial support to assist them in their research work. This support may be used for a variety of activities: travel, research and clerical assistance, computer time, etc.

Once the scholar/scientist is able to engage in the gathering, recording and processing of information, which is the basic ingredient of his activities, there emerges quite early in the research cycle a primary product, a training effect: learning by the principal investigator and his/her assistants if any. This is what we have labelled output 1. This primary product together with some compilation of useable information finds an echo most of the time in the form of some intermediate output (output 2): the compilation and description of results from the search process presented in a preliminary form, work in progress statements, presentations at conferences, discussions at seminars and colloquia, etc. Finally, the search process will take the form of publications formally presenting the results in a synthetic form and developing an explanatory product to be used by the broader community of scholar and perhaps the broader society. This is labelled output 3.

But, in the same manner that professional hockey organizations do not produce hockey games as their ultimate products, but rather audiences for those games as their real output, the whole research cycle is not really closed until its output has an impact on the broader community in a form useable both for consumption and heuristic purposes: new questions and personal endeavours, another round of research activities, a product contributing directly or indirectly to the knowledge base and to the welfare of the community at large.

Any or all of these activities may require additional funding beyond that provided to the scholar by his/her institutional setting: more training, more time, more overhead capital, more research assistance, more technical help, more help to publish, or more help to translate findings into a tangible social product. And within agencies like the SSHRC there are, in fact, programs to assist the scholar in most of these areas. The RGP, then, is only one of many programs to assist the scholar, but its role is basic: it finances additional activities within the research cycle.

Still the question remains, how, or on what basis, should the RGP money be inserted to ensure a maximum of additional productive activities in the research process? The research cycle makes more explicit the points at which agency funding could interfere in scholarly activity, and provides some sense of the chain of activities that leads from the scholar/scientist (upstream) to the point of interference, as well as that which leads from the point of interference to scholarly product and impact (downstream).

The RGP in the Research Cycle

Any research grants program provides only marginal funding to energize the research cycle in a very specific way. As such, this intervention is based on important implicit assumptions about the nature of the research process and its dynamic. Indeed, it is for that reason that research grants are awarded on the basis of specified requirements and only for certain types of activities.

SSHRC awards research grants mainly on the basis of an evaluation of a project, i.e., a proposed bundle of research activities. There is a presumption or expectation that all activities made possible by the grant should generate some primary, some secondary/intermediate output and then some final output. But there is no explicit obligation to do so attached to the funding of those activities. The existence of facilities and research time upstream and the commitment of additional research time downstream are presumed by the funding agency when it funds certain research activities of a gathering/processing/recording type.

NSERC (Natural Sciences and Engineering Research Council) does not interfere with the research process so much on the basis of the evaluation of the project, but in terms of the quality of the scholar/scientist. It bases its decision on some quality reading of what is upstream, i.e., at the scholar/scientist level. Other agencies like the Cleveland Foundation have abandoned any effort to provide ex ante evaluation of scholar/scientist or project and have simply developed a monitoring procedure based on an explicit contract for the generation of a particular product.

In a broad sense, this latter approach applies also to in-house government research, or to the private sector programs: planned output dominates the agenda, and researchers are hired and facilities provided that are deemed likely to help generate this output.

One, at the least, may attempt to operationalize research objectives via one or the other of those three targets: scholar/scientist, project/activities or product. The RGP of the SSHRC has mainly focussed on the project. The question is: is this an effective target?

The Effectiveness of the Research Grant Program

The triple E measurements (effectiveness, efficiency, economy) have been used to gauge the performance of many types of policies or agencies. They refer to the capacity of the agency or policy to do the right thing, to do it right, and to do it economically.

Different funding agencies have different criteria in their programs which have been translated into a greater emphasis on one performance gauge or another. Such choices have had major impact on the effectiveness, efficiency and economy of programs, often without its being fully realized.

For instance, the emphasis on process, which has emerged from the insistence on "curiosity-oriented projects" as sanctioned by peers, has obviously minimized the possibility of enforcing effectiveness criteria. On the other hand, the request that effectiveness criteria be met has given rise to objections that short-run targeting and undue specification would interfere with the creative play of autonomous scholarship, which is assumed by many to be the most productive strategy.

Some questions remain central: whether a RGP has generated a substantial net increase in the aggregate amount of resources devoted to research, and to what extent the structure and rules of the research grants program have triggered the maximum "bang-for-the-buck".

A Displacement Effect?

It is not untoward to suggest that there may be a displacement effect of public funds simply replacing private resources already invested or likely to be invested in unsubsidized research activities. In a sense, the appropriation of public funds to research activities that would otherwise have been financed from other sources (and thus would have gone on anyway) is most certainly not uncommon. However, the magnitude and importance of this effect is unknown.

Such a displacement effect is probably not inconsequential. Certain historical studies have shown that the aggregate amount of resources allocated to education by a society has often been reduced when compulsory public-funded schools were introduced. While one might venture the guess that such absolute reduction may not be the case with the research grants programs, it is also plausible that the aggregate net increase in research activities generated by the programs may not be as high as one might initially have been led to believe.

The Influence of the Filter

The net positive effect of the RGP obviously depends on the manner in which projects are selected: how accurately does the RGP select projects that are likely to have an important significant pay-off in terms of the production of new knowledge.

The overall net effect of any RGP can be measured, according to Helmer and Helmer, by the product of indicators for these two elements (pj . bk), i.e., the probability (pj) that, without a grant, the project would not have been undertaken times the net benefit (bk) ascribable to the project, i.e., to the bundle of subsidized research activities. The greater the two elements, the greater the benefits from the RGP and the costlier the lost opportunities when the grant is denied.

AN EXPERIMENT

We have used this framework experimentally in the examination of research grants programs of the SSHRC. This experiment could not be conducted under ideal conditions because of enormous data problems. Consequently, it should be clear that the focus of this work is the development of an instrument rather than the evaluation of a particular program. While we cannot attach a great deal of credibility to the specific numbers we have produced, we feel that the approach suggested below holds rich promise for the evaluation of research grants programs.

The Basic Questions and the Operational Questions

Under ideal conditions, one would have liked to design two sets of questions corresponding to the p and b components explained in the last section. Segment p would gauge the *force de frappe* of the RGP in generating new activities (questions 1 and 2), while the b component would attempt to deal with the new knowledge (questions 3 and 4) generated by the activities funded by the RGP, and the direct and indirect impact of that knowledge in Canada.

1. Has the RGP generated a net increase in the research effort?
2. Has the RGP chosen the appropriate projects and supported appropriate technologies, i.e., those likely to generate the greatest *force de frappe* in research?
3. Has the RGP generated an increase in outputs 1, 2 and 3?
4. Has the RGP had any impact directly or indirectly on Canadian society?

It has not proved feasible to formulate our questions in this neat compartmentalized and complete way.

First, it has not been possible to determine unambiguously exactly how much research would go on without funding from the RGP. Some experiments on the basis of assumptions about the extent and types of activities likely to be financed privately by the scholar/ scientist (up to $2,500 per year for activities likely to benefit largely if not exclusively the researcher himself) would appear to show that the displacement effect of the RGP is not extremely high. Consequently, one would be led to conclude provisionally that the RGP has generated a net increase in the research effort. However those results are very preliminary and cannot be validated without a much more thorough analysis of the actual and probable private financing of research activities by scholars/scientists.

Second, it is not always possible to distinguish neatly the forces triggering more research activities from those ensuring more efficient research activities from those generating better value for money in terms of results and impact. Consequently, our preliminary testing has dealt with operational questions which often blend somewhat the p and b components. The choice to fund appropriate or inappropriate technologies of research has, for instance, an echo effect on both the level of activities and on their effectiveness. A scholar/ scientist may be more likely to incur personally costs for travel to Europe than for computer time; these in turn may also prove to be channels of activities with different probabilities of generating more output and impact on the same scale.

Finally, there exists at this time no reliable measure of impact. Again, some experiments with the tallying of contents of reading lists in courses, of citation of indexes, etc. have provided some preliminary impressions but nothing deserving formal reporting at this stage. Such a gap could only limit dramatically the possibility of a meaningful test of the b component.

For the purpose of our experiment, we have therefore transformed our basic questions into a number of operational questions which probed the combined product pj x bk:

1. Was there any difference between the productivity of funded and unfunded projects, i.e., in terms of pj x bk, has the RGP generated a net increase in the research output?
2. In choosing to fund projects, has the RGP selected the most appropriate ones, i.e., those likely to be most productive in terms of pj x bk?

Mark I

To answer those questions, we have constructed an architecture of four data bases pertaining to the scholar/scientist, the project, the peer-evaluation of the project, and the output. A fifth component which would be essential in any complete evaluation, has to do with impact. This could not be developed at this stage.

From the very beginning, it was decided to make use of internal information at the SSHRC: first, the only way to generate a useful evaluation instrument is to make it part of the routine of administration; secondly, any specific instrument developed exclusively for evaluative purposes (calling upon clients of an organization to state what portion of their activities or output is ascribable to a grant) is likely to suffer from a fundamental flaw: there is a greater moral hazard problem built into such instruments than in routine reporting since the clients are more likely to overstate the extent of the output as well as to overemphasize the centrality of the grant in achieving such output.

Data were gathered from a sample of 237 files from 1973; applicants were chosen from four disciplines (two in social sciences, SS1 and SS2, two in the humanities, H1 and H2). Of these 237 applicants, 163 were successful.

The basic information (gathered in the summer of 1981) can be grouped under four headings: first, a profile of the scholars/scientists (academic tenure, sex, language, corporate address); second, a profile of the project (duration, cost, location, sector, 'technology' used); third, data on peer-assessment (evaluation grid of assessors, recommendations of assessors and project officers); fourth, information on output (training effect, output in the informal domain, working papers, and the like, and papers, articles, books, etc.).

The quality of the data is quite low. It is not always clear what output can be identified as grant-related. Some standard rules were developed but there is much room for judgment in this process. Nor could we be certain we captured all grant-related output, as the SSHRC has not insisted that all output generated by the activities related to a grant always be acknowledged properly. Finally, since we wished to use only internal data, the re-appearance of a scholar/scientist in the SSHRC's files between 1973 and 1981 implied that for each grant different periods occurred over which some output might have materialized. This forced us to standardize our measures of output somewhat, using a deflation factor corresponding to the number of years between the grant and the last available curriculum vitae. All this has meant that the reliability of the existing measurement is very much in doubt: its presentation here is mainly for illustrative purposes. For the instrument to bear reliable fruit, better data would have to be collected within the agency. It should be clear, however, that it is feasible to collect such data routinely.

Analysis

We have developed a number of tests of hypotheses on the basis of this data bank. To illustrate the potentialities of the instrument, we are presenting a number of simple tests of hypotheses that appear to raise interesting policy questions.

Has the RGP Generated a Net Increase in the Research Output?

It is clear by definition that those receiving grants have spent money hiring assistants, buying material, travelling, etc., but can it be established from our data that they have produced a higher level of output 3 (papers, books, etc.) than if they had not received the grant? This could be an indication that the RGP has generated a net increase in research output.

Since our output 3 information is especially weak because of poor reporting and difficulties in ascribing output to grant, one must be very cautious in interpreting the results, but it would appear that on the average, successful applicants have produced more output 3 than unsuccessful applicants; however, a quick look at the standard deviation of those mean measurements shows that the variance is too large to make these differentials appear statistically significant.

Has the RGP Chosen the Appropriate Projects?

It may be asked whether the RGP has been funding projects of the appropriate size, in the appropriate technology. Appropriate in this instance does not refer to anything normative beyond the proximate indicator of productivity generated by our measures of mean output per grant and mean output per dollar x 10^4.

There is not a simple linear relationship between the amount of money made available and either mean aggregate output per project or productivity per $10,000 for the successful subsidized projects. In fact, more detailed analyses have revealed that outputs 2 and 3 per dollar x 10^4 would appear to be much larger (although not significantly so) for smaller to middle-sized grants. The same holds true, but less consistently, for output 1.

Table I suggests that the mean output per project and mean output per dollar x 10⁴ are quite different from one discipline to the next, and for different areas of study. It should be clear that our measure of aggregate output strongly biases the level of total output in favour of the social sciences, which use more assistants: mean output in the social sciences is therefore greater than in the humanities. This shows up also in the measures of productivity per dollar.

One might note that for output 2, the humanities would appear to perform better, while for output 3 the situation is less clear. SS1 and H1 would appear to have better mean output 3 per project, while the humanities perform relatively better there than in the other measurements.

It is clear that one is faced with different production processes, revealing that H1 might be, in certain respects, closer to the social sciences than to the humanities.

In terms of areas of focus of research projects, geographically neutral, theoretical, methodological studies (that we have labelled neutral) and Canada-related studies would appear to fare better than studies focussing on other geographical areas in general, with productivity per dollar being greater in Canadian studies. Non-Canada geographically-focussed studies show, like the humanities in general, a relatively stronger performance in output 2.

One can analyze the budget of each project in order to unearth different ways in which researchers in different areas, disciplines, or fields have chosen to conduct their research activities in order to reveal either whether the RGP has unconsciously favoured certain technologies, or even favoured technologies less likely to produce the best value for money in terms of measured output.

For illustrative purposes, we have chosen to classify projects in terms of their degree of emphasis on travel and subsistence expenditures and according to the relative importance they give to computer use.

In virtually all cases for all disciplines, the greater the degree of travel and subsistence relative to the overall budget, the lesser the mean output and the productivity per dollar x 10⁴. The results are almost exactly the reverse but somewhat weaker when one deals with the degree of importance of the computing budget within the total budget: the greater the degree of computer use relative to the overall budget, the greater the mean output and the productivity per dollar x 10⁴. Once again, output 2 is an exception to this general tendency.

Table I Output 3: By discipline and by category of verdict

VALUE LABEL	SUM	MEAN	STD. DEV.	VARIANCE	N.
	161.6012	0.6819	3.1840	10.1380	(237)
SS_1					
Unsuccessful Applic.	22.7167	0.5978	1.7903	3.2053	(38)
Successful Applic.	0.8786	0.0628	0.1333	0.0178	(14)
	21.8381	0.9099	2.2069	4.8704	(24)
H_1					
Unsuccessful Applic.	104.6036	0.9868	4.5876	21.0463	(106)
Successful Applic.	6.0833	0.2645	0.5900	0.3481	(23)
	98.5202	1.1870	5.1642	26.6693	(83)
H_2					
Unsuccessful Applic.	24.0083	0.4365	0.8363	0.6995	(55)
Successful Applic.	2.7500	0.1719	0.3502	0.1227	(16)
	21.2583	0.5451	0.9508	0.9040	(39)
SS_2					
Unsuccessful Applic.	10.2726	0.2703	0.4183	0.1749	(38)
Successful Applic.	3.6083	0.1718	0.3811	0.1452	(21)
	6.6643	0.3920	0.4411	0.1946	(17)

Table II **Mean Output and Output Per Dollard By Discipline and Funding Level**
(Successful Applications)

Funding Level By Discipline	Mean Output	Mean Output per dollar$\times 10^4$	N.
Total Population	4.1480	11.0026	163
SS₁	8.8812	16.3041	24
$1-$1499	0.5000	6.6050	1
$2000-$2999	4.7500	23.9875	6
$3000-$4999	6.7108	15.9981	9
$5000-$7999	3.7083	7.1121	2
$10,000 OR MORE	19.3889	13.7602	6
H₁	2.6612	9.3398	83
$1-$1499	0.9343	8.5156	24
$2000-$2999	2.8070	13.2644	34
$3000-$4999	1.9257	5.0919	16
$5000-$7999	0.7500	1.2563	1
$10,000 OR MORE	8.9323	4.6391	3
H₂	2.3933	6.8813	39
$1-$1499	0.9881	10.1113	12
$2000-$2999	0.6944	3.0402	15
$3000-$4999	3.7736	9.4645	7
$5000-$7999	3.2167	4.7649	3
$10,000 OR MORE	17.5000	10.4421	2
SS₂	8.7506	21.0918	17
$1-$1499	0.0	0.0	1
$2000-$2999	6.0298	26.1652	4
$3000-$4999	10.7559	26.9445	7
$5000-$7999	11.7500	18.7097	3
$10,000 OR MORE	7.0500	4.5794	2

Table III **Mean Output By Discipline**
(Successful Applications)

Discipline	Mean Output 1*	Mean Output 2*	Mean Output 3*	Mean Output All	Mean Output All Per Dollarx10[4]	N
Total Population	9.3742	0.1136	0.9097	4.1480	11.0026	163
SS_1	23.7500	0.0546	0.9099	8.8812	16.3041	24
H_1	3.9880	0.1449	1.1870	2.6612	9.3398	83
H_2	5.2564	0.0961	0.5451	2.3933	6.8813	39
SS_2	24.8235	0.0841	0.3920	8.7506	21.0918	17

*Output 1 = Training
Output 2 = Output in the "Informal Domain"
Output 3 = Output in the "Formal Domain"

Table IV	Mean Output by Area (Successful Applications)		
Area		**Mean Output**	**Mean Output Per Dollarx10^4** N
Total Population		4.1480	11.0026	163
Neutral		11.3824	13.8974	9
Canadian		7.2289	18.0200	46
Other		2.2329	7.7725	108

Table V   Mean Output and Output Per Dollar According to Relative Expenditure on Travel and Subsistence

Discipline and Relative Expenditure	Mean Output	Mean Output Per Dollar×10^4	N
Total Population	4.1480	11.0026	163
SS₁	8.8812	16.3041	24
Below Mean*	9.4991	17.1671	22
Above Mean	2.0833	6.8110	2
H₁	2.6612	9.3398	83
Below Mean*	4.3196	12.8956	40
Above Mean	1.1185	6.0321	43
H₂	2.3933	6.8813	39
Below Mean*	3.4774	9.1692	20
Above Mean	1.2522	4.4728	19
SS₂	8.7506	21.0918	17
Below Mean*	9.2975	22.4100	16
Above Mean	0.0	0.0	1

* Projects were classified according to whether the percentage of the grant devoted to travel and subsistence was found to be above or below the mean percentage for travel and subsistence for all grants awarded in the discipline.

Table VI   **Mean Output and Output Per Dollar According to Relative Expenditure on Computers**

Discipline and Relative Expenditure	Mean Output	Mean Output Per Dollarx10^4	N
Total Population	4.1480	11.0026	163
SS$_1$	8.8812	16.3041	24
Below Mean*	5.3000	13.2362	12
Above Mean	12.4623	19.3720	12
H$_1$	2.6612	9.3398	83
Below Mean*	2.1471	9.3390	79
Above Mean	12.8155	9.3563	4
H$_2$	2.3933	6.8813	39
Below Mean*	2.4579	6.6817	35
Above Mean	1.8286	8.6274	4
SS$_2$	8.7506	21.0918	17
Below Mean*	7.6986	19.6515	11
Above Mean	10.6794	23.7323	6

* Projects were classified according to whether the percentage of the grant devoted to computer-related services was found to be above or below the mean percentage for computer-related services for all grants awarded in the discipline.

CONCLUSION

At the center of our work is the view, derived from our analysis of the origin, evolution and practices of SSHRC, that the RGP is an instrument designed to stimulate the production of new knowledge directly and indirectly useable in Canada.

Our p factor measures the extent to which the RGP is likely to trigger new activities and our b factor measures the extent to which such activities are likely to produce new knowledge.

It has been our contention that both factors can be operationalized and that it could be done even in a preliminary way from existing data available in the granting institutions.

Our limited experiment had no other purpose but to show that this was feasible. We do not think that our Mark I is useful as anything but an illustration of what is possible. It is clear that much more work would have to be done internally to improve the quality of the data, and externally to develop better tracking systems for the different outputs and impacts, before policy decisions can be based on such evaluative procedures.

Perhaps the most immediate application of our framework might be to provide a guidance system for the refurbishment of the data gathering process. Indeed, one of the difficulties of such activity, and the reason why so little has been done up to now in this area, might have been the absence of a conceptual scheme likely to be of help in the design of the data gathering process.

But even in this preliminary stage, the very imperfect instrument we have developed enables one to pose and answer many other interesting questions:

1. What are the differences in the pattern of output from sub-sidized research activities and in the time-profile of such output between disciplines?
2. What would be the consequences of a shift from a project-focus to a scholar-focus in the RGP of the SSHRC?
3. What are the differences in the production processes of new knowledge in the humanities and the social sciences and to what extent should the same evaluation procedures be used to gauge their prospects?
4. Is there any way to identify pressure points for affirmative action in the research enterprise (sex, region, linguistic group, institutional size, etc.)?

While it is clear that no reliable instrument can be expected to emerge without much additional work, we are convinced that one can be developed, and that no agency disbursing public monies for research grants can legitimately avoid allocating a portion of its resources to the development of an improved guidance system of that sort.

Otherwise, one might legitimately question whether these agencies are making prudent use of public monies. To the question as to whether effectiveness, efficiency and economy will soon ensue from the use of such a guidance system, one might venture a plausible yes. To the question as to whether such changes as might be triggered would call for a serious restructuring of our existing research organizations and even of our mores in research activities, the answer is also yes and, on this front, our hopes would appear to be as great as some of our colleagues' fears.

REFERENCES

BAKER, W., "The Triple E Movement and Productivity in Canada's Federal Public Service," *Optimum*, Vol. 11, (3), 1980, pp. 5-20.

COLE, S., COLE, J.R., and SIMON, G.A., *Peer Review at the National Science Foundation: the Results of an Experiment*, Center for the Social Sciences at Columbia University, April 1981.

HELMER, O, and HELMER, H., *Future Opportunities for Foundation Support*, Institute for the Future, Middletown, Connecticut, June 1970.

MILLIGAN, F., "The Canada Council as a Public Body," *Canadian Public Administration*, Summer 1979, pp. 269-289.

MILLIGAN, F., "Program Planning and Control in the Canada Council, 1957-78," *Canadian Public Administration*, Vol. 23, (4), Winter 1980, pp. 577-597.

PAQUET, G., and TAYLOR, J.H., "On Marksmanship: a Preliminary Look at the Evaluability and Evaluation of Resources Grant Programs," Rapport du Conseil en Sciences Humaines, Fall 1983, 128 pp.

TUSSMAN, J., *Government and the Mind*, New York, 1977, pp. 11-19.

Psychology and Public Policy

DAVID ZUSSMAN

Traditionally, public policy analysis, drawing from its roots in the area of political science, has been based on the examination of the perceived distribution of winners and losers as they are affected by a particular policy change. During the 1960s public policy as an academic discipline widened its analytical and theoretical base through the rapid development of applied theories of economics, operations research and computer modeling. All of these developments sought ways of uncovering systematic predictors of economic and social change in society while maintaining the basic appreciation that public policy, de facto, is the product of a political environment.

Historically, psychologists have had limited interest in public policy, either as interveners or as active participants in the policy making process. Their lack of interest is more likely related to the way in which psychology has developed as an academic discipline than it is to a natural bias of psychologists against policy analysis or politics. Quite simply, psychologists, as a general rule, view policy making as imprecise, and too unscientific for their liking. As a consequence, they have taken little interest in examining the political process. The purpose of this paper is to demonstrate the usefulness of psychological research in defining federal policies regarding energy conservation. In presenting examples of its value in this policy area, it should become apparent how useful applied psychology might be in other economic and social policy areas.

The first section of the paper defines the problem of energy conservation and how it is as much a psychological orientation as an economic issue. Sections two and three describe the psychology of information exchange and diffusion as an illustration of how applied psychological principles might help to bridge an understanding between theoretical and actual human behavior. The last section is an appeal for greater involvement of psychologists in the development of public policy.

ENERGY CONSERVATION:
THE PROBLEM AND THE PROGRAMS

Energy conservation is one of the most promising solutions to the nation's energy problems. The goal is not controversial, the means to achieving it are. Some conservation advocates argue for a strong government role. Other observers believe that the most effective approach is to rely on supply and demand to allow rising prices to reduce consumption. Most government policy makers, social scientists, and physical scientists believe that widespread conservation is attainable through the development of social and cultural institutions, values, and norms which foster energy conservation at the societal and individual levels.

Energy used in the home for such purposes as home (electric, hot air or water) and hot water heating, air conditioning and operating home appliances offers energy analysts an especially attractive target for the overall reduction of energy consumption and costs in Canada. These uses account for more than one fifth of the total energy consumed in Canada on an annual basis. While advanced technology already exists for effecting great energy savings in these categories through technology transfer, there is scope for savings through changes in consuming behavior and converting from one energy source to another (e.g., oil to natural gas). Most people believe that the motivation for the consumer to change his behavior and to convert to new sources of energy depends simply on price elasticity: high energy prices would dampen demand or would force people to find ways to reduce energy demands.

Some have challenged the theory of consumer demand: consumers' responses to the change in market prices have been disappointing in several ways. First, one might have hoped that a near quadrupling of crude oil prices would produce a greater decline in household consumption than has been observed. In fact, in the US, the modest decrease in energy use brought about by the market discipline was not the result of improved conservation measures for residential or commercial buildings, or of cost saving investments. Ten years of experience since the 1973 oil crisis have raised doubts about the likelihood that a large number of consumers is likely to invest in conservation as a short-term energy strategy.

This poor response to the historically high energy prices makes it critical for psychologists to become involved in the design of schemes to moderate energy consumption without resort to draconian measures such as rationing. Under prevailing conditions of low energy costs, when elasticity arguments no longer apply over the short-term, there remains a critical need for a better understanding of the dynamics of conservation behavior in Canada.

The principles which govern this type of decision-making behavior are essentially psychological in nature. Although social scientists cannot predict individual behavior with great certainty, the research of Tversky and Kahneman demonstrates that, when the same problem is presented in different ways, depending on the way a problem is "framed", decisions often result in complete reversals of preference. The context used by the Canadian government to frame the energy crisis problem of the early 1980s has obviously had much to do with the results obtained.

During the energy crisis of the mid 1970s, the Canadian federal government rejected total reliance on a market-oriented solution. Instead, it devised two government administered programs known as CHIP and COSP to trigger residential energy conservation in an attempt to reduce the overall level of energy consumption. The principal feature of both of these programs were the cash inducements offered to individuals to invite them to modify their energy consuming behavior.

CHIP

The Canadian Home Insulation Program (CHIP) was expanded in 1977 to a national scale after results from a pilot project yielded encouraging results about potential energy savings. During each of its various phases, one of the principal objectives of this program was to modify consumption behavior, in general, by "stimulating action on the part of individual Canadians to upgrade the thermal efficiency of the existing housing stock." A rebate scheme, which has varied over the past seven years, was used as the prime motivator. The most recent program rules allowed for the federal government to pay 60% of eligible material costs up to a maximum amount of $500 for various insulation and other conservation related materials. As of 1984, CHIP had cost a total of $900 million to Canadian taxpayers. The program is due to terminate at the end of 1987.

COSP

The Canadian Oil Substitution Program was designed to encourage home owners to replace their oil fired furnaces with devices using lower cost alternative sources of energy such as natural gas and wood. This was accomplished by providing a cash rebate of up to $800 towards the capital costs of converting oil heating systems to alternative energy sources and by the federal government pegging gas prices at 65% of oil prices. COSP cost approximately $150 million annually and should terminate at the end of 1990.

On November 8, 1984, the Mulroney government decided to honour one of its principal campaign promises by cancelling both of these grant programs in an effort to reduce federal spending. There is some evidence to suggest that many of the Conservative Ministers saw the programs as ineffective ways of achieving their policy goals of lower energy consumption in the residential sector. Moreover, many of the new government members also harbored some skepticism about the use of financial incentives likely to create barriers to the natural functioning of the marketplace.

Initially, both of these programs were designed to radically change individual behavior in two different ways. CHIP was dedicated to decreasing total domestic energy consuming behavior by altering lifestyle behavior and COSP's main objective was to encourage consumers to choose a less costly energy source. The choices that the consumers were being asked to make were complex ones which required some sophisticated reasoning and, in many cases, consumers were asked to make decisions involving relatively large sums of money in anticipation of energy savings over the lifetime of their capital investment.

For the consumer, this elaborate decision process required a series of complex investment and consumption decisions which entailed implicit calculations of long-term discount rates, gauging the likelihood of significant technological innovations over the period of the capital investment, and testing hypotheses about the value of lifestyle changes.

To make such complex decisions, the consumer must have at his or her fingertips information on the costs and savings of their conservation measure and some notion of what the energy picture will look like over the life of the investment. The key to the success of these programs depended on providing useful information to all consumers. No matter how accurate or reliable the information might be, it is also clear that, if it is not presented in a form that the consumer can easily understand, it will fail to have any impact.

In this regard social psychologists can make important contributions to improving the value of information dissemination. They can make recommendations for modifying the government-consumer interaction in order to maximize the impact of the information exchange on the resident's subsequent behavior. Psychologists may also have some knowledge about factors that can expedite the diffusion of innovation throughout the community.

PSYCHOLOGY AND INFORMATION EXCHANGE

It has been assumed by policy-makers that producers and consumers are rational decision makers. Producers and consumers are believed to make choices by, first, surveying the available alternatives; second, collecting and accurately weighting all the information relative to each alternative; third, considering this information to determine the costs and benefits associated with each potential strategy and making probability judgments about the risks and uncertainties associated with the adoption of any given course of action; and fourth, selecting the most cost effective strategy that maximizes positive utility while minimizing costs.

Based on this rational economic model, major energy policies to date have tended to assume that rising prices and technological improvements would produce the needed shifts towards lower consumption. Indeed, there is considerable evidence that such behavior patterns have materialized; energy demand has moderated over the last few years. However, much of the decrease in demand is probably due to the recession and the trend towards smaller family sizes.

Developing more advanced technologies to lower consumption is acknowledged by many to be a cost effective model for decreasing energy consumption. However, known effective and cost efficient technologies have not necessarily and automatically been accepted by the public. Without an effective program to facilitate the diffusion of these innovations, this strategy is likely to fail to have an impact on energy supply problems. For example, although it is clear that insulating, weather stripping, caulking, and installing setback thermostats are cost effective measures with a payback time of less than five years, in most cases, the vast majority of people have been slow to make use of these and other innovations.

Similarly, individuals has been reluctant to borrow money for conservation devices and materials even after their cost effectiveness has been demonstrated. How is it possible that rational agents act systematically in ways that are not in their own best interest? The answer is that individuals act in ways which are consistent with their perception of the situation. Human behavior is best understood in terms of individual desires taking into account the cognitive, social and personal forces that shape the perception of economic realities defining a given situation. The failure to reach conservation goals cannot be viewed as a purely technical and economic problem. It is a perception problem.

As Frieden points out in his review of public policy on household energy consumption:

> The claim that conservation will make big reductions in our energy needs is premature. An implied assumption is that a conservation strategy would yield big payoffs if everyone would cooperate. But since everyone almost never cooperates with any national policy, this is not a strong foundation for an energy policy.

Several studies have shown that people tend to weight information in proportion to its vividness. People tend to believe personal stories told in clear unequivocal terms more than they believe information presented in an impersonal manner with supporting statistical information. One practical consequence of this research is to present information not only completely and accurately but also in the most vivid and personal manner possible. Therefore the use of real personal data instead of fictitious data and the presence of a smoke pencil to illustrate the real situation will have its desired impact.

The fact that people are frequently swayed more by the report of a single individual than they are by a comprehensive data summary reflects, in part, people's tendency to overweigh low probabilities and underweigh large ones. As well, data collected by Kahneman and Tversky indicate that people respond more seriously to reports of financial losses than to reports of financial gains. This suggests that information supplied to consumers might have a greater impact on conservation behavior if energy information were presented in terms of how much more it would cost if a home was not converted to gas or if the walls were not insulated.

Evidence also suggests that people have trouble integrating quantitative information for their own use. As a consequence, they appear to disregard components that the alternatives seem to share and to focus on the components that would appear to contrast them. From another perspective, there is a considerable body of knowledge about the importance of feedback in the learning process. Feedback to the consumer regarding energy costs appears to be a highly cost effective procedure, yielding short-term energy savings ranging from 10% to 20% above previous consumptions levels.

Although incentive or grant programs such as CHIP and COSP may appear attractive because of the considerable cash inducements involved, there is considerable social psychological research which finds that people do not assign weights to information in strict accordance to its economic properties. Consumers do not necessarily value highly or participate more in programs which pay more or provide larger cash bonuses. Thus, the various grant schemes which constituted the heart of the government's conservation policy may have failed to have the motivational impact its planners expected.

Further evidence provided by Stern and Gardner point out that a doubling of the price for energy produces only about a 10% reduction of consumer demand, at least in the short-term. Long-term effects arising from the purchase of more energy efficient appliances and the like may be more substantial but they have not yet been studied by psychologists.

Stern and Gardner also observe that behaviors involving adoption of energy efficient technology generally offer more potential for conservation than behaviors involving curtailed use of existing energy systems. This finding is of psychological importance because people may be relatively more receptive to behavior changes that are not perceived as involving curtailment. Much of the current energy research may therefore have ignored the class of behavior that offers the greatest potential savings in energy in the near future.

Finally, Stern and Gardner warn that one-shot actions have greater potential to conserve energy than do conservation decisions that must be frequently repeated or constantly monitored. Some work on the relative importance of initial versus operating costs in appliance purchases have yielded interesting findings in this connection.

PSYCHOLOGY AND INFORMATION DIFFUSION

Another critical step in the process of increased energy conservation and lower energy demand is to ensure that the appropriate and vivid information is effectively disseminated to potential consumers. One of the most powerful ways of ensuring the rapid acceptance of new ideas is for people to come into contact with others who have successfully adopted them. One refinement to this procedure is to encourage those who have "been converted" to participate in peer tutoring programs as a way of demonstrating the value of energy conservation. Peer tutors have at times been better than specially trained experts. Another related way of addressing the problem of diffusion is by trying to devise ways of increasing the esteem which the community would have for those who conserve energy or for those who change to more plentiful energy supplies. This approach would offer substantial energy savings if the key factors to lifestyle attitudes and behavior could be discovered.

The theory of cognitive dissonance offers some evidence on how conservation behavior might be enhanced by first soliciting a smaller commitment from people before asking them to change their behavior more radically. Building on consumers' modest commitments to energy conservation initially might over the long haul result in more permanent changes in consumption patterns than demanding radical behavioral changes at the outset.

One finds that people, as a general rule, are particularly prone to increase their commitment to a cause, beyond the level one might originally expect, once they have attempted to persuade another to adopt the cause. Therefore, providing people with some encouragement for engaging in whatever energy efficient behavior they choose should plant the seeds for the continuation of energy efficient behavior in the original participants.

The cognitive dissonance theory also suggests another effective way of encouraging diffusion through increased levels of commitment. Research has shown that when consumers are given much decision control they begin to see themselves as having made a commitment to conservation. This approach, generally, results in long-term behavioral change. Other approaches that rely on active consumer involvement have been more consistently successful than simple persuasion attempts which rely simply on information packages which extol the virtues of conservation.

While general findings do suggest ways in which public policy might be formulated with some assurance, there are, unfortunately, some complicating factors which must be considered. In a recent study, Black, Stern and Elworth found that both economic self interest and internalized personal norms affect behavioral responses to the energy situation but that the relative importance of these influences varies with the type of energy saving behavior. Thus, the fewer constraints on a given energy saving action, the more likely a consumer will act on personal norms.

CONCLUSION

It should now be obvious that the issue of energy conservation and energy substitution depends on a large number of factors, some economic, others psychological. According to sources, in the United States the residential conservation service proceeded with almost no basic knowledge of the economic and noneconomic factors which would determine its success or failure. The same is most likely true for Canada for the government's attempts at encouraging long-term energy conservation by offering cash inducements. These programs have failed to consider the powerful interaction between psychological and economic factors in individual decision making and behavior.

In essence, the problem which policy analysts were faced with was to find a way to persuade consumers to act in their own long-term social and economic interest and in the public interest rather than in their short-term individual interest.

To deal with this problem policy-makers should have found it helpful to know to what extent individual decisions were determined by consideration of some of the following factors: the impact of initial and operating costs, consumer expectations of price changes or availability problems, consumer desire for independence from a fragile or volatile energy system. All of these issues could have been studied by psychologists as members of teams of public policy analysts.

To find a place among these interdisciplinary teams, psychologists will have to make a number of important adjustments to their traditional career paths. First, psychologists will have to seek out opportunities to work with other social scientists with similar research interests. This will mean learning new skills in economics, political science and in sociology, which at the outset may appear to place them at a disadvantage. Second, they will have to take a sober look at their methodological tool kit to see which of their techniques are relevant in the applied world of policy analysis. In the public policy arena, the facts are difficult to collect, hard to measure and almost always explained in the context of a political environment. Many of these limitations may make it difficult for psychologists to use their traditional "outillage mental". However, the opportunities for relevant research abound in the public policy arena. The challenge is for psychologists to rise to the occasion.

REFERENCES

ARBUTHNOT, J., "The Induction of Sustained Recycling Behavior Through the Foot in the Door Technique," *Journal of Environmental Systems*, 1976, Vol. 6, pp. 355-368.

BLACK, J.S., STERN, P., and ELWORTH, J., "Personal and Contextual Influences on Household Energy Adaptations," *Journal of Applied Psychology*, 1985, Vol. 70, (1), pp. 3-21.

BORGIDA, E., and NISBETT, R.E., "The Differential Impact of Abstract vs Concrete Information Decisions," *Journal of Applied Social Psychology*, 1977.

FISHER, R.B., "An Each One–Teach One Approach to Music Notation," *Grade Teacher*, 1969, Vol. 86, p. 120.

FREEDMAN, J., and FRASER, S., "Compliance Without Pressure: the Foot in the Door Technique," *Journal of Personality and Social Psychology*, 1966, Vol. 4, pp. 195-202.

FRIEDEN, B., *Household Energy Consumption: the Record and the Prospect*, Cambridge, MIT, 1981.

HAMILL, R., WILSON, T.D., and NISBETT, R.E., "Insensitivity to Sample Bias: Generalizing from a Typical Case," *Journal of Personality and Social Psychology*, 1980, Vol. 39, pp. 578-589.

HAUSMAN, J.A., "Individual Discount Rates and the Purchase and Utilization of Energy-Using Durables," *Bell Journal of Economics*, 1979, Vol. 10, (1), pp. 33-54.

HIRST, E., "Understanding Energy Conservation," *Science*, 1979, pp. 206-513.

KEMPTON, W., and MONTGOMERY, L., "Folk Quantification of Energy," *Energy*, 1982, Vol. 7, pp. 817-827.

LITTLE, A.D., Home Improvement Financing, Office of Policy Development and Research, US Department of Housing and Urban Development, Washington, DC, September 1977.

NEL, E., HELMREICH, R., and ARONSON, E., "Opinion Change in the Advocate as a Function of the Persuasibility of his Audience: a Clarification of the Meaning of Dissonance," *Journal of Personality and Social Psychology*, 1969, Vol. 12, pp. 117-124.

STERN, P.C., and GARDNER, G.T., "Psychological Research and Energy Policy," *American Psychologist*, 1980, Vol. 39, pp. 578-589.

TVERSKY, A., and KAHNEMAN, D., "The Framing of Decisions and the Psychology of Choice," *Science*, January 1981, Vol. 211.

International Management
Gestion internationale

New Directions in International Business Research

A. LOUIS CALVET

International business, as a field of inquiry, is concerned primarily with the study of the international operations carried out by business firms and the interrelations between these business activities and the international environment. Conducting business across national borders requires a decision as to the kind of institutional arrangement that will best suit the corporation's objectives. The range of alternatives goes from, at the one extreme, establishing administratively-controlled affiliates in foreign countries — becoming a multinational enterprise (MNE) — to the setting-up of market-like relationships with a minimum of managerial control, as is more often the case in licensing or minority joint ventures. Business transactions, and the institutional channels through which they take place, exist in an environment which is continually evolving. Hence the endless combinations of situations and business arrangements that arise and are subjects for study and research.

One particular combination has, however, been the center of attention in international business research: the U.S. multinational manufacturing enterprise. The decade of the seventies brought about a myriad of studies concentrating on the period in the sixties when, under the so-called Pax Americana, U.S. firms expanded overseas in the manufacturing industries.[1]

Various projections emerged from these studies, the most publicized perhaps being the Global Reach scenario, which portrayed MNEs as tentacular, power-maximizing firms spanning the globe and imposing their will on weak nation states. More serious discussions of the multinational phenomenon dealt with the economic and political implications of the growth of U.S. business abroad. Overall, most studies warned about the MNEs being on a collision course with nation states and made recommendations for control of these firms' activities.

---

1. Foreign direct investment, i.e., the establishment of equity-controlled subsidiaries, was predominantly initiated in the sixties by manufacturing firms (Caves, 1971; Dunning, 1979).

The purpose of this paper is to describe the recent evolution of the international environment as it affects the research conducted in international business. We will tackle in turn the multinational firm in the eighties, specific Canadian issues, and conclude with other areas of interest.

THE MNE IN THE 1980s

From a brief review of the research of the past decade, it appears that, at least in North America, a great deal of attention was devoted to understanding the reasons why domestic firms in general, and U.S. firms in particular, would prefer to expand into international markets via the establishment or acquisition of foreign affiliates.

This search for the motivational forces behind foreign expansion led to the following rationalization of the MNE phenomenon: if MNEs exist and survive, it must be that the creation and subsequent operation of an administrative and hierarchical machinery across borders is at times a more efficient way to transfer resources than the reliance on external market mechanisms of a contractual nature. Furthermore, not only must a firm choose to internalize its foreign transactions, but it must possess some firm-specific advantage which allows the firm to be competitive in relation to indigenous entrepreneurs. In a nutshell, MNEs must have a monopolistic advantage that they find more profitable to exploit overseas via controlled subsidiaries.

These insights into the nature of MNEs should have led to research in three main directions:

1. how firms develop ownership or firm-specific advantages;
2. how a global network permits better exploitation of these unique skills; and,
3. how MNEs design their international management processes to maintain a lasting edge over simpler, and presumably less costly, market-like arrangements.

Unfortunately, thorough work is still missing in these three areas. Little is known about the internal operations of the MNEs, in part because of the difficulty of collecting hard data and categorizing MNEs' internal processes. To make things worse, the concept of firm-specific advantage remains as elusive as ever. This elusiveness originates in the fact that not only may MNEs have advantages of a monopolistic nature, e.g., a patented and well-protected blueprint, but the internalization of their transactions can be considered in itself a further advantage (Casson, 1984). It would seem that the distinction between knowing how to do something other firms don't know — the ownership advantage — and merely being a global network of equity-controlled firms — a MNE — is hard to draw. In a world of frequent and sudden changes, the flexibility that the MNE's global network provides, for instance through the use of transfer pricing, is in itself a firm-specific advantage.

So much for theory. It should also be pointed out that the particular scenario chosen in studying MNEs was built on the assumption of an ever-expanding world economy. The realities of recent years have reminded us how limited that view was and how a phenomenon so seldom heard of, such as a divestment, can take major proportions. In contrast to the earlier fear of a growing multinationality, nowadays one hears the opposite worry of not enough foreign direct investment. Research in the area of divestment in an international setting has already begun (Boddewyn, 1983).

A further bias in the early research on the MNE resided in the disproportionate emphasis on privately owned U.S. multinationals. The emergence of European, and even Third World, MNEs led to the dual realization that:
1. MNEs are not a unique U.S. invention, and
2. most non-U.S. MNEs are either controlled by national governments or closely intertwined with them (Franko, 1976).

As a result, two of the old clichés about MNEs have to be revised, i.e., the imperialist view of the U.S. MNEs extending their corporate domination over less-developed countries, and the MNEs vs the nation states. The former stereotype is an oversimplification of a quite complex international environment, which no longer serves much purpose, while the latter is a confusing picture of the power relations at play internationally, for what lie behind many MNEs are simply other nation states.

Technology transfer played a major role in the seventies. It was perceived by many, in particular in developing countries, as the key to harmonious world development and received a great deal of attention in international organizations such as the United Nations. The argument was that if technology and technological knowledge could flow freely to developing nations, we would do away with the need for trading manufacturing goods against raw materials and the inescapable deterioration of the terms of trade experienced by the developing world.

Multinational firms were at the center of this polemic since they were seen as major roadblocks to the release of technological know-how. The whole thrust of technology transfer appears to have lost its momentum, partly because of the growing realization that the transfer of technology is not a costless activity, as it was long thought to be. Furthermore, the gradual diffusion of skills and knowledge, and the appearance of competitive firms from the semi-industrialized nations, have removed some of the political arguments surrounding the technology transfer issue.

The eighties have brought a growing concern about the employment effects arising from the multinational phenomenon. American policymakers had already faced this problem earlier when U.S. foreign direct investment abroad dominated the international scene. More recently, the spread of non-U.S. MNEs has shifted the interest on this topic to the other major countries of the world that have experienced the largest increases in outward foreign direct investment. There is a major difference though: while U.S. MNEs were free to "export" jobs abroad,[2] non-U.S. MNEs, because of their tight links with their governments, are faced with a politically-determined impossibility of allocating resources on the basis of worldwide opportunities: witness the French government interference in the operations of its MNEs.

All these changes in the international arena open promising avenues for research. State-owned MNEs have already been the center of numerous international conferences, and further research is necessary on the managerial processes of these large firms which appeal to so many constituencies. Little is known of the operations of Third-World MNEs, particularly the way in which their more rigid cultures influence managerial processes. The same is true of Japanese firms, although more attention has been paid to their particular business philosophy.

THE CANADIAN SCENE

The Canadian realities of the eighties are also quite different from those experienced in the sixties and seventies, and so are the topics for research. The early literature reflected the aftermath of the foreign "invasion" by U.S. MNEs and the political and cultural implications of a foreign-dominated economy (Gray, 1972). With the growth of Canadian-owned MNEs in the mid-seventies, we saw an opposite trend of Canadian direct investment abroad of quite a large magnitude. In this respect, Canadian firms were part of the main trend characterized by the emergence of non-U.S. MNEs. Government policy, though, remained focused on the foreign domination part of the global equation and tried to lessen the negative impact of having, at home, a "replica" of the larger U.S. economy. In this respect, world product mandates, e.g., the specialization by a foreign-owned affiliate in the development, production, and marketing of a particular product on a worldwide basis, were promoted as a way to make up for the short and inefficient production runs that allegedly made Canadian products non-competitive abroad. Looking back at the results, it would seem that world product mandates, although they may alleviate some of the shortcomings of a foreign-controlled economy, are not a panacea that will in itself resolve the perceived problems. Recent comments suggest in fact that world product mandates have failed on several accounts. First of all, world product mandates are mostly given for products at the end of their life cycle, thus not allowing Canadian indigenous research and development activities to develop as initially expected. Second,

---

2. Challenge by labor unions was relatively minimal.

Canadian senior management seems in general unaware of the decision-making process of the headquarters staff and hence does not participate fully in the strategic choices. And third, even when a world product mandate is granted, it is seldom exclusive and hence, strictly speaking, not really a world product mandate. Note that these are not surprising comments if we recall that the logic of a MNE is to operate a network of integrated subsidiaries to gain flexibility and alter the allocation of resources in response to or anticipation of external changes. Accordingly, if each affiliate in a particular country were fully specialized, the flexibility of the global network would be seriously hampered, and by the same token, the MNE itself.

At present, the Canadian situation differs dramatically from the concerns expressed previously. The indications are that Canada is presently witnessing a substantial migration or exodus of Canadian-owned firms, as exemplified in Table I.

Table I	Canadian Direct Investment Abroad (CDIA)	
Book value CDIA (millions of $)	CDIA as a % of FDI in Canada*	CDIA as a % of Domestic Assets**
1971	6132	24.73	6.95
1975	9695	29.57	7.7
1979	17501	37.00	8.20
1983e	34309	54.27	10.66

* Ratio of book values, FDI: Foreign Direct Investment.
** Book value of CDIA as a % of the book value of all $10+ million Canadian corporations.
Source: Statistics Canada, International Balance of Payments Statistics and International Investment Position — various issues.

Large increases in Canadian direct investment abroad have been taking place in the last few years, as seen by the growing value of Canadian-controlled assets held abroad (column 1). Also CDIA represents nowadays over 50% of the book value of domestic assets held by foreigners (column 2). Preliminary data show that there has been a tendency for capital to migrate to the U.S. in larger proportions, to the point that two-thirds of all new outward flows are directed to our southern neighbor. Note also the steady rise in the proportion of CDIA to the book value of domestic assets, which indicates that foreign investing represents a larger percentage of total, domestic and foreign, investment carried out by Canadian corporations.

The U.S. experience had been that while U.S. firms expanded abroad, they tended to maintain R&D and upper administrative jobs at home in the U.S. while exporting "lower" type activities. As once described by Hymer (1970), the MNE phenomenon was one of substituting white collar employment at home for blue collar employment, since blue collar jobs were lost in favor of the foreign affiliates. In a sense, production moved overseas but research, development, managerial and upper-echelon administrative positions remained and even increased at home. It was not envisioned that everything would move abroad! However, this is the phenomenon that appears to be taking place among Canadian corporations. Large Canadian MNEs have shelved plans for expansion at home while opening R&D departments, high-tech laboratories, and large regional offices in the U.S. It is no longer that a local firm engages in foreign direct investment; it is more as if the firm gradually becomes an expatriate ready to lose its national roots so as to grow new ones south of the border.

This phenomenon has many implications, but the most publicized one is without any doubt the loss of employment at home. The U.S. studies had found no definite proof as to whether total employment in the U.S. had suffered from the waves of U.S. foreign direct investment (Bergsten, Horst and Moran, 1978). The employment impact in the Canadian case would seem less ambiguous and probably negative.

Certainly these new aspects of the international business environment and their implications for Canada are areas of extreme importance for research. At the public policy level, the question is whether the government should interfere with its own firms' decisions, and whether it should formally screen outward foreign investment or use incentive schemes to influence location decisions by Canadian firms. This situation is far removed from the one presently discussed by some groups about whether the agency in charge of screening foreign incoming investment should be scrapped or not. While this last issue may be of some interest, the stakes are nowadays somewhere else.

TOWARD MORE PRODUCTIVE RESEARCH

Our discussion has isolated only a few, but I believe rather important, points in the field of international business. Many other issues await further study. In North America the topic of exporting is becoming increasingly important. Not enough research has gone into understanding the managerial processes involved in the initiation and success of an exporting activity within a previously domestic-oriented firm. The importance of this topic transcends the domain of theoretical concepts and has immediate application in knowing how to target public monies and programs to encourage exporting by firms. It is also in accordance with the growing interest in small and medium-size firms, which were somewhat forgotten in the research and policy making of the earlier years.

In the same vein, it is also true that while MNEs provide a relatively well-defined area of study, many international business arrangements involve other types of relationships such as consortia, franchising, etc. Learning more about them is certainly necessary and calls for further research.

At a more macro level, the question of free trade between Canada and the United States has regained vitality with the notion of sectoral free trade, i.e., the suppression of tariff and non tariff barriers within a particular industry.

Also, attempts to bypass the monetary means of payment, at least in part, in order to cancel international business transactions have been recently on the rise. This entire domain, often named countertrade, in which firms and/or governments engage in a two-way exchange of goods, if pursued further will bring major changes in the way international trade is conducted. New marketing vehicles may have to be devised to cope with a complex system that avoids the monetary channels.

Interest is also high in the area of international finance, in particular concerning the behavior of exchange rates, the effects of the international diversification of large pools of money, such as pension funds, and the internationalization of the owner-ship of large firms, not to mention the question of Third World indebtedness.

Finally, on a different front, it seems that the kind of interna-tional business research needed is concrete analysis of business situations rather than theory. A more balanced approach, which focuses on clearly identified problems, should lead in the future to more productive research and avoid the extreme prophecies which characterized the research of the seventies and are of little help in international business management.

158   A. LOUIS CALVET

REFERENCES

BARNET, R., and MULLER, R., *Global Reach*, New York, Simon and Schuster, 1974.
BERGSTEN, C.F., HORST, T.O., and MORAN, T.H., eds., *American Multinationals and American Interests*, Washington, D.C., The Brookings Institution, 1978.
BODDEWYN, J.J., "Foreign and Domestic Divestment and Investment Decisions," *Journal of International Business Studies*, Winter 1983, pp. 23-35.
BUCKLEY, P.J., and CASSON, M., *The Future of the Multinational Enterprise*, London, Holmes and Meier, 1976.
CALVET, A.L., "A Synthesis of Foreign Direct Investment Theories and Theories of the Multinational Firm," *Journal of International Business Studies*, Special Issue, Spring/Summer 1981, pp. 43-59.
CASSON, M., "General Theories of the Multinational Enterprise: A Critical Examination," University of Reading, Discussion Papers in International Investment and Business Studies, No. 77, January 1984.
CAVES, R.E., "International Corporations: The Industrial Economics of Foreign Investment," *Economica*, February 1971, pp. 1-27.
DHAWAN, K.C., and KRYZANOWSKI, L., "Characteristics and Experiences of Canadian-Based Export Consortia," in K.C. Dhawan, H. Etemad, and R.W. Wright, eds., *International Business: a Canadian Perspective*, Don Mills, Ontario, Addison-Wesley Publishers, 1981.
DUNNING, J.H., "Explaining Changing Patterns of International Production: In Defence of the Eclectic Theory," *Oxford Bulletin of Economics and Statistics*, November 1979, pp. 269-295.
FRANKO, L.G., *The European Multinationals: A Renewed Challenge to American and British Big Business*, London, Greylock, 1976.
GILPIN, R., "The Politics of Transnational Economic Relations," in R. Keohane and J.S. Nye, eds., *Transnational Relations and World Politics*, Cambridge, Mass., Harvard University Press, 1971.
GRAY, H., *Foreign Direct Investment in Canada* ("The Gray Report"), Ottawa, Information Canada, 1972.
HYMER, S.H., *The International Operations of National Firms: A Study of Direct Foreign Investment*, Cambridge, Mass., The MIT Press, 1976.
HYMER, S.H., "The Efficiency (Contradictions) of Multinational Corporations," *American Economic Review*, May 1970, pp. 441-448.
KINDLEBERGER, C.P., *American Business Abroad: Six Lectures on Direct Investment*, New Haven, Yale University Press, 1969.
KOGUT, B., "Foreign Direct Investment as a Sequential Process," in C.P. Kindleberger and D.B. Audretsch, eds., *The Multinational Corporation in the 1980s*, Cambridge, Mass., The MIT Press, 1983.
RUGMAN, A.M., "Internalization as a General Theory of Foreign Direct Investment, A Re-Appraisal of the Literature," *Weltwirtschaftliches Archiv*, No 116, 1980, pp. 365-379.
Science Council of Canada, *Multinationals and Industrial Strategy: The Role of World Product Mandates*, Ottawa, Supply and Services, 1980.
TEECE, D.J., *The Multinational Corporation and the Resource Cost of International Technology Transfer*, Cambridge, Mass., Ballinger, 1976.
VERNON, R., *Sovereignty at Bay: The Multinational Spread of U.S. Enterprises*, New York, Basic Books, 1971.

La sélection des marchés d'exportation: inventaire et évaluation des méthodes

JEAN-ÉMILE DENIS
JEAN LAMOTHE

Les efforts des gouvernants en vue d'inciter les entreprises à exporter, en particulier les petites et moyennes, ont porté leurs fruits. Nombreuses sont-elles en effet à tenter de pénétrer les marchés étrangers.

Pour une entreprise, l'une des premières décisions à prendre concerne le choix des marchés-cibles. Quelles sont les démarches et les méthodes suggérées et recommandées aux entreprises dans les publications en marketing international ? Sont-elles adaptées à leurs besoins, en particulier à ceux des PME ? Quelles démarches peut-on suggérer aux entreprises canadiennes désireuses de sélectionner leurs marchés-cibles de manière rigoureuse ?

Telles sont les questions auxquelles répond ce texte qui comporte trois parties. En premier lieu, un cadre de classification des démarches et approches est proposé et celles-ci sont succinctement commentées. La pertinence de ces approches en fonction des besoins des PME est abordée dans une deuxième partie. En dernier lieu, une démarche est proposée et des recommandations sont formulées dans le but de faciliter la tâche des entreprises dans la sélection des marchés d'exportation.

Un certain nombre de points doivent être précisés avant d'entreprendre la classification des démarches et méthodes de sélection des marchés.

CLASSIFICATION DES MÉTHODES

Par démarche, on entend une manière générale d'aborder le problème de la sélection des marchés. Ainsi peut-on distinguer deux démarches possibles. D'une part, l'entreprise peut rassembler des renseignements divers sur les marchés étrangers en vue de déterminer ceux qui sont les plus intéressants pour elle. Pour ce faire, elle peut s'adresser aux services gouvernementaux de promotion des exportations, tant au niveau provincial que fédéral. Elle peut aussi avoir recours à divers agents privés tels que les associations professionnelles, les banques, les transitaires internationaux. Cette démarche « renseignement », qui consiste essentiellement à rassembler les avis éclairés de spécialistes du commerce international, ne possède pas toujours une grande rigueur d'analyse ou de réflexion. Elle est néanmoins celle qu'adoptent sous une forme ou sous une autre un bon nombre d'entreprises exportatrices.

À cette démarche s'oppose celle qui consiste à rassembler des données secondaires chiffrées et à traiter ces données au moyen de diverses techniques, certaines très élémentaires et d'autres beaucoup plus sophistiquées. Cette démarche est donc plus formalisée que la première, le texte portera essentiellement sur l'examen des diverses méthodes qui s'inscrivent dans cette démarche que l'on qualifiera ici de « statistique ».

À ce point, il est bon de noter que certaines des méthodes qui seront examinées n'ont pas le degré de rigueur que le terme « méthode » implique. Les auteurs anglo-saxons ne s'y trompent pas puisqu'ils les dénomment assez vaguement *approaches*, ce qui reflète bien le manque de précision qui les caractérise.

L'approche renseignements et l'approche statistique ne sont pas mutuellement exclusives. Au contraire, elles peuvent avantageusement se compléter, ce qui sera démontré à la fin de ce texte.

La démarche statistique se divise en deux familles distinctes de méthodes (voir figure I). D'une part, celles qui consistent à effectuer des regroupements de pays selon un critère de similarité et, d'autre part, celles qui estiment les marchés selon divers critères comme ceux de la taille ou de la croissance par exemple.

Les regroupements de marchés

Dans la plupart de ces méthodes, les unités d'observation sont les pays pour lesquels on s'efforce de rassembler une grande variété d'indicateurs socio-économico-politiques. Depuis les premiers efforts de Liander et de ses collaborateurs du Marketing Science Institute (1967), les algorithmes utilisés dans ce type d'analyse ont considérablement évolué. Les travaux de Sethi (1971), qui ont fait école, consistent à réduire un très grand nombre de variables décrivant les pays à quelques facteurs à partir desquels des groupes homogènes de pays sont constitués. Ces regroupements révèlent quelques surprises. Des pays de divers continents sont réunis dans une même grappe. La classification n'est ni strictement géographique ni strictement fonction du niveau de développement économique comme l'était celle de Liander et de ses collaborateurs.

Parmi les critiques adressées à cette méthode, le manque de spécificité quant aux produits est l'une des plus fréquentes. Les pays sont en effet regroupés selon des indicateurs qui peuvent caractériser adéquatement peut-être un environnement de marketing global, mais qui sont insuffisants pour cerner l'état du marché pour un produit donné.

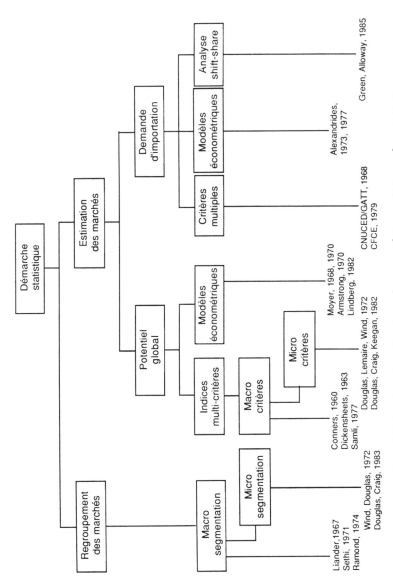

Figure I — Méthodes de sélection des marchés — Démarche statistique

Dans une variante de cette méthode, Raymond (1974) parvient à combler cette lacune. Il réduit les variables en facteurs à partir desquels il établit des grappes de pays. Disposant de données sur les ventes et sur certains éléments du marketing mix d'une multinationale pour trente-deux pays, il isole, à partir de l'analyse précédente, les effets des différences d'environnement sur la performance de l'entreprise et parvient alors à rendre compte des différences de performance d'un pays à un autre en termes de variations dans la composition du marketing mix.

Les techniques qui viennent d'être discutées portent, comme on l'a indiqué, sur des regroupements de pays. Une autre approche plus en accord avec l'esprit du marketing consisterait selon Wind et Douglas (1972) à procéder d'abord à une macro-segmentation (par pays) puis ensuite à une micro-segmentation sur des bases plus spécifiques, telles que les attitudes ou le genre de vie des consommateurs. Douglas et Craig (1983) offrent une illustration de cette méthode, l'exemple donné portant sur les montres-bracelets.

L'estimation des marchés

La démarche précédente s'appuie sur le postulat que les marchés les plus intéressants pour une entreprise sont ceux qui ressemblent le plus à ceux où elle est déjà implantée (hypothèse de succès). La démarche de l'estimation des marchés consiste à évaluer les marchés étrangers en fonction d'un ou de plusieurs critères et à retenir ceux dont l'évaluation est la plus élevée selon les critères envisagés. Alors que la première démarche consiste à regrouper des pays en se basant sur leur similarité, la seconde consiste au contraire à distinguer les pays les uns des autres en établissant un ordre de préférence entre eux.

Les critères adoptés varient selon les méthodes. Ils peuvent être des indicateurs de richesse, de taille, d'accès ou de degré de concurrence. Ils peuvent être utilisés pour effectuer des évaluations de marchés actuels ou futurs.

Les méthodes qui s'inscrivent dans cette démarche sont assez diverses (voir figure I) et peuvent se diviser en deux sous-groupes majeurs : d'une part, les méthodes visant à une évaluation globale du potentiel des marchés étrangers et, d'autre part, celles qui ne s'adressent qu'à l'évaluation d'une des composantes du potentiel global d'un pays, à savoir les importations.

Potentiel global

Dans ce sous-groupe, on retrouve les méthodes qualifiées selon certains auteurs de méthodes multicritères ou multifacteurs. L'origine de ce vocable est liée au recours dans les années soixante aux indicateurs macro-économiques pour évaluer les marchés. Moyer (1968) définit les mesures d'indices multifacteurs comme des mesures indirectes de marchés sur la base de variables « proxy » que l'intuition ou l'analyse statistique révèlent étroitement corrélées avec le potentiel d'un produit étudié. Cette méthode est fréquemment utilisée en marketing domestique pour estimer le potentiel d'un territoire donné. L'un des exemples les plus connus est l'indice du pouvoir d'achat publié dans Annual Survey of Buying Power par Sales Management Magazine (Kotler, 1980). Transposée au marketing international, cette méthode est utilisée lorsque des données statistiques sur les potentiels de marché ne sont pas disponibles.

L'analyste sélectionne donc les indicateurs les plus appropriés selon son expérience et son jugement, décide de leurs poids relatifs et génère des indices de potentiel qui lui permettent de classer les marchés étrangers par ordre d'intérêt.

Conners (1960) est probablement l'un des premiers à exposer l'utilisation de cette méthode à partir d'indices macro-économiques pour le compte de la compagnie 3M. Dickensheets (1963) décrit, sans toutefois l'illustrer, une méthode similaire alors appliquée chez General Electric.

Plus récemment Samli (1977), s'inspirant fortement des travaux de Conners, compare les potentiels des pays de l'Est. Dans un premier temps, il retient un certain nombre de macro-indicateurs (revenu national, consommation d'acier, consommation d'électricité, véhicules de transport, etc.). Il en tire ensuite un indice pondéré qu'il exprime en pourcentage de l'indice du marché américain. En multipliant cet indice relatif (appelé indice de qualité) par un indice relatif de taille (pourcentage de la population d'un pays étudié par rapport à celle des États-Unis), il dérive un indice de potentiel exprimé en pourcentage du potentiel du marché américain. On remarque donc qu'il s'agit bien d'une transposition de la méthode de l'indice du pouvoir d'achat mentionnée précédemment.

L'une des principales faiblesses de la méthode de Conners et de Samli réside, comme l'a déjà souligné Denis (1978), dans le fait qu'un bon nombre de ces macro-indicateurs sont fortement redondants. Les travaux de Sethi (1971) montrent par exemple que plusieurs de ces indicateurs sont colinéaires et appartiennent à une même grappe de facteurs. Beckerman (1966) parvient à estimer le revenu per capita presque entièrement par l'un ou l'autre d'entre eux. Estimer la qualité des marchés en additionnant ces critères revient donc à mesurer plusieurs fois la même chose. Cette lacune dans les travaux cités n'est pas fondamentale puisqu'il suffit de choisir judicieusement les indicateurs pour y remédier.

Une autre faiblesse de ces méthodes est de recourir à des macro-indicateurs qui ne sont pas spécifiquement reliés à des produits particuliers. Pour pallier cette insuffisance, Douglas, Lemaire, Wind (1978) suggèrent une approche adaptée aux besoins des entreprises. Cette dernière consiste à recourir à des macro-indicateurs ainsi qu'à des facteurs qui conviennent exactement aux produits en cause et à pondérer indicateurs et facteurs en fonction du jugement des gestionnaires. Il s'agit là d'un modèle conceptuel (cité à nouveau dans Douglas, Craig et Keegan, 1983 et dans Douglas et Craig, 1983) qui ne semble pas avoir fait l'objet d'application concrète et publiée.

Les méthodes économétriques

Ces méthodes portent sur la constitution de modèles d'estimation de la demande dont les paramètres sont estimés par régression. La démarche consiste habituellement à estimer les paramètres du modèle à l'aide des données disponibles (sur les pays industrialisés par exemple) et à les transposer ensuite dans les pays où les données sont plus limitées. Bien que certains auteurs comme Ferguson (1979) suggèrent une certaine similitude dans les déterminants de la demande pour les marchés étrangers, une telle pratique peut mener à des estimations très imprécises.

Moyer (1968) propose une application très simple des méthodes économétriques. Il estime la demande pour des pays où les données sont très limitées à l'aide d'un modèle testé là où les données le permettent (données sur la demande primaire d'un produit particulier). Il teste cinq modèles d'estimation de la demande de cinq produits différents en fonction du PNB. La qualité des résultats est plutôt modeste (R^2 variant de ,50 à ,78), ce qui n'est pas surprenant étant donné la simplicité du modèle adopté.

Armstrong (1970) fournit un autre exemple d'utilisation des méthodes économétriques. La méthodologie comprend l'élaboration d'un modèle théorique visant à préciser la nature des variables « causales » ainsi que la forme mathématique du modèle. Il est bon de noter que ce type de réflexion, tout à fait dans la ligne méthodologique des travaux classiques en économie sur l'analyse de la demande, est rarement présent dans ceux des chercheurs en marketing international.

Armstrong estime la demande nationale apparente d'appareils photographiques pour 19 pays sur une période de cinq ans. Le modèle, avec un R^2 de ,99, permet d'estimer la demande de tout pays pour lequel les données statistiques des variables explicatives sont disponibles et permet donc, en fin de compte, de classer les pays par ordre de taille de leur marché.

Comme le soulignent Douglas et Craig (1983), ce genre d'approche est surtout efficace pour un produit ayant atteint le stade de maturité. Il faut également espérer qu'aucun changement majeur ne vienne modifier la relation établie et que cette relation soit similaire sur tous les marchés.

Lindberg (1982) s'attaque au problème des difficultés causées par les disparités entre pays dans l'analyse internationale de la demande. Dans son étude sur la demande de postes de télévision, il adopte comme variable dépendante la proportion de la consommation personnelle dépensée pour le produit étudié (demande relative) et comme variable indépendante le niveau de saturation. Ce modèle pourrait donc servir à prévoir la demande lors de la sortie d'un nouveau produit de même qu'à comparer les potentiels de différents marchés où le produit pourrait être commercialisé.

L'analyse de la demande d'importation

Les diverses méthodes entrant dans cette catégorie ont comme point commun l'utilisation des statistiques du commerce international et essentiellement celles sur les importations. Les sources utilisées sont le plus souvent celles des Nations-Unies ou de l'OCDE. Par opposition à la sous-catégorie précédente où l'on cherchait à évaluer l'ensemble du potentiel d'un pays, on ne veut, dans ces méthodes, qu'évaluer le potentiel du marché exprimé par les seules importations.

On peut distinguer trois groupes de méthodes d'analyse de la demande d'importation : les méthodes multicritères, les modèles économétriques et enfin, l'analyse des parts de marché.

Parmi les méthodes multicritères, figure celle proposée par le Centre du commerce international CNUCED/GATT de Genève. Cet organisme suggère (CNUCED/GATT, 1968) d'analyser les marchés en termes de taille (importations), de croissance (importations), de couverture de marché (rapport importation/exportation) et de concurrence. À ces critères de base, à partir desquels d'autres critères sont dérivés, sont associés des seuils d'acceptation ou de rejet établis subjectivement par l'analyste.

Cette méthode élaborée à l'intention des pays en voie de développement désireux d'exporter a été adoptée et adaptée par le Centre français du commerce extérieur (CFCE, 1979) et s'avère, dans sa nouvelle version, beaucoup plus simple que la première.

Si elle présente l'avantage d'être facile à appliquer, elle comporte aussi quelques inconvénients. Le premier se situe au niveau de la classification des produits. Pour un produit dont la classification est trop large, l'analyse des statistiques du commerce international ne donnera que des indications imprécises sur les marchés potentiels. Le retard dans la publication des données constitue aussi un problème sérieux. Entre temps, la situation peut avoir beaucoup changé.

Les modèles économétriques peuvent aussi être appliqués aux données du commerce international. Alexandrides (1973), par exemple, estime une relation de demande d'importation pour un produit industriel. La méthode consiste à rassembler les données relatives au produit étudié, à retenir les variables pertinentes, puis à élaborer le modèle. Malheureusement, le substrat théorique fait défaut et la qualité des estimations en souffre.

L'analyse de l'évolution des parts de marché constitue une autre approche à la sélection des marchés fondée sur des statistiques d'importation. Cette méthode dont les promoteurs sont Green et

Allaway (1985) consiste à identifier les changements relatifs dans les parts des marchés internationaux. Pour la période étudiée, on calcule le taux de croissance moyen d'un produit donné pour l'ensemble des pays considérés et l'on compare le taux de croissance effectif pour chacun des pays par rapport au taux de croissance moyen. L'écart net qui résulte de cette comparaison permet d'identifier les marchés en croissance ou en décroissance réelle relativement à l'ensemble des pays de référence. Cela permet donc là encore de classer les pays cette fois-ci non pas selon leur taille, mais en termes de progression dans la part de marché détenue par un pays. Cette méthode n'examine pas l'ensemble des dimensions qui concernent celui qui doit sélectionner les marchés étrangers. Elle est unidimensionnelle, mais elle a au moins l'avantage d'être simple.

Autres méthodes

Certaines méthodes mentionnées parfois dans des ouvrages de marketing international n'ont pas été retenues ici, par exemple celles de Carr (1978), d'Erickson (1963), de Winjholds (1981). Ces travaux ne portent que sur un pays à la fois et non pas sur plusieurs. Il ne s'agit donc que d'études de niveau national, qui offrent parfois des aperçus intéressants sur des méthodologies qui pourraient peut-être s'appliquer à la sélection des marchés étrangers, mais qui ne l'ont pas encore été.

Ayant couvert les différentes méthodes de sélection des marchés, certaines observations peuvent être faites. Premièrement, si l'on constate une relative diversité des méthodes proposées, on remarque aussi qu'elles font l'objet de très peu de publications à caractère empirique. Deuxièmement, elles datent de la fin des années soixante et du début des années soixante-dix, à deux exceptions près, Lindberg (1982) et Green et Allaway (1985).

L'importance des stratégies d'exportation quant à la performance sur les marchés étrangers a souvent été évoquée et démontrée très récemment encore par Cooper et Kleindschmidt (1985). Mais comment établir des stratégies d'exportation sans sélectionner rationnellement les marchés-cibles ? Cette question, il faut bien l'admettre, n'a pas préoccupé beaucoup les chercheurs comme en témoigne cette revue des publications. Reste à examiner la pertinence de ces méthodes pour les entreprises.

UTILITÉ DES MÉTHODES POUR LES ENTREPRISES

L'utilité des méthodes pour les entreprises en général dépend de deux critères fondamentaux (Denis, 1978) : d'une part, leur adéquation aux particularités des produits et, d'autre part, leur capacité de prendre en compte les dimensions stratégiques des marchés, c'est-à-dire non seulement leur taille, mais aussi la croissance, la nature et le degré de concurrence sur ces marchés ainsi que leur accessibilité.

Quant à leur pertinence pour la PME, il faut ajouter aux critères précédents ceux de la simplicité et de la modicité des coûts d'utilisation. Il n'est pas nécessaire de s'étendre sur ce dernier point : les ressources humaines et financières sont rares dans les PME et leur dirigeants résistent mal à la tentation de choisir des marchés-cibles impulsivement (surtout quand les programmes d'expansion des exportations les soutiennent presque automatiquement dans leurs tentatives internationales).

Les méthodes de regroupement des marchés (voir figure I) se caractérisent par un niveau de généralité élevé puisque les indicateurs utilisés sont rarement ceux d'un produit en particulier. De par leur nature, elles ne tiennent pas compte des dimensions stratégiques des marchés puisqu'elles n'ont pour objet que de regrouper les pays selon un critère de comparabilité socio-économique. Elles seraient donc surtout utiles aux entreprises fortement diversifiées du point du vue des produits et présentes d'une manière ou d'une autre sur au moins un marché étranger. Les PME, et en particulier celles qui débutent dans l'exportation, leur trouveront donc peu d'intérêt d'autant plus qu'elles sont complexes et relativement coûteuses à manipuler.

Parmi les méthodes d'évaluation du potentiel global, les modèles économétriques présentent l'avantage d'être adaptés aux produits, mais par contre ils ne tiennent que peu compte des caractéristiques stratégiques des marchés. Du point de vue de la PME, leur inconvénient majeur réside dans leur degré de complexité. On voit mal les dirigeants des PME se livrer à des analyses de régression ou même, dans bien des cas, interpréter celles que des consultants pourraient effectuer pour eux.

Les méthodes ayant recours à l'élaboration d'indices multi-critères souffrent à la fois de leur généralité et du fait qu'elles ne portent que sur une dimension des marchés, la taille, laissant de côté croissance, concurrence et accessibilité. Mais, au moins, ces méthodes ont l'avantage d'être facilement compréhensibles et applicables.

Restent les méthodes d'analyse de la demande d'importation. Les modèles économétriques d'estimation de la demande d'importation présentent les mêmes écueils que les modèles d'estimation du potentiel global dont on a déjà parlé. La méthode d'analyse shift-share a l'avantage de s'appliquer à des produits en particulier, mais elle ne porte que sur la dimension croissance des marchés. Elle est, par contre, facile d'utilisation.

En ce qui concerne les méthodes à critères multiples d'analyse de la demande d'importation du type GATT/CNUCED ou CFCE, on peut observer qu'elles tiennent compte des dimensions stratégiques des marchés : taille, croissance, concurrence, accessibilité, mais qu'elles ne sont adaptées aux caractéristiques des produits que dans la mesure où ceux-ci s'inscrivent dans une catégorie CTCI (classification type du commerce international) qui ne soit pas trop agrégée. Il faut espérer de surcroît, lorsque l'on utilise ces méthodes, que les données sur les pays étudiés soient disponibles et récentes. Si elles ne le sont pas, il faut alors qu'elles ne soient pas trop difficiles à mettre à jour.

Cet exercice d'évaluation des méthodes de sélection de marchés-cibles dans le cadre d'une démarche statistique permet de tirer deux conclusions. La première est que, si chacune de ces méthodes possède certains mérites, aucune d'entre elles n'est entièrement satisfaisante. La seconde est que la méthode d'estimation de la demande d'importation par les critères multiples serait celle qui est à la fois la plus satisfaisante et la plus accessible aux PME pour autant que les données secondaires appropriées soient disponibles.

Ces conclusions plutôt décevantes expliquent, du moins en partie, pourquoi les entreprises en général, et les PME qui désirent exporter en particulier, sélectionnent les marchés étrangers d'une manière moins rigoureuse que les universitaires le souhaitent. Dans ces conditions, quelles recommandations peut-on proposer pour que le processus de sélection soit plus rigoureux ?

UNE DÉMARCHE POUR LA SÉLECTION DES MARCHÉS PAR LA PME[1]

Confrontée à plus de cent quatre-vingts marchés potentiels, la PME ne peut les analyser tous de façon détaillée et, de surcroît, en ayant recours à des méthodes qui ne sont pas entièrement satisfaisantes. Plusieurs auteurs suggèrent donc une sélection préliminaire des marchés, notamment Root (1966) et Douglas, Craig et Keegan (1982). Cette étape permet de réduire sensiblement le nombre des marchés qui doivent faire l'objet d'analyses plus approfondies.

Recours à la démarche renseignements

Pour cette étape de sélection préliminaire, Alexandrides et Moshis (1977) suggèrent à l'exportateur d'utiliser les sources de renseignements disponibles (agences gouvernementales ou autres) pour établir la liste des marchés nécessitant des recherches additionnelles. La figure II illustre les principales sources de renseignements accessibles à l'exportateur canadien.

En ce qui concerne les services offerts par le système fédéral, la démarche à adopter, qui est sensiblement la même que celle proposée par l'Association canadienne d'exportation (1984), est la suivante :

1. Cette partie de l'article s'appuie sur un article antérieur publié par les auteurs. Voir Lamothe et Denis (1986).

1. prise de contact avec le bureau régional du ministère de l'Expansion industrielle régionale (MEIR) le plus proche ;
2. prise de contact avec les directions sectorielles du MEIR à Ottawa ;
3. prise de contact avec les directions géographiques du ministère des Affaires extérieures (MAE) à Ottawa ;
4. prise de contact avec les délégations commerciales à l'étranger (s'il y a lieu).

À l'exploitation de cette filière fédérale peut s'ajouter, bien sûr, le recours aux services d'assistance provinciaux ainsi qu'à des organismes privés (voir figure II).

Cette démarche renseignements aura pour résultat d'identifier un nombre restreint de pays qui, du point de vue des experts consultés, présentent un potentiel d'exportation intéressant pour une compagnie canadienne.

Il y a lieu de s'arrêter un instant sur la nature des critères utilisés par les experts en question pour recommander tel ou tel pays. Il est bien évident que ces critères n'ont pas le caractère d'objectivité que l'on pourrait souhaiter. Ils sont entièrement subjectifs, varient d'un expert à l'autre et finalement se résument au jugement des personnes interrogées qui lui-même dépend, entre autres, de la qualité de leurs informations et de leur expérience des marchés et des produits concernés. Ainsi donc l'approche renseignements permet de réduire considérablement l'éventail de choix dans un laps de temps assez court et à assez peu de frais (en particulier si l'on a recours aux services gouvernementaux). Cette présélection n'est valable que pour autant que les experts fassent preuve de la plus grande objectivité.

Cette démarche présente cependant quelques avantages majeurs si on la compare à la démarche statistique. D'une part, elle est adaptée aux produits en cause ; d'autre part, elle tient compte des dimensions stratégiques des marchés, les experts fondant leurs recommandations non seulement sur la croissance, la concurrence étrangère, mais surtout sur l'accessibilité pour les entreprises canadiennes.

Compléter la démarche renseignements

L'approche renseignements aura permis d'identifier un certain nombre de pays intéressants, en général environ une dizaine. Il s'agit maintenant, dans une deuxième étape, d'identifier les meilleurs. Les dirigeants de l'entreprise faisant face à ce problème peuvent toujours classer les pays retenus selon des critères plus ou moins subjectifs. Mais, mieux encore, ils peuvent avoir recours à certaines des méthodes appartenant à l'approche statistique.

À titre d'illustration, une recherche (Lamothe, 1985) visant à identifier les marchés potentiels pour un exportateur canadien de purificateurs d'eau et pour un exportateur d'équipement lourd de

170 J.-É. DENIS & J. LAMOTHE

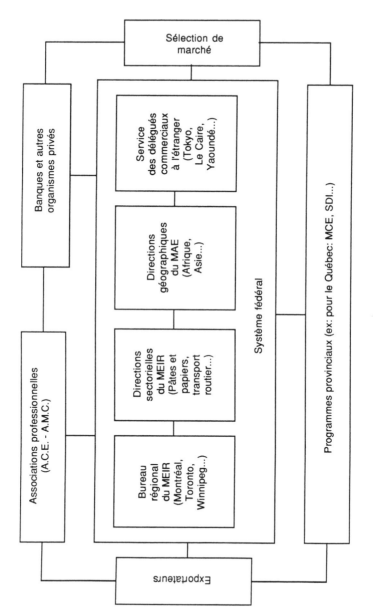

Figure II — Sources de renseignements pour la sélection de marchés étrangers

travaux publics remis en état a permis de retenir, en ayant recours aux services du gouvernement fédéral, neuf pays pour le premier produit (Japon, Belgique, Pays-Bas, États-Unis, Royaume-Uni, France, Allemagne, Australie et Nouvelle-Zélande) et dix pays pour le deuxième (Malaisie, Singapour, Égypte, Liban, Israël, Mexique, Colombie, Chili, Équateur et Arabie Saoudite). Il restait alors à poursuivre le processus de sélection afin de réduire les choix aux deux ou trois marchés les plus intéressants, puis à arrêter le choix sur un seul marché après une prospection sur le terrain. C'est à ce stade que le recours aux méthodes statistiques s'est avéré approprié. Dans les deux cas, la méthode de l'analyse de la demande d'importation par les critères multiples fut employée.

Pour les équipements remis en état, les données d'importation qui dataient de 1982 furent réestimées pour 1985 au moyen d'une régression. Compte tenu de ces nouveaux éléments, trois marchés furent finalement sélectionnés. Il s'agit, dans l'ordre, de l'Égypte, du Mexique et de Singapour.

En ce qui concerne le purificateur d'eau, l'analyse de la demande d'importation par les critères multiples fut utilisée, mais celle-ci se révéla difficile car la catégorie CTCI la plus appropriée qui fut utilisée était insuffisamment désagrégée. Elle fut complétée par la méthode des indices multicritères. En dernier lieu furent retenus respectivement les États-Unis, la France et la Belgique.

À partir de ces deux cas pratiques, Lamothe suggère un modèle de sélection des marchés étrangers pour la PME qui intègre l'approche renseignement et l'approche statistique (voir figure III).

Ce modèle privilégie la méthode d'analyse de la demande d'importation par les critères multiples. Si la classification CTCI ne correspond pas d'une manière satisfaisante au produit en cause, on propose d'utiliser comme indicateur la classe de produit CTCI qui s'en rapproche le plus. Si les données sont incomplètes, elles doivent être reconstituées à partir d'autres sources statistiques.

Le modèle montre enfin comment, le cas échéant, la sélection des marchés peut gagner en rigueur par le recours à d'autres méthodes statistiques. Il va de soi que le recours à ces autres méthodes dépendra des ressources en personnel, en temps et en argent que l'entreprise peut consacrer à cet exercice.

CONCLUSION

L'examen des diverses méthodes de sélection des marchés proposées dans dans les publications de marketing international révèle qu'elles souffrent de diverses lacunes et que, si elles peuvent être utiles dans certains cas, elles ne peuvent l'être dans tous. Il apparaît aussi que très peu d'entre elles sont susceptibles d'être utilisées par la PME, étant donné leur complexité.

Par comparaison, la démarche qui consiste à avoir recours à des experts, qu'ils soient du secteur public ou du secteur privé, permet

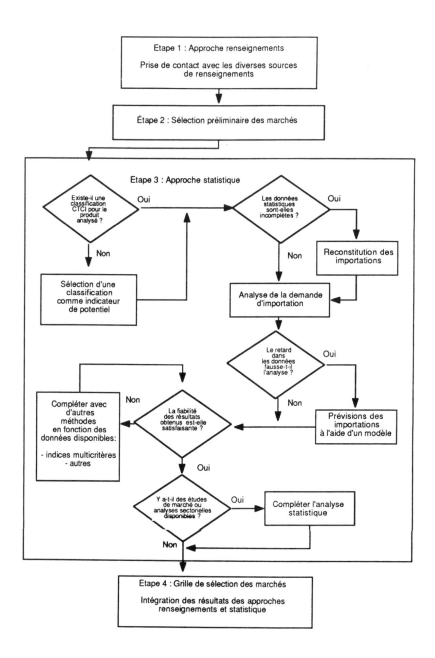

Figure III — Méthode de sélection des marchés étrangers pour la PME

de réduire rapidement et à moindres frais le choix des marchés à un très petit nombre d'entre eux.

C'est alors que le recours à certaines méthodes plus formelles peut être approprié. La première à envisager est celle de l'analyse de la demande d'importation par les critères multiples. Si les données sont disponibles, elle permet de réduire efficacement le choix des pays à quelques-uns seulement, quitte à arrêter le choix définitif après prospection sur le terrain. Si les données sont insatisfaisantes, la PME a alors deux choix : ou bien s'en tenir aux jugements des experts et arrêter sa sélection sur cette base, ou bien poursuivre l'analyse au moyen d'une ou plusieurs méthodes statistiques à déterminer en fonction des ressources dont elle dispose.

La démarche générale qui est proposée ici souligne l'importance de bien informer les entreprises s'orientant vers les marchés étrangers sur les services publics dédiés à la promotion à l'exportation. S'il existe tant au niveau fédéral qu'au niveau provincial des dispositifs partiels d'assistance, aucun mécanisme global n'est en place à l'heure actuelle à notre connaissance. Autrement dit, il n'est pas possible pour une entreprise voulant exporter de s'adresser à un endroit et à un seul, au niveau fédéral ou au niveau provincial, pour savoir quels sont les quelques marchés étrangers les plus intéressants pour ses produits. D'où la nécessité pour l'entreprise d'extraire dans un premier temps autant de renseignements que possible des services gouvernementaux et des organismes privés, et de poursuivre le processus de sélection au moyen des méthodes exposées dans ce texte qui lui paraissent les plus abordables.

BIBLIOGRAPHIE

ALEXANDRIDES, C. G., « A Methodology for Computerization of International Market Research », *International Business Systems Perspectives*, Atlanta, Georgia State University, 1973, 185-193.
ALEXANDRIDES, C. G., MOSHIS, G. P., *Export Marketing Management*, New York, Praeger, 1977.
ARMSTRONG, J. S., « An Application of Econometric Models to International Marketing », *Journal of Marketing Research*, vol. 7, mai 1970, 190-198.
ASSOCIATION CANADIENNE D'EXPORTATION, *Les exportations : feuille de route*, Ottawa, Expansion industrielle régionale et Affaires extérieures, 1984.
BECKERMAN, W., « Comparaison internationale du revenu réel », *Études du Centre de développement*, Paris, Centre de développement de l'Organisation de coopération et de développement économique, 1966.
CARR, R. P., « Identifying Trade Areas for Consumer Goods in Foreign Markets », *Journal of Marketing*, vol. 42, octobre 1978, 76-80.
CENTRE FRANÇAIS DU COMMERCE EXTÉRIEUR, *Selexport*, Paris, 1979.
CNUCED/GATT, *Manuel des méthodes d'élaboration d'information de base sur les marchés étrangers*, Genève, CNUCED /GATT, 1968.
CONNERS, R. J., « World Market Potential as Developed for 3M's Overseas Operation », *Dynamic Marketing*, Chicago, American Marketing Association, 1960, 461-466.
COOPER, R. G., KLEINDSCHMIDT, E. J., « The Impact for Export Strategy on Export Sales Performance », *Journal of International Business Studies*, vol. 16, (1), printemps 1985, 37-55.
DICKENSHEETS, R. J., « Basic and Economical Approaches to International Marketing Research », *Proceedings, American Marketing Association*, Chicago, American Marketing Association, 1963, 359-377.
DOUGLAS, S. P., CRAIG, C. S., *International Marketing Research*, Englewood Cliffs, Prentice-Hall, 1963.
DOUGLAS, S. P., CRAIG, C. S., KEEGAN, W. J., « Approaches to Assessing International Marketing Opportunities for Small and Medium-Sized Companies », *Columbia Journal of World Business*, automne 1982, 26-32.
ERICKSON, L. G., « Analyzing Brazilian Consumer Markets », *Business Topics*, vol. 11, été 1963, 7-26.
FERGUSON, C. E., « International Commonality of Demand Determinants : A Reappraisal », *Academy of Marketing Science Annual Conference Proceedings*, 1979, 93-97.
GREEN, R. T., ALLAWAY, A. W., « Identification of Export Opportunity : Shift-Share Approach », *Journal of Marketing*, vol. 49, hiver 1985, 83-88.
LAMOTHE, J., *Méthode de sélection des marchés étrangers à l'usage des PME*, travail dirigé de M.Sc., Hautes Études Commerciales, Montréal, 1985.
LAMOTHE, J., DENIS, J.-É., « Comment les PME peuvent-elles sélectionner les marchés étrangers ? », *Revue internationale de gestion*, vol. 11, (1), février 1986, 27-32.

LIANDER, B. C., TERPSTRA, V., YOSHINO, M. Y., SERBINI, A. A., *Comparative Analysis for International Marketing*, Boston, Allyn and Bacon, 1967.

LINDBERG, B. C., « International Comparison of Growth in Demand for a New Durable Consumer Product », *Journal of Marketing Research*, vol. 19, août 1982, 364-371.

MOYER, R., « International Marketing Analysis », *Journal of Marketing Research*, vol. 5, novembre 1968, 353-360.

RAYMOND, C., *The Art of Using Science in Marketing*, New York, Harper & Row, 1974.

ROOT, F. D., *Strategic Planning for Export Marketing*, Scranton International Textbook Company, 1966.

SAMLI, A. C., « An Approach for Estimating Market Potential in East Europe », *Journal of Internataional Business Studies*, vol. 8, automne/ hiver 1977, 49-53.

SETHI, S. P., « Comparative Cluster Analysis for World Markets », *Journal of Marketing Research*, vol. 8, août 1971, 348-354.

WIND, Y., DOUGLAS, S. P., « International Market Segmentation », *European Journal of Marketing*, vol. 6, (1), 1972.

WINJHOLDS, H. B., « Market Forecasting for Dual Economies : The Application and Accuracy of Income Elasticities », *Journal of International Business Studies*, hiver 1981, 89-98.

Turning a Joint Venture
into a Successful Marriage

JEAN-LOUIS SCHAAN

Managers in many Canadian firms face a strategic dilemma. They generally want to have full management control over their companies' subsidiaries and affiliates at a time when there are mounting political and economic pressures for setting up joint ventures (JVs). On the one hand host governments, responding to social and economic forces in their own countries, are enforcing more and more arrangements which require sharing ownership and control. On the other hand the rapidly changing competitive structure of several industries is pushing firms to join forces in order to share in the costs and risks associated with large-scale projects or to share expertise as they enter new markets. As a result, JVs are becoming more and more unavoidable and their numbers worldwide are increasing at a growing pace. Figures from the U.S. Commerce Department show that from 1981 to 1982 the number of JVs, as a proportion of foreign direct investments in the U.S., grew from 3.9% to 6.7%. Similarly, the number of JVs entered into by U.S. companies worldwide has sharply increased in the last three years. "Mergers and Corporate Policy" reports that the number of new JVs involving U.S. companies rose from 219 in 1981 to 281 in 1982 and 348 in 1983.

In spite of the growing infatuation with JVs, one fact remains: they are not an automatic route to success. Historically, JVs have had a high failure rate. The lack of success of JVs can be explained by two sets of factors. First, JVs may be unsuccessful for the same reasons that any business might perform poorly: general economic conditions, depressed demand, increasing competition, sudden shifts in exchange rates, or poor management. Second, JVs may be unsuccessful for reasons inherent in their being JVs. Chief among those reasons are the inability of parent companies to control the JVs and/or the inability of the partners to develop a sound working relationship.

Since the relationship between parent and JV success has been examined elsewhere (Killing, 1983; Schaan, 1983), this paper will analyze why and how JV success or failure is tied to how well the partners can work together. There is widespread evidence that this is an important issue for managers involved in JVs. For instance, the inability of the partners to work together has led to the termination of JVs which were financially successful. That was the fate of a JV between CP Hotels and a large Mexican bank that was terminated after two and a half years of operation because the partners could not agree on the JV's future strategy. It was also the fate of a JV between BASF and Dow Chemical that was dissolved after twenty years of successful operations. Further, three recent publications discussing the growing trend toward JVs agree that a key ingredient to the JV's success is the ability of the parties to work together:

> "There is more to a joint venture than money and technology", says Gulf's Walker. "Both sides have to be able to work together in a common purpose. There has to be compatibility among the key people." (*Financial Post*, January 22, 1983)
>
> If a joint venture is not set up in a way that forces the partners to work together, the risk of failure is heightened. (*Industry Week*, February 20, 1984)
>
> Success or failure depends not on a venture's underlying strategic rationale, Ohmae says, but on how well companies, with different blood types, different ways of doing things can work together. (*Business Week*, May 28, 1984)

However, not one of the articles provides insights into the managerial implications of the issue. Drawing from the experience of close to thirty successful and unsuccessful JVs, this paper presents some guidelines which should help parent company managers deal with their partner and with the JV. The paper begins with an examination of the factors which most often lead to a deterioration of the relationship between partners, then presents key elements in the successful management of a long-term relationship, and concludes with a discussion of some managerial implications.

SOURCES OF PROBLEMS IN THE RELATIONSHIP BETWEEN PARTNERS IN A JOINT VENTURE

Like the long-term survival of a marriage, the long-term survival of a JV is tied, to a certain extent, to the partners' ability to develop a working relationship. JVs are an organizational arrangement which is prone to creating conflicts. The parents' unwillingness or inability to deal with such conflicts may lead to irreversible outcomes. Important decisions may be postponed or not made at all, one partner may end up buying the other one, or the JV may simply be terminated.

Significant financial and goodwill costs are usually associated with such events. An understanding of why conflicts between partners arise is a first step towards minimizing or avoiding those costs altogether. This section examines four factors which may hinder the development of a long-term relationship between partners in a JV: differences in management philosophy, differences in expectations, lack of parent commitment to the JV, incompatibility between the people involved in the JV.

Differences in Management Philosophy

Each parent company approaches a JV with its own organizational culture, its own character, and its own management style. As a result, each may have its own views regarding which problems are important and how to deal with them. In fact, each has its own concept of what constitutes a problem in the first place. Such differences are further heightened in JVs involving parents operating in different core businesses and/or of different nationalities. The following examples illustrate the nature of such differences:

A Mexican JV involving a major US chemical company and a Monterrey capitalist underwent a lengthy deadlock period following the takeover of the capitalist's shares by a Mexican conglomerate. Both partners had the same philosophy of active participation in their JV's operating matters by appointing parent company personnel to the JV's managerial positions. Finally, the US parent, which had successfully been running the JV until then, handed the JV's operating responsibility to its partner and played a passive role from then on.

Another Mexican JV was simply terminated after three unprofitable years when the Canadian parent decided that from then on it would run the JV "the way we do it in Canada." The Mexicans responded that this was Mexico and that the JV had to be managed by Mexicans. The JV was liquidated following seven months of unfruitful discussions.

The decision-making process of a JV between a giant government-owned oil and gas company and a small Canadian petrochemical firm was seriously hampered by differences in the parents' mentalities. The Canadian JV general manager was frustrated by his inability to respond promptly to competitive pressures because of lengthy board discussions over issues such as the purchase of a plane for the JV, which was seen as a waste of resources by the Canadians but was a routine decision for their partner. Another source of frustration and conflict was the emphasis placed on social considerations by the government parent. It took the JV eleven years to show its first profit.

It took two and a half years for the board of a JV in the petrochemical industry to approve the switch from an outdated technological process to a state-of-the-art process developed by the US parent. The local parent was a bank, and it took one year before it was convinced of the economic benefits of the move. Once the investment was approved, it took a year and a half to resolve the financing issue. The conservative bankers wanted the parents to

inject more equity into the venture, while the Americans pushed
for debt financing. In the end a compromise was struck by using a
combination of debt and equity.

A dispute between CGE and GSW Inc. over business strategy
and management of Canco Inc., an appliance maker they jointly
own, eventually ended up in the Supreme Court of Ontario (*Financial Post*, January 22, 1983, p. 18).

A difficulty for managers is that such conflicts can seldom be
predicted at the time the JV is set up. To come back to the marriage
analogy, the two partners discover each other's philosophy as they
share experiences. Further, one's philosophy is not static. It evolves
and it can change in the light of one's experiences. Such differences
in philosophy between parent companies in a JV are not necessarily
detrimental to the success of a JV, as long as the parents understand
and can live with each other's differences and as long as compromises can be reached.

Differences in Expectations

Another source of conflicts between parent companies is that
they often have different expectations regarding what the JV should
do for them or regarding how to measure JV success. Such differences appear in the criteria of JV success used, in the time orientation, in the level of achievement, and in the degree of specificity.

Differences in the Criteria of JV Success

Probably the most frequent disagreements are over dividends.
Typically one parent would like to receive a dividend while the
other would prefer to see the money reinvested in the JV. This is
particularly prevalent in JVs in which dividends are the only tangible benefit to one parent while the other parent receives financial
revenues from the sale of goods, components, technology, or management services to the JV.

Once the parents have agreed to pay a dividend, the next sources
of contention are: how much should be paid out? In what form? In
order to answer the first question, many JV contracts include clauses
which state, for example, that if the parents cannot agree on the
dividend payment in a given year, 50% of the preceding year's
profits will be paid out.

Another dilemma faced by managers involved in JVs is that of
growth versus profits. Differences between the parents over these
criteria are very important because they lead to potential conflicts
over the JV's strategy, capital expenditure decisions, financing decisions, and transfer pricing. An example will help to illustrate the
point. In a JV in the textile industry one of the partners was the
JV's single largest customer, accounting for 40% of the JV's sales.
This parent was not interested in profits but rather in minimizing
the transfer price from the JV. On the other hand, the other partner,

which had contributed capital and its nationality, wanted to maximize the transfer price in order to maximize profits and in turn the dividends it received. The same situation occurs when one parent is a supplier to the JV.

Still another conflict area is exports. Typically, the local partner will want to use its comparative advantage in international markets while a multinational parent company will be very reluctant to see the products from the JV compete on third markets with products coming from subsidiaries from which it receives 100% of the profits.

Differences in Time Orientation

In many JVs one parent is interested in short-term performance (e.g., yearly or even quarterly ROI), while the other is interested in building a strong earning stream base. Obviously, such differences in objectives lead to very different strategies. For instance, in a petrochemical JV the Mexican partner threatened its US partner with bringing a conflict over the timing of a major project to the attention of public officials. The Americans wanted to postpone the project because "it would not look good on the numbers" at that point in time.

Differences in the Expected Level of Achievement

Even if the parents agree on the criteria to measure the JV's performance, they may disagree over what constitutes a satisfactory level of performance. In a study of thirteen Mexican JVs, the author observed that managers in the local parent companies had higher expectations regarding sales growth than managers in foreign companies. Foreign parents often had difficulties in understanding that the Mexican JV could grow at rates of 30% or more when they were experiencing stagnating sales on their domestic and other foreign markets. This situation led to numerous conflicts over the aggressiveness of the JV's expansion plans.

Differences in the Degree of Specificity

Finally, the criteria of success applied to a particular JV differ according to their specificity. Some parents tend to use broad criteria of success while others use very precisely defined criteria. In one JV, for example, the foreign parent had a broad set of expectations (to optimize long-term shareholders' value through consistent real growth in earnings and ROE), while the local parent evaluated growth by comparing it to industry average standards.

Lack of Parent Commitment

To be successful, most JVs require the commitment of both parents (see Beamish, 1985). This is particularly true of JVs which have been created in order to take advantage of complementary skills or resources provided by the parent companies. At first sight, it would appear obvious that a company which decides to allocate resources to a JV would, by the same token, make a commitment to make it work. In reality, this is not always the case. And in many instances, managers explain difficulties with a JV — or the failure of a JV — by saying: "We did not pay enough attention."

Dealing with a partner who does not show much commitment to the success of a joint undertaking can, and often does, become a very upsetting experience for the partner who counts on the other's contribution. Therefore, a lack of parent commitment can lead to very tense situations between the partners. It usually occurs when a parent does not have enough resources to allocate to a JV or when a JV is simply not important enough in its strategic game plan.

Incompatibility between Personalities Involved

JVs involve a significant amount of interaction between people from the parent companies, if only at Executive Committee or Board of Directors meetings. Conflicts that arise between personalities are probably the most common, but also the most difficult to manage. Some factors which lead to clashes between people are differences in personalities, differences in professional background and training, and differences in culture and language.

Having to deal with such differences is not unique to JVs. What is unique, though, is that personality conflicts can have devastating effects on the trust between partners. Trust is particularly important when things go wrong. It is less important if the JV is doing well and both parents' expectations are met. But if it is not there when problems arise, the JV's survival can be seriously threatened. And once trust has been destroyed, it is very difficult to rebuild.

MANAGING RELATIONSHIPS IN A JOINT VENTURE

On the one hand there is a tendency among the larger parent companies to expect that the JVs they are involved in will adopt their own management policies and procedures (i.e., that they be managed as if they were a wholly-owned subsidiary). On the other hand, smaller parent companies lack the resources to play an active role in the JV's day-to-day operations. Whatever the stance taken towards the JV, managers from the parent companies have come to realize that their relationship with their partner is not something that can be left to chance. A relationship with a partner can be managed.

This section examines some of the proactive moves undertaken by some parent companies in an attempt to shape the quality of their relationship with their JV partner. Then it discusses the management of the parent-JV relationship and ends with an examination of the role of the JV general manager in influencing the nature and quality of the relationship between the partners.

Relationship with the Partner

The author has observed that managers with the most experience with JVs tend to have a more positive attitude towards their partners than managers with little experience. The defensive attitude is probably caused by the uncertainty in becoming involved in a new type of business relationship with a partner who is not really known (i.e., the uncertainty of not knowing what to expect and how to behave).

One way management in a parent company shows its commitment to a JV is by the involvement and support of its top management. This is the case when, for example, the presidents of two companies initiate the idea of a JV (TELKO, a JV between Northern Telecom and Grupo Alfa, was born at a Conference Board meeting in New York where the presidents of the two companies met and signed a letter of intent) or when they are actively involved in part of the negotiations leading to the establishment of the JV.

Top management's failure to understand when and how to be involved in a JV can be very upsetting for a partner. Several Latin American JVs have gotten off to a bad start because the foreign partner failed to recognize that in those countries the decision-making process is centralized at the top. In many cases the president of the local parent company has been offended because its partner would send middle managers to negotiate with him and because those managers typically had limited decision-making authority. Such practices, although not uncommon in North America, can jeopardize the development of a working relationship. In an extreme case it led to the breakdown of the negotiations between a Canadian hotel company and its Brazilian counterpart.

Some parent companies resort to symbolic manifestations of their union. One such symbolic gesture occurs when the two partners decide to purchase a minimal number of shares in each other's company. The intent is simply to show the mutual commitment to the JV. As one manager put it: "In that way we get their Annual Report and we acquire some knowledge as to what our partner does. We get to know each other better."

Another commonly used vehicle to promote a better relationship between partners is the invitation of one parent by its partner to attend all public announcements made by the head office. It could be to announce the introduction of a new technology or the launch of a new product, neither directly related to the JV's business. What seems to be important here is the gesture. Managers invited to such events, even though they may not attend, feel favorably predisposed towards their partner. The same is true for invitations to visit a plant or the parent's headquarters. To risk another analogy with a marriage, the partner is made to feel welcome in the family.

Another opportunity to strengthen the ties between partners is provided by the JV's executive committee or board of directors meetings. In Mexico, for instance, there is a general rule to avoid conflicts between the parent companies during the board meetings. Issues are resolved at a breakfast meeting before the board meeting, or they are not discussed. According to managers who have adopted this approach, it contributes to a smoother relationship between the partners. Another interesting approach was followed by the V-P in charge of Latin America at Alcan. He made it a point, every time he attended a JV's board meeting, to allocate 50% of his time to business and 50% to other activities such as visiting historical sites or going fishing with top managers from the partner. Getting to know the people socially helped him gain a better understanding of whom he was dealing with.

Relationship with the JV

To manage the relationship with the JV itself also plays an important role in the development of a working relationship between the partners. For one thing, a parent can develop a good appreciation of its partner's commitment to the JV through discussing the JV's affairs. In such circumstances it is easy to find out whether the partner knows and/or understands what is happening to the JV.

One factor which contributed to the collapse of a JV was the foreign parent's V-P International's failure to develop any sort of a relationship with its JV. In two and a half years the V-P never came to discuss the JV with the JV general manager or with its partner. Many issues remained unresolved, to the frustration of the local parent. In the end, the local partner decided to terminate the JV. The V-P's first visit coincided with the signing of the termination documents.

Managing the relationship with the JV requires a structure within the parent's organization and the allocation of resources to the performance of the task. This is the "keep in touch" principle. In most parent companies this is done through reports: quarterly and annual reports, strategic planning documents, progress reports on specific projects. . . But in many companies, managers attempt to improve their assessment of the reports through personal visits to the JV and through telephone calls. To many managers, the personal and eyeball-to-eyeball contact are the best way of finding out what is really going on in the JV.

The keep-in-touch strategy is usually perceived as a sign of commitment by the partner as long as it does not mean interference in the JV's affairs. In that case it would have a negative impact on the partners' relationship by making the other parent suspicious.

Role of the JV General Manager

The JV general manager plays an absolutely essential role in helping the partners in a JV develop and maintain a sound working relationship. In addition to his management responsibilities he has to play the role of a middleman and a diplomat. These tasks make his job all the more difficult and challenging. It should come as no surprise that when asked about their JV's success, JV general managers respond by referring to the absence (or existence) of conflicts between the parents.

Conflicts between partners may arise if the JV general manager is perceived to favor one partner to the detriment of the other. This is more likely to happen in JVs in which the JV general manager comes from one parent and his future promotions are decided by that parent.

The JV general manager often plays the role of a buffer between the two partners. For example, if one parent wants him to do something that he knows the other parent would not agree with, he will negotiate a compromise with the two parents separately. Or he can present a sensitive issue in a favorable light by using arguments that are acceptable to both partners. Knowing how to talk to the partners is a skill that JV general managers develop over time through a trial and error process as they learn what to say and what not to say, how to say it, to whom, and when.

IMPLICATIONS FOR MANAGERS

This paper shows that an important determinant of the long-term success or failure of JVs is the parents' ability to develop a working relationship. Of course not all JV failures are the result of poor relationships between the partners. JVs may fail because of poor economic conditions, competitive factors, poor management, or because they no longer fulfill the role for which they were originally created.

Similarly, parents do not need to see eye to eye on every single issue to maintain a good working relationship. Some JVs may even involve parent companies that have a very poor relationship and still survive because they are successful in meeting both parents' expectations and/or because each partner needs the other one badly enough to avoid breaking the JV up. What is important, though, is that the partners be prepared and willing to deal with disagreements. The parents need to recognize, understand, and accept each other's role, expectations, and contribution with respect to the management of the JV (whether a parent is passive and the other active, or whether both are active in the JV's management).

In the long run it is difficult to predict and control the relationship between two partners in a JV. Philosophies change, the general conditions (economic, competitive, etc.) surrounding the JV change, and so do the general circumstances in which the parent companies operate. However, the following guidelines should help managers develop a working relationship with their partner in a JV.

Commitment and Trust

As in a marriage, commitment and trust are key to the development of a long-term working relationship between the partners in a JV. These two elements are particularly important when things go wrong. If there is no trust and no commitment from at least one parent, chances are that the JV will be terminated or that one parent will buy the other one's share. If there is no trust but both parents are committed, a typical scenario is that both partners will fight over the management of the JV, but no decisions will be made, putting the JV in a weak competitive position.

If trust and commitment are important, managers need to work on these two ingredients of a successful relationship:

Show your commitment by allocating resources to the management of your relationship with your partner and with the JV. In other words, keep in touch and try to understand why your partner thinks and acts the way it does.

Show your commitment by transferring knowledge and skills that the JV may lack. It is in your best interest to provide support to the JV, and you build goodwill vis à vis your partner.

By showing your commitment you contribute to building trust, which is important for solving conflicts to the mutual satisfaction of the parents.

Avoid anything that may destroy your partner's trust. Once it is destroyed, it is extremely difficult, if not impossible, to restore.

Implementing the suggestions above is no guarantee of a trouble-free JV. Circumstances change, people change, and relationships change. However, these suggestions are an important step towards avoiding major surprises, and that alone is a major concern of managers involved in JVs.

Selecting a JV Partner

Before even thinking about selecting a partner, managers should satisfy themselves that a JV is the best alternative for achieving their objectives. All too often JVs are set up after a company approaches another one with a proposal, and the two get down to business without really taking the time to get to know each other or to establish the feasibility of the JV. If a JV is the best way to take advantage of a market opportunity, the next question is: Who would be a suitable partner?

Look for a partner who has complementary skills and resources to yours. In looking for a potential JV partner managers should first develop a clear understanding of what they can contribute to the JV in terms of skills and resources and then of what they expect their partner to contribute. The rationale for this recommendation is that there is more pressure on the parents to develop a working relationship if they need each other to maximize the chances of JV success.

Look for a partner for whom the JV is as important as it is for you. Many conflicts can be avoided by choosing a partner for whom the JV represents a significant stake. In JVs with large multinational corporations, the local partners are often frustrated when they realize that their particular JV receives a very low priority compared to the foreign parent's domestic operations.

Look for a partner who is of a size comparable to yours. It increases the likelihood of compatibility in management styles and of similarity in availability of financial resources to allocate to the JV. Too great a disparity leads to conflicts about how fast and how much to grow, with the smaller parent unable to provide his share of the required resources.

Look for a partner with a value system as close as possible to yours. This is obvious, but quite difficult to do in practice. Find out what your potential partner's philosophy, reputation, and managerial practices are before signing the JV contract.

Should your partner be in the same business as you are? The answer to this question is a matter of judgment. Some companies systematically look for partners outside their area of business in order to be able to control the JV's management. A drawback to this approach is that it sometimes takes a lot of convincing to get important decisions approved by a partner who does not understand the rules of the game. On the other hand, many companies look for partners in the same line of business so that both parents speak the same language. Sometimes the question does not even need to be addressed. This is the case in many developing countries where there are few, if any at all, suitable potential business partners. In those cases the only options are a bank, a government agency, or a consortium of local investors.

Obviously, finding the ideal partner is seldom possible. The issues discussed above are really intended to help managers in thinking about the kinds of compromises that have to be made in screening potential JV partners. Each one will have its strengths and weaknesses, its idiosyncracies, and in the end it is up to managers to decide which ones they can live with and which ones they cannot.

Planning a JV

Planning a JV refers to the set of activities undertaken by the parent companies from the time they decide to pool their resources together in a common venture to the time when the JV contract is signed.

The single most important recommendation with respect to this phase is: do not think that you can delegate it to your lawyers. Lawyers play a very important role in the process, but JVs whose parents do not meet, after agreeing to set up a JV, until it is time to sign the contract, are not those which create the most harmonious relationships between partners. And this has nothing to do with the quality of the legal document. One observation that stems from the study of successful and unsuccessful JVs is that, if you have to resort to the contract to solve a particular disagreement with your partner, your relationship is in trouble.

The importance of the planning phase lies in the opportunity that it provides the parents to get to know and understand each other better. By involving themselves in the discussions leading to the preparation of the JV contract, the partners can clarify their respective expectations and roles in the management of the JV and in the process develop a good understanding of each other's management philosophies and ways of doing business.

Clarifying the expectations makes it easier for the partners to agree on a set of common JV objectives and hence on the JV's strategy. It also helps managers in deciding how the payoffs are going to be distributed (i.e., who gets what?). This will minimize the likelihood of conflicts such as the distribution of dividends since clauses can be built into the bylaws which specify distribution rules (e.g., 50% of the previous year's profits).

Clarifying the role of each parent minimizes the likelihood of conflicts resulting from one parent believing that its partner is interfering in areas where it should not. This is done by allocating areas of influence on the basis of the parents' distinctive competence. In many JVs such an allocation is done in response to specific conflicts rather than being planned. For example, the Canadian parent in a JV in the hotel business with a bank convinced its parent, following an ill-fated experience in a previous JV, to concentrate on the marketing problems while its partner concentrated on financial as well as "local" problems.

Clarifying the role of the JV's board helps in identifying the important decisions for the JV's success and for the parents. Also, it helps in reaching agreement on how best to make those decisions.

The recommendations above contribute to enhancing the level of comfort between the partners. They tend to create a sense of commitment and trust which in turn helps in avoiding surprises as the JV unfolds. Further, they help managers from the two parents learn how to talk to each other, which is more effectively done in a positive non-threatening context than in the heat of a serious conflict.

Managing Relationships in a JV: the Parent's Perspective

This paper argues that the development of a working relationship with a partner is an important ingredient for the long-run success of the JV. It means that managers in parent companies need to work on developing such a relationship on an on-going basis. This is usually done in two ways: (i) by having a structure at the parent level to manage the process and (ii) by having an intelligence system which helps managers in managing the process effectively and efficiently.

Having a structure to manage the process means allocating resources to the management of the relationship with a partner. Someone at a general management level in the parent organization should be responsible and accountable for that.

Having an intelligence system means developing an approach to gathering and processing information on which management can act. This can involve formal periodic reports, planning documents, but also and more importantly, direct contacts with managers from the partner's organization or from the JV. A major difficulty is deciding how to obtain sufficient information to avoid asking dumb questions and to avoid surprises and at the same time to avoid appearing to interfere with the partner or with the JV. Doing so successfully requires a lot of interpersonal skill and judgment.

CONCLUSION

To develop a working relationship with a JV partner requires a positive approach. All too often managers enter JV arrangements worrying what their partner is going to do next or whether their partner has a hidden agenda in setting up the JV. If this is the case, the JV should probably not be created at all. Conflicts are unavoidable in JVs and both parents need to be prepared to compromise. This is more likely to be done to the benefit of both partners if the climate is conducive to compromise.

Managers need to pay attention to the relationship they maintain with their partner. Sometimes a big gap exists between what a manager believes — or wants to believe — the relationship to be and what it really is. Taking a proactive approach to the establishment of a working relationship by looking for opportunities to reinforce it (by taking initiatives which are valued by the partner) is a step towards enhancing the chances of the JV's long-term success.

REFERENCES

BEAMISH P., *Joint Venture Performance in Developing Countries*, Unpublished doctoral dissertation, The University of Western Ontario, 1984.
KILLING J. P., "How to Make a Global Joint Venture Work," *Harvard Business Review*, May-June 1982, pp. 120-127.
SCHAAN J-L, *Parent Control and Joint Venture Success: the Case of Mexico*, Unpublished doctoral dissertation, The University of Western Ontario, 1983.
The Financial Post, "High-Tech Firms Team up on New Projects," Jan. 22, 1983.
Industry Week, "Joint Ventures: for Better or for Worse?", Jan. 20, 1984.
Business Week, "Are Foreign Partners Good for U.S. Companies?", May 28, 1984.

Section II
DIVERSITY OF FUNCTIONS
DIVERSITÉ DE FONCTIONS

Human Resources
Ressources humaines

Human Resource Management:
A Strategic Approach Needed

AREMANDA V. SUBBARAO

"Productivity is both a central and an elusive challenge," according to the Mcdonald Commission's Interim Report on Canada's Future. It is a challenge today particularly in view of the fact that the rate of productivity in Canada has been falling. "In the ten years immediately after the Second World War, Canada's productivity advanced at an annual rate of 3.5%. In the next ten years, it proceeded at a more moderate 2.1% a year. Between 1967 and 1973 it moved ahead at a rate of 2.5%. For the remainder of the 1970s," as the Mcdonald Commission notes, "Canada had negligible productivity growth and from 1979 to 1982, productivity declined." If declining trends in productivity are not reversed, our ability to compete in international markets may be jeopardized. Canada ranked seventh among seven summit nations in terms of production per person. Our performance in international markets and the rate of productivity growth in Canada will determine the living standards of Canadians in the future.

The question that confronts every management professional is how to improve productivity in Canadian organizations. The objective of this paper is to describe the importance of human resources and suggest a strategic approach to the management of human resources in order to improve productivity over the longer term in Canadian work organizations.

Fortunately, Canada is blessed with a work force which is relatively more educated and mature now than at any time in the past. The proportion of workers in the Canadian labor force with post secondary education, which constituted only about one-twelfth in 1961, has risen to one-third today. This trend is expected to increase to 40% by the end of the decade and to 50% by the end of the century. The participation rate among young (15-24 age group) workers is declining and the rate among the 25-34 year olds will begin to shrink in the 1990s. The 35-54 age group of mature and experienced workers is expected to constitute a majority of the Canadian labor force in the near future. These mature, educated workers and the Canadian organizations that employ them face the challenge of increasing productivity in order to improve and maintain the standard of living of Canadians.

IMPORTANCE OF HUMAN RESOURCES

Management's proper use of human resources does contribute to productivity growth, according to a recent New York Stock Exchange Study. Productivity is both a confusing and a controversial topic and its measurement has become complex, varying from one organization to another. For the purposes of this paper, productivity is defined as output per person, and its change is measured in terms of the ratio of output to input of labor employed in a work organization. Productivity can be improved by increasing the efficiency of labor inputs and the efficiency of labor inputs, in turn, can be improved through better management of human resources. Efficiency in management of human resources is of particular importance for improving productivity in labor-intensive work organizations such as those in the service sector. The service sector is, in fact, the fastest-growing sector in Canada and now employs over 60% of the Canadian labor force as against the 6% engaged in the primary sector which, three decades ago, employed over one-third of the labor force.

Unit labor costs are often referred to as indicators of the efficiency of management of human resources in a work organization. Increasing labor costs add to the inputs, and if the output does not increase proportionately, the resulting ratio indicates declining productivity growth. Unit labor costs in the commercial service sector increased along with its expansion. The annual percentage changes in unit labor costs in the commercial service sector were 4.7 in 1971-72; they increased to 10.1 in 1980-81. In the manufacturing sector (which currently employs about 20% of the Canadian labor force), unit labor costs changed from 2.6% in 1971-72 to 10.7% in 1980-81.

Human resource problems such as employee absenteeism, accidents, turnover, and work stoppages contribute to unit labor costs and they seem to be on the rise in Canadian work organizations. In 1978, 83 million working days were lost in Canada due to employee absenteeism. Absenteeism is estimated to cost the Canadian economy $7.7 billion annually. In 1976, Canadian work organizations lost 14 million working days due to work injuries and illnesses and 11 million days due to strikes. Employee turnover increased from 16% in 1978 to 19% in 1980. The service sector in Canada experienced the highest turnover rate in 1980. In contrast, employee turnover in the U.S. declined from 19% in 1978 to 17% in 1980. In the U.S. the percentage of working days lost on account of absenteeism, accidents, and strikes was also low in comparison with the situation in Canada.

The changing characteristics of the Canadian labor force, as discussed above, are expected to intensify these human resource problems in Canadian work organizations in the future. In addition to changes in educational level and age composition, the future Canadian work force will consist of more Canadian-born workers than immigrants and more women than in the past. The labor force participation rate of immigrants decreased from 68% in the 1951-56 period to 17% in the 1976-81 period while that of women increased from 21% in 1961 to 49% in 1981. Employment expectations of these educated and mature Canadian-born men and women will be different from those in the past. These workers will expect safety, security, and equal opportunities in employment and will not hesitate to express their dissatisfaction with work. Different studies in 1974 and in the 1977-81 period indicated that employee dissatisfaction with work in Canada increased over that period of time. The level of dissatisfaction was more significant among the 30-44 age group, which is expected to constitute a large majority of the Canadian labor force in the near future. Increased employee dissatisfaction may contribute to increased absenteeism, turnover, and work stoppages.

The Canadian labor force may also demand new social policies as well as changes to existing employment policies through legislative amendments. Recent amendments to employment standards, health and safety, human rights, and labor relations legislation indicate the trends that can be expected to continue into the future. Changes in legislation and in labor markets are two of the most important environmental influences that Canadian work organizations are expected to cope with in managing human resources. In addition, technology is changing fast and some employers are replacing human resources by technology in order to reduce unit labor costs. Developing and implementing human resource policies and programs that are compatible with expected environmental changes and which are capable of accomplishing long-term labor productivity goals is the challenge that confronts the management of every Canadian work organization. If we fail to meet the challenge, we may fall behind our competitors and may be managing our way to economic decline in the future.

STRATEGY FOR MANAGING HUMAN RESOURCES

To meet the challenge discussed above, work organizations need to develop a strategy for managing human resources. Strategy, according to Chandler, a business historian, is "the determination of the basic long-term goals and objectives of an enterprise and the adoption of courses of action and the allocation of resources necessary for carrying out these goals." In a strategic approach, identification of higher labor productivity as a long-term goal is the first and the most important step. Second, specific intermediate-term targets such as reduction in absenteeism, accidents, turnover, work stoppages, and performance problems need to be identified. The intermediate term targets should be of such a nature that their realization should contribute to accomplishment of the long-term goal. In a strategic approach to management of human resources, realization of intermediate term targets results in human resource outcomes such as improved employee attendance, safety, health, security, commitment, performance, and industrial peace.

Only the top management of an organization is capable of determining a long-term goal and of committing organizational resources for accomplishing it. A committed top management guides the development and implementation of human resource policies and programs compatible with the external environment and appropriate for attracting, accommodating, developing, and utilizing employees to improve human resource outcomes in the intermediate term and to achieve labor productivity over a longer term. A flow chart indicating the important components in a strategic approach to human resource management is presented in Figure I.

Human Resource Policies

The three most important policies that are relevant to human resource management in any work organization are commitment, fairness, and participation. Top management commitment to employee health, safety, and employment security and employee commitment to the organization are essential for the survival and prosperity of a work organization. With mutual commitment, managers and workers participate in developing and implementing human resource programs that are not only fair but also are perceived as equitable. In other words, commitment, fairness, and participation are the policies — pronounced and accepted — on the basis of which strategic human resource programs are based.

Human Resource Programs

A number of human resource programs in different organizations have been developed over a period of time, and the following five are considered the most important in anticipation of expected environmental changes:
Human resource planning,
Staffing and career planning,
Appraising and developing,
Rewarding and protecting,
Consulting and cooperating.
Human resource planning involves forecasting demand and supply of both internal and external human resources and accommodating them along with technological changes. Forecasting and ac-

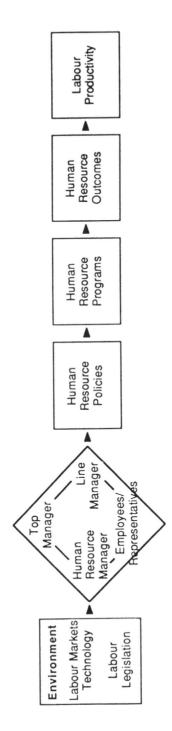

Figure I — Human Resource Management

commodation are likely to be smooth and effective if managers and workers participate in the process with a commitment to be fair to each other's interests. With commitment, they could plan to accommodate those human resources found to be in surplus against positions in demand, and employees with potential could be considered for higher positions on the career ladder. Managers and employees participate in appraising performance and in assessing potential of employees for promotions. They also participate in designing training programs and developing employees for careers in organizations. Those companies which adopt quality circles and other participatory programs also encourage managers and employees to participate in the selection of workers from both external and internal sources to ensure not only that the selection process is fair but also that those selected are compatible with the group with which they have to work. Participation in the job evaluation process and the design of compensation programs has become a common feature in a number of organizations. Employees perceive the fairness of the reward programs when they participate in designing them.

Employee participation in safety and health committees is mandated by law. It is an established practice in those organizations that recognize employees' ability to detect unsafe situations and to prevent them from becoming safety hazards. In all these human resource programs employees have an interest and, in recognition of the fact, employers of nonunionized companies as well as those with unions are adopting innovative schemes of consultation and labor-management cooperation. Consultation and cooperation schemes require appropriate organizational structure. Structure is also important for strategic human resource management to achieve long-term labor productivity growth.

STRUCTURE OF WORK ORGANIZATIONS

According to Chandler, strategy without structural adjustment leads to inefficiency. He defined structure as "the design of organization through which the enterprise is administered." Traditional hierarchical and bureaucratic organizational designs may not be appropriate for developing and implementing human resource management strategies appropriate to the ever-changing environments in which Canadian work organizations will be required to function in the future. Different organizations in different sectors functioning in different environments may be required to make appropriate structural adjustments to suit their specific situations. In the future, organizations will need flexible structures which facilitate "matching of organizational competences with the opportunities and risks created by environmental changes" for accomplishing desired results.

A traditional organizational structure that prescribes the responsibility for human resource management to a personnel specialist is not compatible with a strategic approach. The strategic approach requires structural adjustments to involve top managers, human resource management specialists, line managers and employees or their representatives (see Figure I). In the strategic approach, top managers provide leadership and take full responsibility for human resource management. Human resource managers, who are specialists by virtue of their training and occupation, are competent to understand and respond to expected environmental changes. They are responsible for providing assistance in formulating and implementing appropriate human resource policies and programs for achieving desired human resource outcomes.

Line managers are responsible for implementing human resource programs. Implementation is more likely to be effective if line managers are involved in formulating human resource policies and programs. Employee involvement and participation in both the formulation and implementation of human resource policies and programs is becoming more acceptable in practice in both unionized and nonunionized organizations. Evidence indicates that employee participation enhances achievement of human resource outcomes and accomplishment of long-term productivity growth.

A strategic approach requires a flexible organizational structure with a team led by committed top managers and followed by competent human resource managers, involved line managers, and employees or their representatives committed to achieving long-term productivity growth. Team structure facilitates identification of specific human resource problems such as absenteeism, accidents, turnover, work stoppage, and poor employee performance. It also facilitates analysis and appreciation of environmental changes which vary from time to time and from one location to another.

A team with an understanding of the internal problems and an appreciation of external pressures is better equipped than a hierarchical structure for formulating and implementing human resource policies and programs that are capable of accomplishing an organization's intermediate-term targets and long-term goals. Thus, a team structure is essential for a strategic approach, and a strategic approach is needed in the management of human resources for solving human resource problems and for improving labor productivity in Canadian work organizations. It is hoped that such an approach at the micro level will reverse the trend of productivity decline and will improve Canadians' standard of living in the future.

REFERENCES

ATKINSON, T., "Changing Attitudes Toward Work in Canada," *The Canadian Business Review*, Spring 1983, pp. 39-44.

BURSTEIN, M., TIENHAARA, N., HEWSON, P., and WARRENDER, B., *Canadian Work Values*, Ottawa, Manpower and Immigration, 1975, 104 p.

CHANDLER, A.D. Jr., *Strategy and Structure: Chapters in the History of the Industrial Enterprise*, Cambridge, Massachusetts, The MIT Press, 1962, pp. 13-14.

DEZANNA, M.A., FOMBRUN, C., TICHY, N., and WARREN, L., "Strategic Planning and Human Resource Management," *Human Resource Management*, Spring 1982, pp. 11-17.

DRUCKER, P.F., "Behind Japan's Success," *Harvard Business Review*, January-February 1981, pp. 83-90.

DYER, L., "Bringing Human Resource into the Strategy Formulation Process," *Human Resource Management*, Fall 1983, pp. 257-271.

The Financial Post Magazine, September 27, 1980.

FOSSUM, J.A., and PARKER, D.F., "Building State-of-the-Art Human Resource Strategies," *Human Resource Management*, Spring/Summer 1983, pp. 97-110.

FOULKES, F. K., *Personnel Policies in Large Non-Union Companies*, Englewood Cliffs, N.J., Prentice-Hall, 1980.

FRENCH, W.L., *The Personnel Management Process*, Boston, Houghton Mifflin, 1982.

HAYES, R.H., and ABERNATHY, J., "Managing our Way to Economic Decline," *Harvard Business Review*, July-August 1980, pp. 67-77.

HOFER, C.W., and SCHENDEL, D., *Strategy Formulation: Analytical Concepts*, St Paul, Minnesota, West Publishing, 1978, pp. 4-20.

KANTER, R.M., "Frontiers for Strategic Human Resource Planning and Management," *Human Resource Management*, Spring/Summer 1983, pp. 9-25.

KATZ, H.C., KOCHAN, T.A., and GOBEILLE, K.R., "Industrial Relations Performance, Economic Performance and QWL Programs: an Interplant Analysis," *Industrial and Labor Relations Review*, October 1983, pp. 3-17.

Labor Market Developments in the 1980s, Employment and Immigration, Ottawa, 1981.

Market Research Handbook 1983, Statistics Canada, Tables 1-15.

MYERS, H.E., "Personnel Directors are the New Corporate Heroes," *Fortune*, February 1976, pp. 84-88.

NININGER, J.R., *Managing Human Resources: a Strategic Perspective*, The Conference Board of Canada, 1982, 171 p.

People and Productivity: a Challenge to Corporate America, A Study from the New York Stock Exchange Office of Economic Research, 1982, 53 p.

PIGOT, G., *The Changing Educational Profile of Canadians, 1961-2000*, Ottawa, Statistics Canada, 1980, Table 6.

PRAHALAD, C.K., "Developing Strategic Capability: an Agenda for Top Management," *Human Resource Management*, Fall 1983, pp. 237-254.

RESCHENTHALER, G.B., *Occupational Health and Safety in Canada: the Economics and Three Case Studies*, Montreal, Institute for Research on Public Policy, 1979, p. 2.

Royal Commission on the Economic Union and Development Prospects for Canada, *A Commission on Canada's Future: Challenges and Choices*, Ottawa, Ministry of Supply and Services, 1984, p. 39.

SANDERSON, G.I., *Absenteeism, its Extent, Causes, and Costs*, CCH Ltd, 1980, pp. 8153-8163.

SCHUSTER, M., "The Impact of Union-Management Cooperation on Productivity and Employment," *Industrial and Labor Relations Review*, April 1983, pp. 415-430.

SEIGEL, I.H., and WEINBERG, E., *Labor-Management Cooperation: the American Experience*, Kalamazoo, Michigan, W.E. Upjohn Institute for Employment Research, 1982, 316 p.

SRINIVAS, K.M., *Human Resource Management: Contemporary Perspectives in Canada*, Toronto, McGraw-Hill Ryerson, 1984.

U.S. News and World Report, June 6, 1983, p. 32.

Workstoppages, Labor Canada, January 1980.

1980 AMS Office Turnover Survey, *Management World*, September 1981, pp. 25-27.

Perceptual Errors in Organizations: An Attribution Theory Approach

ANDRÉ DE CARUFEL
JAK JABES

Effective managerial behavior is influenced to an important degree by the ability to interpret the actions of others and to predict their future behavior. The operation of these perceptual and cognitive processes has recently become the focus of important research in human resource management in the areas of performance appraisal (Feldman, 1981; Ilgen and Feldman, 1983); leadership (Mitchell, Green and Wood, 1981); decision-making (Einhorn and Hogarth, 1981), and performance (Staw, 1975). It is well known, however, that perception reflects not only external stimuli, but also the psychological state of the perceiver. As such, perceptions are subject to errors, biases, and distortions. While the operation of certain specific perceptual errors is well known to organizational theorists, the literature in this area is seriously deficient in two ways: the standard reference (Zalkind and Costello, 1962), one which is still being reprinted in new books, is now more than 20 years old; and there is a lack of theoretical coherence to work in this area.

The errors themselves have been drawn from diverse research traditions and have been "tacked on" to our understanding of person perception. Accordingly, the major aims of the present paper are:

1. to provide for an organizational audience an up-to-date review of the area of perceptual errors;
2. to present a theoretical framework to organize the study of perceptual errors based on attribution theory; and
3. to present some management implications of the study of perceptual errors from an attributional perspective.

ATTRIBUTION THEORY: AN OVERVIEW

This overview will be brief, since the major purpose is to analyze perceptual errors. (Detailed theoretical statements of attribution processes may be found in the following sources: Heider, 1958; Jones and Davis, 1965; Kelley, 1967; Bem, 1972; Jones et al., 1972; Jones and McGillis, 1976; Lord and Smith, 1983; Weiner, 1974; Shaver, 1975; Harvey, Ickes and Kidd, 1976, 1978, 1981).

Attribution theory treats the perceiver as a "naive scientist" searching for the causes of events that occur in the social environment to enable more effective behavioral responses and prediction of future events. Since the social environment is complex and the individual's ability to comprehend and store perceptual information is limited, the perceived environment is simplified into meaningful cause and effect sequences. This causal analysis is done by the perceiver based on imperfect knowledge of the social environment and the use of naive causal principles as the tools of analysis (Kahneman, Slovic, and Tversky, 1982). Attribution theory specifies three major tasks for the perceiver in the analysis of action sequences.

The Signification of Action

The perceiver begins by selecting from the continuous flow of action in the social environment a specific "act" significant enough to require explanation. These acts, which may be as momentary as a sarcastic grin or as drawn out as a leadership struggle, form the raw material for the attribution process. Two criteria for acts that will motivate explanation via the attribution process are:
1. that the act departs from the perceiver's expectations; and
2. that the act has important hedonic consequences for the perceiver.

Causal Judgment

The perceiver tries to identify the cause, or set of causes, to which the act can be reasonably attributed. Attribution theorists have categorized the causes of social behavior into three main classes:
1. those that are the result of the internal "dispositions" (e.g., personality traits or abilities) of the target person;
2. those that are the result of stable aspects of the external environment (e.g., the nature of a task or peer pressure); or
3. transient combinations of situational variables and states of the target person (e.g., the employee who drunkenly assaults his boss's wife at the office Christmas party).

There is a strong preference on the part of perceivers to explain a target person's behavior with reference to internal dispositions. This is because transient acts and responses to powerful situational pressure may allow confident prediction of the target's future behavior but tell the perceiver little about the target person's unique dispositions. In the process of making causal judgments, it is necessary for the perceiver to decide what the target person intended by the behavior. Any given behavior may have several consequences. Deciding which of these the target intended provides a necessary link in the chain of inferences from acts to dispositions.

All intentional acts are not equally informative about the target person's underlying dispositions because most actions occur within a social context in which there may exist facilitatory and/or inhibitory situational influences. For example, an employee who works very well while under surveillance may be performing well because of high levels of internal motivation or because of the surveillance itself. This aspect of social situations brings about the third task for the perceiver.

Social Inference

The crucial aspect here is the amount of information that the perceiver gains about the target's unique dispositions as a result of having observed the act. A useful criterion for the perceiver in the task of social inference is the extent to which the behavior reveals aspects of the target person that go beyond what is typical of individuals in general. For example, if an employee's expense account claim is extremely low, the employer (i.e., the perceiver in this case) may conclude that not only was the employee trying to be economical (i.e., complying with norms) but also that this person is "cheap." The perceiver may infer the disposition to account for that portion of the behavior which exceeds the normal range. Further inferences that the perceiver might make could involve predictions about the target's future behavior and generalizations about the target person in other settings.

In sum, the attribution process is concerned with the rules of "naive psychology," that is, how individuals explain events in their environment. These "attributions" are then processed via feedback loops to prepare the perceiver for the next attribution sequence. A critical concern for the perceiver, since his/her subsequent behavioral responses will be based on these inferences, is that of accuracy.

A FRAMEWORK FOR ANALYZING ATTRIBUTION ERRORS

The framework suggests that perceptual errors are not simply features that are "tacked on" to the perceptual process, but rather reflect systematic distortions that are associated with specific stages of the attribution process itself. In the different stages of the attribution model there exists the potential for the inferences of the perceiver to go away and result in judgments that are too extreme, inappropriate, or unfounded. The perceptual errors may be divided into three general classes, which are linked to the major stages in the attribution sequence. The framework is diagrammed in Figure I.

The Failure to Seek Out and/or Use Adequate Information

Before any causal analysis or social inference can take place, there must be some informational "input" into the attribution sequence. It is impossible for an individual manager to be constantly

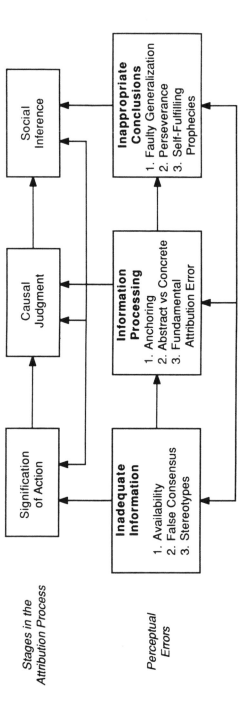

Figure I — Stages in the Attribution Process and Associated Perceptual Errors

aware of everything going on in the organizational environment. Certain aspects will be attended to and others ignored. This is the phenomenon of perceptual selectivity (Dearborn and Simon, 1958; Benton, 1970). Information selected by the perceiver as a basis for attribution will not necessarily be biased. However, the criteria for sampling information from the action environment is often based upon the perceiver's past history, needs, and expertise. Errors may occur at this stage because the perceiver may fail to notice or to appreciate the significance of events and may rely too heavily upon his or her imperfect knowledge of the target person and the social environment.

There are three major points in the analysis of the action sequence where the failure to obtain or use adequate information is likely. This stage underlies all of the others in the sense that without adequate information it is unlikely that accurate and meaningful conclusions will be drawn.

Availability

Tversky and Kahneman (1974) used the term "availability" to describe a major influence upon individuals' judgments of the probability of past and future events. Individuals are rarely able to retrieve every single instance of past events from memory. The perceiver's subjective estimate of the likelihood of events will be strongly affected by the ease with which vivid examples can be brought to mind.

The availability bias may manifest itself in a variety of organizational seetings. Foremost among these is the area of performance appraisal. Relatively objective data usually exist on productivity and absenteeism, but there may be whole other classes of appraisal for which records do not exist, e.g., interpersonal skills, cooperativeness, initiative, attitude, or appearance. Managers may have to scan their memory for concrete instances of the employee's behavior along these dimensions. Another similar situation occurs when records do in fact exist but the managers decide that they "are the best judge." In general, individuals' skills as intuitive estimators of the likelihood of events are quite poor (Tversky and Kahneman, 1974). To the extent that the individuals rely on their memories, biases such as availability may affect the judgments they reach because they are relying on a small, and likely biased, sample of the target person's behavior.

The False Consensus Effect

The false consensus effect is defined (Ross, 1977, 188) as the tendency of individuals "... to see their own behavioral choices and judgments as relatively common and appropriate to existing circumstances while viewing alternative responses as uncommon, deviant, and inappropriate." A major consequence of this for attribution purposes is that the perceiver will judge those behaviors that differ from his or her own choices as more revealing about the target's dispositions than those which are similar to his or her own choices. This is because these "deviant" choices depart from what the perceiver believes to be normative.

The implications of this effect for organizational behavior are numerous. One is that managers may feel more confident about decisions than is warranted because they imagine that others in a similar circumstance would have done the same. Another is that they may be less tolerant of dissenting opinions because they are falsely attributed to "cranks" who are in the minority and are acting for purely personal (i.e., dispositional) reasons. Pressures to uniformity in decision-making groups may stifle dissenting opinions and give rise to a false consensus effect (Janis, 1972; Huseman and Driver, 1979). It may also limit flexibility in decision-making to some degree once a preliminary decision has been reached because of the tendency to overestimate the appropriateness of this decision and the consequent lowered ability to perceive viable alternatives.

Stereotypes

The concept of stereotype was originally used to describe judgments made about individuals based on their ethnic group membership but has been broadened in current usage to include judgments made about members of any social category (e.g., sex, age, occupational status). Stereotypes may short-circuit the attributions of the target person derived from the causal analysis or cause traits to be attributed on the basis of the restricted information that social category membership typically provides.

The most recent work in this area has concerned "sex-role stereotypes," i.e., the traits that are commonly attributed to males and females (Bass, Krusell and Alexander, 1971; Rosen and Jerdee, 1973; Rosen and Jerdee, 1974a, b; Cohen and Bunker, 1975; Dipboye, 1978). Broverman et al. (1972) reviewed the evidence and suggested that the male sex-role stereotype included traits such as independent, dominant, active, and logical, while that for females included traits like gentle, tactful, and aware of their own feelings. These stereotypes have been implicated in the explanation of successful and unsuccessful performance by males and females in achievement situations. Deaux and Emswiller (1974) and Feather and Simon (1975) have indicated that success by a male is likely to be explained by a stable disposition such as ability, while success by a female is attributed to more transient causes and failure by a female is explained by lack of ability. These relationships are particularly strong in traditionally masculine tasks, as most managerial tasks are thought to be. In a study in which female managers rated male and female managers described in bogus personnel files, Jabes (1980) demonstrated that the stereotype may reverse itself due to organizational socialization. In the study, female managers were perceived to be more successful, more intelligent, more likeable, and less conservative than their male counterparts.

The consequences for the organization are quite clear. Judgments based on stereotypes may hamper selection and placement decisions, leading to a waste of human potential as well as possible legal problems. Further, the target of the stereotypes may become disaffected and leave the organization or remain but be less than optimally efficient. Erroneous impressions of individuals based on stereotypes may cause managers to be less effective in a broad range of duties regarding these employees, such as performance appraisal, discipline, and training, as well as daily interactions.

Information Processing Errors

Once the perceiver has information about the target person and the action context, there may be several processing errors which may bias the conclusions drawn from the input. These errors typically result from tendencies to systematically overestimate the importance or representativeness of certain kinds of information and underestimate or ignore other relevant inputs. These biases occur most clearly in the "analysis" phases of the attribution model, where the perceiver judges the intentions, dispositions, and abilities of the target person. The tendency to place too much emphasis on certain kinds of information to the exclusion of other, perhaps equally valid inputs may operate on its own or may compound the errors based on inadequate information discussed above.

Anchoring

Individuals are typically faced with data about other individuals' behavior over time. Other things being equal, this information should carry equal weight in the formation of an overall impression. However, an initial impression is usually formed very early in the sequence and is then adjusted in light of new information. The adjustment, though, is often inadequate, with the result that the final estimate is biased or anchored by the initial information. Jones and Geothals (1971) argued that this anchoring effect should be especially pronounced when judgments are being made about relatively stable attributes (such as ability). Early information may be unreliable and/or invalid for a number of reasons (e.g., nervousness, lack of experience, etc.) yet these reasons may be underestimated in the course of forming an early impression. This bias may result in selection decisions that do not contribute to organizational effectiveness and evaluations of performance that fail to reward and motivate "late bloomers."

The Use of Concrete and Abstract Information

Nisbett et al. (1976) have investigated a bias in the processing of information and the intuitive psychology of prediction and judgment. They suggest that individuals' predictions and judgments are relatively impervious to information presented in the form of abstract statistical baselines and overly influenced by specific concrete cases. They give the example of someone vacillating between purchasing a Saab or a Volvo automobile. The individual decides to buy a Volvo after reading Consumer Reports. At a party he attends he has a conversation with a man who vividly describes the tremendous problems his brother-in law has had with his Volvo. As Nisbett et al. point out, the logical status of the information provided by the person at the party is that one's impressions based on Consumer Reports should be shifted an iota on several dimensions. However, it is likely that this single case will cause the potential car buyer to seriously reconsider the choice.

The impact of this processing bias is that vivid, concrete events which may not be representative at all of the individual's dispositions or future behavior may outweigh more representative information presented in more abstract form. This may be important in selection interviews or unsystematic attempts to evaluate the impact of training. The manager as judge may form an impression based on an unrepresentative occurrence to the relative exclusion of "dry" data such as attendance or performance. One often encounters this bias in the evaluation of the performance of an athlete when stellar statistics accumulated over an 80-game schedule may be dismissed if the athlete should have a bad playoff game. This overreliance on concrete information also has direct implications for the marketing of products and for advertising strategies. Borgida and Nisbett's (1977) work suggests that concrete instances of excellent product functioning may be more effective than presenting information in the form of "97% of those surveyed..."

The Fundamental Attribution Error

The fundamental attribution error refers to the process by which observers tend to underestimate the role of situational factors in explaining the cause of an observed act and overestimate the importance of personal dispositions. Milgram (1974) has aptly demonstrated that obedience to a superior's orders often is a result of situational determinants. Nevertheless, psychiatrists and laymen alike, when reading or witnessing enactments of such order-following episodes, invariably attribute the cause to personal dispositions (Bierbrauer, 1973; Milgram, 1974).

This bias may lead to erroneous impressions of others in the work setting. An important situational influence that is often ignored is the organizational role. The expectations created by this role are powerful determinants of behavior in the organizational environment (Lieberman, 1956). However, they may not really reflect the individual's underlying dispositions. Imagine a manager's surprise when it is discovered that an employee relatively low in the hierarchy is an important figure in a local charity drive. This really should not be surprising, however, unless the manager has inferred the employee's personality from the highly constrained work situation.

When behaviors are attributed to the person rather than the situation, an unrealistically high level of consistency in behavior is expected. This may reinforce the "anchoring" effects discussed earlier: first impressions become "traits" which may be difficult to explain away in the face of contradictory information.

Inappropriate Use of Conclusions

This is the stage at which the conclusions based on earlier analyses may be inappropriately used to make behavioral responses, judgments, and predictions. Once the attribution process results in a conclusion that the observed act reflects the environment or the target person's dispositions, the perceiver uses this information as a basis for action and prediction which may condition the possible responses of the perceiver. Attributional conclusions may also compound earlier errors, as in the case of the "self-fulfilling prophecy" (Merton, 1948; Jones, 1977), where individuals develop expectations about how others will behave and then act towards them in terms of these expectations. The result may be that the target person, responding to the behavior of the perceiver, comes to behave in exactly the way expected by the perceiver, thus fulfilling the prophecy. These errors often occur in: (1) the assignment of dispositions where the major attribution conclusion is made; and (2) the feedback stages where inappropriate revisions of earlier judgments are made.

Faulty Generalization

This refers to several processes which have in common inappropriate generalization from knowledge about the target in one area to dispositions in another. One of these is the "halo effect" (Zalkind and Costello, 1962), which is the tendency to attribute, on the basis of a single inferred trait, other traits or dispositions to the target person of similar valence (e.g., a "good" person has other "good" traits attributed to him or her). Closely related is the "implicit personality theory" (Schneider, 1973), wherein the individual assumes that certain combinations of traits "go together." An inference of one of the traits leads to the others also becoming part of the target person's "personality." For example, an employee who is perceived to be "honest" may also be attributed related traits such as trustworthiness, fairness, and dependability, for which the perceiver actually has no evidence. Staw (1975) has shown that organizational participants possess a theory of the relationship between organizational characteristics and subsequent performance. Performance becomes a cue, or a central trait, around which characteristics are ascribed to others in the organization. These processes may seem like stereotyping, but whereas stereotyping short-circuits the attribution process by assigning traits solely on the basis of social category membership, the halo effect and the implicit pesonality error represent unwarranted generalization after the attribution sequence has taken place.

The Perseverance of Causal Theories

Erroneous impressions may persist despite possible disconfirming evidence because individuals not only seek information that is consistent with their initial impressions (Haire and Grunes, 1958) but also search for antecedent events that explain them (Ross, 1977). Perceivers often play the role of amateur clinicians, speculating about the reasons why an individual behaves in a certain way and searching for events in that person's life history to account for it. This type of explanation involves the construction of causal theories as to the reasons for another's behavior which may be invoked to explain an event even when the behavior is no longer being manifested. In other words, these causal theories persist, despite the nonexistence of confirming evidence in that person's current behavior, and sometimes even in the face of disconfirming evidence. In newspaper accounts, for example, an individual may be referred to as an "ex-mental patient" or "a former inmate of ..." as if this explains the current behavior! Similar processes may occur in selection decisions, where certain candidates may be stigmatized by a criminal record or a dishonorable discharge from the service, or in financial decisions (Ashton, 1976).

The perseverance of causal theories may result in an insensitivity to a possible reinterpretation of new, incoming information and to an overreliance on them as sources of information for the prediction and understanding of others' behavior in organizational settings.

IMPLICATIONS FOR ORGANIZATIONAL BEHAVIOR

Recently, there have appeared some studies which have begun the process of linking attribution theory to management and organizational behavior. These studies have examined control systems (Birnberg, Frieze and Shields, 1977), promotion (Smith and Hunt, 1978), consumer behavior (Calder and Burnkrant, 1977; Scott, 1978), marketing research (Burnkrant, 1975), and performance (Staw, 1975; deCarufel and Jabes, 1980). We would like to suggest some further areas in which attribution theory, and the study of attribution errors in particular, may be useful to the understanding of behavior in organizational settings.

Personnel Selection and Performance Evaluation

The selection of personnel for the organization, their assignment to tasks and functions, and the evaluation of their performance are processes at the heart of human resource management. Yet, because of their judgmental quality, they are particularly prone to attribution errors.

Personnel decisions such as selection may be reached on the basis of small samples of information (e.g., a resume, a short interview, or a brief work sample). The candidate's behavior in a stressful and sometimes novel setting such as an interview is used to characterize that person's work potential. In order for this process to be considered valid, the observed behavior should be representative of the candidate's work behavior in general. The process is analogous to scientific sampling theory in which samples are used to predict population parameters. The two factors which are crucial in the scientific process of characterizing populations from samples are that the sample be of sufficient size and that it be inclusive of all the relevant aspects of the population itself. In a study by the present authors (deCarufel and Jabes, 1980) undergraduate students were presented with information about a job candidate and were told that the information was based on either a large or small sample of observations and that the information was based on the opinions of one person or reflected the views of a more representative set. Subjects were then asked to make judgments about the stimulus person's personality and potential in a work setting. Subjects made extreme judgments in all conditions and held these opinions with high confidence. They did not make use of the sampling theory information to moderate the extremity of their judgments or the confidence with which they were held, although the information was correctly perceived. These results were replicated in a second experiment using as subjects a group of experienced personnel officers. One can clearly see here the operation of the first category of attribution errors, the failure to use diagnostic information about the sample and appreciate the potential problems of acting with great confidence on unrepresentative information about others.

We would not, of course, suggest that decision-makers use formal sampling principles for gathering information in their daily activities. However, we would like to point out the frequency with which even experienced personnel officers use small and highly unrepresentative samples of information as a basis for extreme judgments. Cautions then are in order both in the process of gathering this information and the use of this information for decision-making. The attributional model presented here provides an integrated perspective on these processes and offers the promise that a careful consideration of the implications of the model may sensitize decision-makers to these errors.

A second aspect related to selection, and one which will lead us into the domain of performance evaluation, concerns the use of selection instruments. Often these instruments require the decision-maker to make trait attributions about the candidate. This process reinforces the perceiver's tendency to make the fundamental attribution error and encourages a simple trait-based approach to the explanation of behavior at the expense of more sophisticated contingency (person x situation) models now favored by organizational researchers. The development of multiple-instance observations and the use of categories that do not exclusively rely on traits would foster more sophisticated personnel selection procedures.

When the performance of personnel is evaluated, many factors in addition to actual performance are included (Feldman, 1981; Ilgen and Feldman, 1983). These include judgments about that person's attitude toward work, cooperativeness, likelihood of future sources, as well as other trait dimensions. The difficulties to which these procedures lead has increased the popularity of behaviorally-based measures. In the behaviorally-based measures, job-relevant behaviors rather than global traits are measured. An interesting variation on this technique would require decision-makers to maintain behavioral records of employees' performance. To facilitate the keeping of records in an environment, sampling procedures over time or events would be established. The compilation of a permanent behavioral record would be an immense improvement over traditional rating scale procedures. These records would allow for the determination not only of the presence or absence of job-related behaviors but also for more sophisticated analyses of frequency, dispersion over time, and situational specificity. These data would enable the decision-maker to determine more directly the cause (internal or external to the person) of the behaviors in question and thus to avoid attribution errors.

Attribution theory is concerned not only with the accurate and representative measurement of performance but also with the interpretation of the behaviors by the decision-maker. As Weiner (1974) has shown, performance is affected by several factors, including ability, effort, task difficulty, and luck. The causes of performance or lack thereof is an attributional question and one over which there may be disagreement between the evaluator and evaluatee. Attribution theory points out the reasons why the two parties may disagree over "objective" data, i.e., disagreements are due to inferences about the causes and significance of behaviors. Attribution theory points out that both parties may be subject to perceptual errors and interpretation errors and that each must examine his assumptions and information processing to account for the differences.

Conflict

A major area of organizational behavior which might benefit from an attribution theory perspective is that of conflict. In his review of the conflict literature Thomas (1976) points out at least two stages where perceptions are crucial aspects. One is in the conceptualization stage, where each party must define for itself the conflict issue. The other is in the interaction stage where each party is influenced by (its perception of) the behavior of the other. In the conceptualization stage, each party uses the information at its disposal, blends it with a motivated self-interest, and arrives at a definition of the problem. Since each party has different information and self-interest, the problem definitions are likely to be quite different as a consequence. The resulting "dialogue" between the two parties may appear rather unusual to a disinterested party since each will be talking about a different "problem." In this aspect as well we see the possible error of inadequate shared information being a contributor to conflict. Each group will indulge in stereotyping and each will be able to find support for its own position — a "false consensus effect." These attribution errors will contribute to the tenacity with which each party will hold to its own position and likely to the difficulty of resolving the conflict.

In the interaction stage, attribution theory is extremely relevant. Judgments about the intentionality underlying events, the inferences drawn about the other party, and the perceptions of the course of the conflict itself all lend themselves to attribution theory analysis. It might be suggested as a hypothesis that hostile actions would be more readily attributed to the other party's dispositions than would conciliatory acts. Furthermore, one can readily see the implications of the "anchoring" literature for judgments about who is retaliating and who is engaging in unprovoked actions. It is likely that both sides will be motivated to see the other as the aggressor and to justify their own actions accordingly. A particularly crucial aspect to this is that each party "knows" the reasons why it is behaving as it does. As such one's own behavior seems entirely reasonable, possibly the result of situational factors (Jones et al., 1972) while the behavior of the other is seen as arbitrary and probably motivated by selfish personal considerations. This interpretive process, whereby the causality for actions is allocated, contributes to the conflict and makes it difficult for the two parties to realize the other's viewpoint. In future studies of conflict, it is recommended that researchers gather data on the perceived meaning of the behaviors of both parties as conceptual underpinnings to their actions.

In the case of managing conflict in organizations, a recent article by Cosier and Ruble (1981) proposes a two-dimensional model. The two dimensions are: (1) assertiveness, defind as behavior intended to satisfy one's own concerns and (2) cooperativeness, defined as behaviors intended to satisfy another's concerns.

This two-dimensional model is an important advance over the previous unidimensional, cooperative-competitive model not only because it identifies previously "hidden" behavior, but also because it makes it clearer that conflict management is an interactive process. The potential for attribution theory as a tool of analysis is particularly evident here when an actor in a conflict situation must make inferences not only about the effects of his or her actions on the other, but simultaneously about the reasons for the actions of the other. It would seem to be a particularly ripe area in which to study errors of social inference, such as the self-fulfilling prophecy.

Communication

Communication is a central area of organizational behavior that is appropriate for the application of attribution theory. The communication of a message from a sender to a recipient and back again (in the form of feedback) is a social interchange that relies heavily upon perceptions of the sender's intent. The message that the source wishes to communicate is influenced by a variety of factors, including the encoding strategy, choice of message channel, and nonverbal context. All of these influence what the recipient perceives the sender's message to be. The trustworthiness and intent to persuade are perceived characteristics, as is the potential clash between verbal and nonverbal cues. It would be interesting to consider attributions about a sender who chooses different channels (e.g., oral, written, telephone) to convey different types of messages (e.g., good vs bad news).

The familiar "barriers and gateways" to communication may be conceived of in many cases as the causes or consequences of attribution errors. For example, in the encoding of the message, an important mediator is the perception of and attributions about the recipient by the source. What the recipient's state of knowledge is on this issue, what the recipient's attitude is toward this issue, and other concerns of this sort are inferences which must be made by the source and, if incorrectly made, will often cause the communication to miss its mark. Similarly, the extent to which the recipient is more influenced by early rather than late information (anchoring) or ignores the representativeness of the basis for statements by a source may result in attribution errors and potentially ineffective message receipt. Thus, communication is a process based largely on inferences about motives and intentions and as such is amenable to analysis by attribution theory and research in the area of perceptual errors.

CONCLUSION

On the basis of attribution theory, which describes the rules of inference used by individuals to explain the causes of others' behavior, a framework was developed to organize the domain of perceptual errors into a conceptual scheme following the stages of inference in the attribution model. Several categories of perceptual errors were discussed, and some implications for organizational behavior were presented. It is hoped that this paper will provide some structure to the highly differentiated area of perceptual errors and will spur researchers to further explore the attribution components of behavior in organizational settings.

REFERENCES

ASHTON, R.H., "Cognitive Changes Induced by Accounting Changes: Experimental Evidence on the Functional Fixation Hypothesis," *Journal of Accounting Research*, 1976, Vol. 14, pp. 1-17.

BASS, B.M., KRUSELL, J., and ALEXANDER, R.A., "Male Managers' Attitudes Towards Working Women," *American Behavioral Scientist*, 1971, Vol. 15, pp. 221-236.

BEM, D.J., "Self-Perception Theory," in L. Berkowitz (ed.), *Advances in Experimental Social Psychology*, Vol. 6, New York, Academic Press, 1972.

BENTON, L.R., "The Many Faces of Conflict: How Differences in Perception Causes Differences in Opinion," *Supervisory Management*, 1970, Vol. 43, pp. 7-10.

BIERBRAUER, G., "Effect of Set, Perspective, and Temporal Factors in Attribution," Ph.D. dissertation, Stanford University, 1973.

BIRNBERG, J.G., FRIEZE, I.H., and SHIELDS, M.D., "The Role of Attribution Theory in Control Systems," *Accounting, Organizations and Society*, 1977, Vol. 2, pp. 189-200.

BORGIDA, E., and NISBETT, R.E., "The Differential Impact of Abstract vs. Concrete Information on Decisions," *Journal of Applied Social Psychology*, 1977, Vol. 7, pp. 258-271.

BROVERMAN, I.K., VOGEL, S.R., BROVERMAN, D.M., CLARKSON, F. E., and ROSENKRANTZ, P.S., "Sex-Role Stereotypes: A Current Appraisal," *Journal of Social Issues*, 1972, pp. 59-78.

BURNKRANT, R.E. "Attribution Theory in Marketing Research: Problems and Prospects," In J. Schlinger (ed.), *Advances in Consumer Research*, 1975, Vol. 2, pp. 465-467.

CALDER, B.J., and BURNKRANT, R.E., "Interpersonal Influence on Consumer Behavior: An Attribution Theory Approach," *Journal of Consumer Research*, 1977, Vol. 4, pp. 29-38.

COHEN, S., and BUNKER, K., "Subtle Effects of Sex Role Stereotypes in Recruiters' Hiring Decisions," *Journal of Applied Psychology*, 1975, Vol. 60, pp. 566-572.

COSIER, R.A., and RUBLE, T.L., "Research on Conflict-Handling Behavior: An Experimental Approach," *Academy of Management Journal*, 1981, Vol. 24, pp. 816-831.

DEARBORN, D.C., and SIMON, H.A., "Selective Perception: A Note on Departmental Identification of Executives," *Sociometry*, 1958, Vol. 21, pp.140-144.

DEAUX, K., and EMSWILLER, T., "Explanations of Successful Performance on Sex-Linked Tasks: What is Skill for the Male is Luck for the Female?", *Journal of Personality and Social Psychology*, 1974, Vol. 29, pp. 80-85.

deCARUFEL, A., and JABES, J., Biases in Intuitive Judgement in Organization: An Attributional Model and Empirical Test, In F.W. Renwich (ed.), *Proceedings of the Atlantic Schools of Business Conference*, Sydney, N.S., 1980.

DIPBOYE, R.L., "Women as Managers — Stereotypes and Realities," In B.A. Stead (ed.), *Women in Management*, Englewood Cliffs, New Jersey, Prentice-Hall, 1978.

EINHORN, H.J., and HOGARTH, R.M., "Behavioral Decision Theory: Processes of Judgement and Choice," *Annual Review of Psychology*, 1981, Vol. 32, pp. 53-88.

FEATHER, N.T., and SIMON, J.G., "Reactions to Male and Female Success and Failure in Sex-Linked Occupations: Impressions of Personality, Causal Attributions, and Perceived Likelihood of Different Consequences," *Journal of Personality and Social Psychology*, 1975, Vol. 31, pp. 20-31.

FELDMAN, J.M., "Beyond Attribution Theory: Cognitive Processes in Performance Appraisal," *Journal of Applied Psychology*, 1981, Vol. 66, pp. 127-148.

HAIRE, M., and GRUNES, W.F., "Perceptual Defenses: Processes Protecting an Original Perception of Another Personality," *Human Relations*, 1958, Vol. 3, pp. 403-412.

HARVEY, J.H., ICKES, W.H., and KIDD, R.F. (eds.), *New Directions in Attribution Research*, Vol. 1 (1976), Vol. 2 (1978), Vol. 3 (1981), Hillsdale, New Jersey, Lawrence Erlbaum Associates.

HEIDER, F., *The Psychology of Interpersonal Relations*, New York, John Wiley & Sons, 1958.

HUSEMAN, C.R., and DRIVER, R.W., "Groupthink: Implications for Small Group Decision Making in Business," In R.C. Huseman and A.B. Carroll (eds.), *Readings in Organizational Behavior*, Dimensions of Management Actions, Boston, Mass., Allyn & Bacon, 1979.

ILGEN, D.R., and FELDMAN, J.M., Performance Appraisal: A Process Focus, In B. Staw and L. Cummings (eds.), *Research in Organizational Behavior*, Greenwich, Conn., JAI Press, 1983.

JABES, J., "Causal Attributions and Sex-role Stereotypes in the Perceptions of Women Managers," *Canadian Journal of Behavioral Science*, 1980, Vol. 12, pp. 52-63.

JANIS, I.L., *Victims of Groupthink*, Boston, Mass., Houghton Mifflin, 1972.

JONES, E.E., and DAVIS, K.E., "From Acts to Dispositions," In L. Berkowitz (ed.), *Advances in Experimental Social Psychology*, Vol. 2, New York, Academic Press, 1965.

JONES, E.E., and GOETHALS, G.R., *Order Effects in Impression Formation: Attribution Context and the Nature of the Entity*, Morristown, New Jersey, General Learning Press, 1971.

JONES, E.E., KANOUSE, D.E., KELLEY, H.H., NISBETT, R.E., VALINS, S., and WEINER, B., *Attribution: Perceiving the Causes of Behavior*, Morristown, New Jersey, General Learning Press, 1972.

JONES, E.E., and McGillis, D., "Correspondent Inferences and the Attribution Cube: A Comparative Reappraisal," In J.H. Harvey, W.J. Ickes, and R.F. Kidd (eds.), *New Directions in Attribution Research*, 1976, Vol. 1, Hillsdale, New Jersey, Lawrence Erlbaum Associates.

JONES, R.E., *Self-Fulfilling Prophecies*, Hillsdale, New Jersey, Lawrence Erlbaum Associates, 1977.

KAHNEMAN, D., SLOVIC, P., and TVERSKY, A. (Eds.), *Judgement Under Uncertainty: Heuristics and Biases*, New York, Cambridge University Press, 1982.

KELLEY, H.H., "Attribution Theory in Social Psychology," In D. Levine (ed.), *Nebraska Symposium on Motivation*, 1967, Vol. 15, Lincoln, Nebraska, University of Nebraska Press.

LIEBERMAN, S., "The Effects of Changes in Roles on the Attitudes of Role Occupants," *Human Relations*, 1956, Vol. 9, pp. 385-402.

LORD, R.G., and SMITH, J.E., Theoretical, Information Processing, and Situational Factors Affecting Attribution Theory Models of Organizational Behavior, *Academy of Management Review*, 1983, Vol. 8, pp. 50-60.

MERTON, R.K., "The Self-Fulfilling Prophecy," *Antioch Review*, 1948, Vol. 8, pp. 193-210.

MILGRAM, S., *Obedience to Authority*, New York, Harper & Row, 1974.

MITCHELL, T.R., GREEN, S.G., and WOOD, R.E., "An Attributional Model of Leadership and the Poor Performing Subordinate: Development and Validation," In B. Staw and L. Cummings (eds.), *Research in Organizational Behavior*, Greenwich, Conn., JAI Press, 1981, pp. 197-234.

NISBETT, R.E., BORGIDA, E., CRANDALL, R., and REED, H., "Popular Induction: Information Is Not Necessarily Informative," In J.S. Carroll and S.W. Payne (eds.), *Cognition and Social Behavior*, Hillsdale, New Jersey, Lawrence Erlbaum Associates, 1976.

ROSEN, B., and JERDEE, T.H., "The Influence of Sex-role Stereotypes on Evaluation of the Male and Female Supervisory Behavior," *Journal of Applied Psychology*, 1973, Vol. 57, pp. 44-48.

ROSEN, B., and JERDEE, T.H., "Influences of Sex-role Stereotypes on Personal Decisions," *Journal of Applied Psychology*, 1974, Vol. 59, pp. 9-14.

ROSEN, B., and JERDEE, T.H., "Sex Stereotyping in the Executive Suite," *Harvard Business Review, 1974, Vol. 52, pp. 45-58.*

ROSS, L., "The Intuitive Psychologist and his Shortcomings: Distortions in the Attribution Process," In L. Berkowitz (ed.), *Advances in Experimental Social Psychology*, 1977, Vol. 13, pp. 279-301.

ROSS, L., GREEN, D., and HOUSE, P., "The False Consensus Phenomenon: An Egocentric Bias in Social Perception and Attribution Process," *Journal of Experimental Social Psychology*, 1977, Vol. 13, pp. 279-301.

SCHNEIDER, D.J., "Implicit Personality Theory: A Review," *Psychological Bulletin*, 1973, Vol. 79, pp. 294-309.

SCOTT, C.A., "Self Perception Process in Consumer Behavior: Interpreting One's Own Experiences," In H. Keith Hunt (ed.), *Advances in Consumer Research*, 1978, Vol. 5, pp. 714-720. Association for Consumer Research.

SHAVER, K.G., *An Introduction to Attribution Processes*, Cambridge, Mass., Winthrop Publishers, Inc., 1975.

SMITH, R.E., and HUNT, S.D., "Attributional Processes and Effects in Promotional Situations," *Journal of Consumer Research*, 1975, Vol. 5, pp. 149-158.

STAW, B.M., "Attribution of the 'Causes' of Performance: A General Alternative Interpretation of Cross-Sectional Research on Organizations," *Organizational Behavior and Human Performance*, 1975, Vol. 13, pp. 414-432.

THOMAS, K., "Conflict and Conflict Management," In M.D. Dunnette (ed.), *Handbook of Industrial and Organizational Psychology*, Chicago, Rand McNally, 1976.

TVERSKY, A. and KAHNEMAN, D., "Judgement under Uncertainty: Heuristics and Biases," *Science*, 1974, Vol. 185, pp. 1124-1131.

WEINER, B., *Achievement Motivation and Attribution Theory*, Morristown, New Jersey, General Learning Press, 1974.

ZALKIND, S.S., and Costello, T.W., "Perception: Some Recent Research and Implications for Administration," *Administrative Science Quarterly, 1962, Vol. 7, pp. 218-235.*

Industrial Relations Revisited

ALTON W.J. CRAIG

Industrial relations have been defined as a complex of private and public activities, operating in a specified environment, which is concerned with allocating rewards to employees for their services and determining the conditions under which work is performed. Taking this definition as a starting point, I have developed a frame for analyzing industrial relations systems which includes environmental subsystems, goal- and value-oriented actors who, through a series of processes, negotiate organizational and worker-oriented "outputs."

What I will attempt to do in this brief paper is to emphasize some of the more pressing needs of the Canadian industrial relations system and to offer some suggestions of both a structural and procedural nature which are necessary to meet these needs. Twenty years ago the following statement was made:

> Our future progress in achieving our goals will depend in very large measure on our ability to innovate new processes, structures and institutions for creative decision-making. This will involve labor, management and government in complex inter-relationships that confront, clarify and resolve multi-dimensional conflicts of interests, rights and expectations.

In reviewing what has happened over the course of these twenty years, I find that statement almost as relevant today as it was then. There is still very little consensus on what our economic and social goals are today, and there is also very little consensus on the most appropriate processes and structural changes which are necessary to achieve them. As I shall point out later, however, there now exists the potential for change that did not exist then.

THE NEED TO BE COMPETITIVE

Perhaps the one goal which the major participants in our industrial relations system now share is the need for Canada to be more competitive in international markets so that we might experience greater prosperity at home. For these twin objectives to be achieved, Canada must improve upon her dismal productivity performance, which has been worse in recent years than that of many advanced industrialized economies. For this shared goal to become

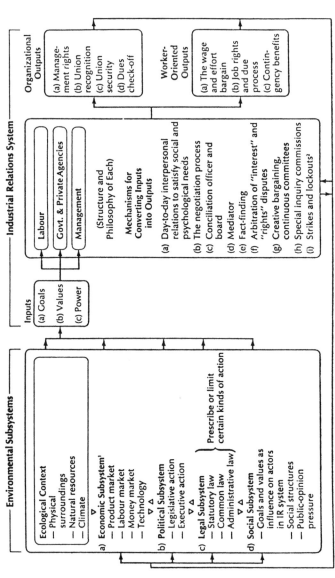

Figure I — A Framework for Analyzing Industrial Relations Systems

Source: Alton W.J. Craig, The System of Industrial Relations in Canada, Scarborough, Ontario, Prentice-Hall Inc., 1983, p. 3.

a reality, there needs to be a fundamental change in our industrial relations system to make the parties acutely aware of the highly competitive environment in which they operate. Presently, our highly decentralized collective bargaining system, with its emphasis on local negotiations, does not encourage the participants to be aware of the competition in international markets or to keep the larger and more complex world view in mind. Under this structure, their concerns are too narrow in scope.

A More Centralized Structure

In my view, the predominance of provincial jurisdiction over labor relations policy in industries such as steel, automotive, and meat packing is one of the fundamental weaknesses in Canada's industrial relations systems. Because of the micro focus of decision-making in most of our industrial relations, except transportation, communications, etc., we have a system built largely on a local and highly decentralized basis. Under such a system it is very difficult for employers and unions to keep the larger world scene — the one in which they must compete — as part of their mental picture. Yet this larger view is a necessity in today's highly competitive world markets. In my view, a more centralized structure of bargaining is necessary if the parties are going to negotiate from the vantage point of a world view. This new structure may come about in one of two ways.

Federal Jurisdiction

First, it may take a major constitutional amendment to bring more industries under federal jurisdiction to make national negotiations possible. Under this scheme, the parties in national negotiations would have to contend with only one set of laws, and they could easily form broader bargaining units which would enable the main participants to negotiate from a world-wide perspective.

Informal Restructuring

Secondly, some flexible and informal arrangements might be worked out between the federal government and the provinces to make more centralized bargaining a reality. This informal restructuring would also allow negotiators in our important export industries to form broader-based bargaining units, which would enable all the participants involved to stand back from the immediate scene and to view their industries in the larger world landscape when negotiating their collective agreements.

If this more centralized restructuring were to occur, it would create an uneasy tension between the parties involved in central negotiations and those in local negotiations. However, this is not an insurmountable problem since the parties could negotiate company- or industry-wide agreements on the major issues, including wages, with the possibility of supplemental agreements to reflect different regional patterns across the country. For example, a good many local issues could be negotiated at the local level, a practice already used in many centralized bargaining structures. In addition, the grievance process could be revamped to make it less costly and time-consuming and to bring it closer to where the action is, namely, to the shop floor. A greater degree of centralized bargaining, even with its few handicaps, is essential for the parties in order for them to acquire a more realistic view of what needs to be done for the survival and growth of their industries, particularly in international markets.

The Canadian Labor Market and Productivity Centre

A second alternative for the development of larger bargaining units through which more centralized negotiations may take place, or at least within which the broad parameters for more centralized negotiations may be formulated, is the Canadian Labor Market and Productivity Centre. The centre was created in the Spring of 1984. If it is properly administered, the centre may form one of the missing structural links that Canada has so desperately needed in the past.

The centre comprises a board of directors which is made up of twelve voting members from management and unions respectively plus a number of non-voting government members. The representatives from management come from the Business Council on National Issues (which was instrumental in getting the centre established), the Canadian Manufacturers' Association, the Chamber of Commerce, and the Canadian Federation of Independent Business, which represents medium and small business organizations. On the union side there are three representatives from the Canadian Federation of Labor and nine representatives from the Canadian Labor Congress, one of whom is the President of the Quebec Federation of Labor, a provincial arm of the Canadian Labor Congress. The centre also comprises a number of non-voting members which includes four senior federal public servants, ten senior provincial public servants, and two members from the academic community. This broadly based membership should give the centre the support that it will need, and it is particularly important that the provinces are represented. Their participation will be critically important should the centre become involved in more centralized bargaining structures. In addition, the centre has expertise among its members for resolving collective bargaining issues at the local level, for many of them have had a good deal of experience in negotiating at that level.

The timing of the newly created Canadian Labor Market and Productivity Centre could not have been more propitious. The tone which the new government sets will largely determine how effective this new structure will be. It is my firm conviction that if the government fails to take advantage of this new structure, it will have missed a golden opportunity for establishing a new link, along with links between the business and labor community and the federal government which have been missing since wage and price controls were introduced in 1975. It is now time that relations between labor and the federal government be "normalized" and that advantage be taken of the newly created centre and the Business Council on National Issues to gain greater cooperation among labor, management, and governments at all levels. Hopefully any benefits of this new potential at the national level will filter down to lower levels of unions and management through the participation of their representatives at the national level. Only time will tell whether the leaders of our country will capitalize on these new structures.

PRODUCTIVE ACTIONS

Adopt New Technology

The pressing need to make Canadian industries more productive and competitive, both for domestic and international markets, makes it imperative that Canadian management adopt the most highly advanced forms of technology. While productivity is usually measured in terms of output per man-hour or per person-hour, it is management that has the responsibility for making Canadian industry more productive, because it is the party in the production process which determines the form of capital to be employed and the most effective means of production. While union leaders and workers accept the necessity for the newest forms of technology, unions are acutely sensitive to any adverse consequences that the introduction of advanced technology might have on the workers they represent. The MacDonald Royal Commission stated its concern about this issue in the following terms:

> We find it a dubious proposition that new technology can be increased without the active support of employees and their unions. The challenge, as we have posed it, implies this active support.

It is my view that governments also have an important role to play in assisting unions and management to adjust to any adverse impact of technological change. At the present time only four jurisdictions, namely, the federal, British Columbia, Manitoba, and Saskatchewan governments, have public policies which require employers to give advance notice of technological changes that are likely to affect substantial numbers of workers. The Ontario government, in the Spring of 1984, established a task force of three union and three management representatives to study the impact of new technology on employment. It is my conviction that existing legislation must be strengthened so that workers will not be alone in paying the price for the adverse human consequences resulting from the introduction of new technology. The need is all the greater with the introduction of less costly forms of hardware which medium and small companies can afford, and the rapidly expanding computer software packages which are becoming less costly and more readily available. Several recent arbitration cases involving workers made redundant by new computer software have held that such software changes do not constitute technological change. This is particularly important since "...software now frequently accounts for 50% of total costs in many systems, a percentage which is expected to reach 80 to 90 by the end of the decade..."

Keep Wages Down

Another important requirement for the Canadian industrial relations system to function properly is the need to keep wages and wage costs down, particularly since about two-thirds of Canada's trade is with the United States. Presently union membership is about forty percent of the nonagricultural labor force while it is only in the low twenties in the United States. As a leading American industrial relations scholar recently told the annual meeting of the Canadian Industrial Relations Association, the high proportion of nonunion workers in the United States enables employers to respond rapidly to conditions in the American economy. With the high unemployment rates in the United States, nonunion companies have been giving relatively low wage increases, and in many cases workers in unionized sectors have opted for wage freezes or wage reductions in a number of industries. Canadian union leaders have not seen fit to take similar action, although there is a growing movement to nonunion work in the construction industry, particularly in the Western provinces.

Negotiated wage increases in collective agreements covering 500 or more workers in Canada were 13.0% in 1981, 10.2% in 1982, 4.8% in 1983, 3.6% in 1984, 3.6% in 1985, and 3.5% for the first quarter of 1986. The relatively high settlements in Canada from 1980 to 1982 were much higher than settlements in the United States for the same years. While we would not argue for a return to a less-unionized society, we suggest that these high levels of wage increases in comparison with U.S. wage settlements may be harmful to both Canadian companies and workers in today's economy. Hence both unions and employers may find it necessary to keep wage settlements somewhat more in line with those in the U.S., and support and encouragement from the centre's board of directors may go a long way in achieving this end. If the parties do not keep a close eye on what is happening on the American scene, they might very well price themselves out of lucrative American markets. While the low value of the Canadian dollar presently makes Canadian-made goods quite competitive in the American market, should the Canadian dollar return to a much higher value relative to the American dollar, Canadian producers will find themselves at a severe handicap in the U.S. market. The time to think and act in terms of what might become a new reality between the two countries is now, not at a much later date when a reactive strategy might see Canadian producers priced out of the American market. Recent negotiated settlements of 3.6% in 1984 and 1985, and 3.6% in the first quarter of 1986 signal the right direction. However, it will require a strong management resolve and a strong union leadership to keep wages much lower than they have been in recent years.

With the introduction of wage and price controls in 1975, when negotiated wage settlements in Canada reached 17.4% annually, and with the introduction of public sector wage restraint in 1982 and 1983, unions and management now realize that free collective bargaining under these restrictions does not exist in Canada. Since unions may not negotiate over wages and other collective agreement provisions which have a cost component in them, they should now realize that a more moderate approach to negotiations may restore free collective bargaining to its rightful place. If wage and price control programs have taught unions and employers that such programs destroy free collective bargaining, they will have taught a lesson that was unintended and probably in the long run one which is more important than any consequences that the wage and price controls programs had as their intended effects, particularly on the price side of these programs. It is now seriously questioned whether there was a need for the recent wage restraint programs in the public sectors.

Utilize Expertise

Another issue that labor and management should address during the remainder of this decade is the development of quality of work projects, quality circles, and labor-management cooperation in order to fully utilize the expertise among their workforces. It seems rather strange that at a time when workers are being encouraged to utilize their full potential in political and other aspects of their lives they should, at the same time, be subjected to very bureaucratic rules at the workplace which treat them as if they lacked maturity and potential. Today's workers, especially the young and more highly educated ones, are seeking challenging jobs in which they are able to use the skills in which they have been trained and that provide them with an outlet for their creative abilities — jobs in which they will be more productive and in which they will find a greater degree of self-fulfillment.

Reduce Duration of Strikes

Canada's work days lost due to work stoppages is about the worst in the world. This phenomenon is due in large measure to the fact that work stoppages in Canada are often of very long duration. In some cases strikes have been called when employers were stockpiled with enough inventory to last for six months or more. The lengthy strike at Inco in 1980 is a good case in point. So is the strike at Stelco in 1981, which occurred about the time that the bottom fell out of the market for steel. Union leaders must be more aware of the economic climate at times when they feel that strike action is necessary. A country with a strike record like Canada's in some industries cannot be counted on to deliver goods in world markets. While there is no hard evidence on this subject, it would not be surprising if some Canadian companies have lost potential contracts in international markets because of Canada's well-publicized strike record. A major task facing unions, management, and specialized government agencies is to reduce the incidence and duration of strikes in the sectors in which they occur frequently.

If the parties truly believe in the shared goals suggested above and if needed structural and procedural changes are implemented, the Canadian economy should become more competitive at home and in international markets. If we should be fortunate enough for these changes to come about, then Canadian society generally will be much better off in the coming years.

REFERENCES

Annual Meeting of the Canadian Industrial Relations Association, Guelph, Ontario, May 29, 1984.

BROOKBANK, C.R., "The Adversary System in Canadian Industrial Relations: Blight or Blessing?", *Relations industrielles*, vol. 35, (1), 1980, pp. 20-40.

CRAIG, A., *The System of Industrial Relations in Canada*, Scarborough, Ontario, Prentice-Hall Canada Inc., 1983.

CRAIG, A., and WAISGLASS, H.J., "Collective Bargaining Perspectives," *Relations industrielles*, vol. 23, (4), p. 571.

DALY, D.J., ed., *Research on Productivity of Relevance to Canada*, Social Science Federation of Canada, 1983, p. 11.

JAMIESON, S.M., *Industrial Conflict in Canada: 1966-1975*, Discussion Paper No. 142, Ottawa, Economic Council of Canada, December 1979.

KUMAR, P., "Recent Public Sector Wage Restraint Programs: The Economic and Labor Market Rationale?", a paper presented to the Canadian Industrial Relations Association's 21st Annual Conference, Guelph, Ontario, May 30, 1984.

Labor Canada, *Major Wage Settlements: Second Quarter 1986*, p. 1.

Royal Commission on the Economic Union and Development Prospects for Canada, A Commission on Canada's Future: Challenges and Choices, Hull, Quebec, Supply and Services Canada, April 1984, p. 41.

World Labor Report 1, Geneva, International Labor Office, 1984, p. 179.

Accounting
Comptabilité

———————

Epistemological Choices for the Development of Accounting Theory

RONALD E. HOYT

Many of the serious problems that have plagued accountants in defining the appropriate information content of financial reports over the past 200 years are related to the philosophical problem of unity and diversity in nature. Nobel Laureate Herbert Simon, in his keynote address at the doctoral symposium on management science at Laval University, discussed human information processing and our procedures for dealing with the unity/diversity problem. His recent research suggests that our mental processes proceed through approximately 10 subconscious steps for each conscious decision step. Using identification of a friend's face as an example, there are many hidden cues which the subconscious mind picks up but of which the conscious mind remains unaware.[1]

The capacity to identify similarities and dissimilarities in objects means that we are able to see the unity of a rosebush in a diversity of cues, including thorns, branches, leaves, and petals, or conversely, to recognize uniqueness in each snowflake that falls. If this capacity is exercised in the area of accounting numbers, we are able with training to separate companies which are performing well from companies which are performing poorly. However, in the area of nature, we have not only the visual sense, but other senses to rely on. These enable us to separate, for example, snowflakes from soap suds by virtue of their physical attributes such as cold, smell, and other characteristics. In the area of accounting, we are forced to interpret from numerical representations. The same process of recognition requires a higher mental level of discrimination in the sense that the numerical representations denominated in an economic value, such as the dollar, are only representative signals of real world attributes. Because of this, certain problems arise in

1. Doctoral seminar given by the Programme du doctorat of the Faculté des Sciences de l'Administration of Laval University during the 1982-83 academic year.

choosing the significant attribute or event, in measuring it, and finally, in interpreting the signals generated.

This paper examines the question of meaning and accountability in the preparation of financial information from the perspective of society's external pressures and influences on accounting. In the first section we discuss the impact of external influences on accounting techniques, the financial attributes which are measured, the numerical measures employed, and the interpretation of financial information. The second section examines the source of these external influences as they relate to the profound debate currently dividing the accounting profession in its choice of objectives. Having examined these influences which result in the choice of certain accounting models and data over others, and after discussing how they may affect the kinds of information on which financial decisions are based, in a final section we will suggest possible alternatives for the production of financial data in the years ahead.

EXTERNAL INFLUENCES ON ACCOUNTING TECHNIQUES

The Choice of Attributes

One area in which external influence is apparent is the choice of the attributes of an economic entity. These attributes may be determined from three different elements.

The Scope of the Enterprise

The growth in scope of the modern corporation from a small proprietorship to a large diversified multinational has drawn attention to different measures of viability. John Kenneth Galbraith has pointed out that the trend toward business combinations stems primarily from the desire to reduce commercial risk by vertical and horizontal integration. This risk reduction trend became popular during the 1960s, which saw enterprises such as Ling-Temco-Vought, Inc. building huge conglomerates in an attempt to obtain financial stability, higher earnings, and less variability in sources of supply. For hundreds of years prior to this, financial measures of the enterprise focused on the balance sheet. Only after the Great Depression of the 1930s did the income statement become considerably more important as a measure of corporate earning power and future prospects. Recently we have experienced a renewal of interest in the balance sheet, but in a modified form with different measures of the same attributes. Each of these trends reflects a different vision of the enterprise as a result of the growing number of people affected by the increasingly large size of operations. External users and their view of what was important for financial decision-making at that particular point in time have molded the concepts of financial reporting employed by the profession.

The Availability and "Hardness" of Data

Computers have not always been available to store a corporation's transactions and to provide real-time compilation of its various transactions and account balances. Consequently, even at the present time, analysts are forced to choose those key characteristics which are not only important for their decision models, but which also are available, in terms of current data. The quality of this data, however, is always a problem. When we speak of the "hardness" of data, we speak of data which are not likely to vary even if management or some other interested party desired a more favorable figure. Availability of useful data is normally limited also to known transactions. It comes as a surprise to many accounting students that many of the financial data produced in accounting are in fact estimated data with some existing range of variability. We do not know, for example, the true value of a used asset. We know the value of an asset when it is first purchased, but as soon as it is put into use, the asset may diminish or increase in value. At this point estimates must be made. The same is true of almost all manufactured products to which costs must be allocated in order to determine profit from sales. Consequently, one of the problems in measuring attributes is to determine which data are truly accurate in the sense of being a representation of the true economic value of the enterprise.

Decision Models of Analysts

In recent years, another source of concern has been pressure from analysts to choose attributes which will fit their decision models. An example of this is the series of financial ratios commonly used to evaluate a corporation's liquidity, its earning power, or its debt servicing ability. The information provided may be a result of what analysts consider necessary for their decision models even though the attribute is not necessarily appropriate in the accounting model. Leasing information is one example. The accounting profession was required to include this information in the financial statements of corporations entering into lease purchase agreements even though, in a classical sense, the lease agreements, shown as assets and liabilities in the accounting statements, do not actually represent completed transactions.

The attributes, therefore, have been chosen in part by external influences such as the scope of the enterprise, the availability and hardness of data, and the decision models of analysts and other users.

The Numerical Measures

External influences have also had a major impact on the numerical measures employed. Historically, many accounting methods have been employed by enterprises. Some are used in a pragmatic effort to do the job as quickly and as easily as possible; others are used because the measure seems to work well for the enterprise in question. There are certain characteristics which numerical measures should have, such as consistency, comparability, and relevance.

Consistency

Consistency in a numerical measure is necessary so that a similar transaction will be measured in the same way each time. If we consider, for example, valuation of a house for real estate purposes, it is helpful if we estimate the value of the house using the same criteria or measures over a period of years. This is even more important in dealing with a corporation because it buys and sells many assets on a regular basis. If its procedures for measuring these assets are uniform from one period to the next, we are able to determine whether the corporation's financial position is improving or deteriorating.

Comparability

Comparability as a characteristic of numerical measures deals, for example, with the relative position of one company to another company. If, in fact, each company uses comparable measures, we are able to tell if one company is in a relatively better position than another.

Relevance

Relevance has to do with whether the measures we use are coherent with the attributes that are measured and with our decision models. The question is whether we should use an economic measure such as current value reflecting today's monetary value of an item rather than the value which was in effect at the time the transaction took place. The unit of measure debate has become particularly important as a result of economic instability in recent years and the well-known effects of inflation on purchasing power. While the subject is vast and there are many views, one can say that if the numerical measure changes from period to period, we do in fact have problems related to the characteristics previously discussed. Comparability is affected when companies are operating in different environments (e.g., the foreign exchange problem); uniformity in comparing one period with another is problematical when the unit of measure has changed. Various solutions which have been proposed for the interperiod problem of uniform presentation can be grouped into two approaches: first, constant dollars, or inflation-adjusted units of measure, and second, unit prices or current value measures.

None of these solutions is free from criticism, but the point of interest in the present context is that the debate focuses on the technical issues, often without recognition of the fact that the source of the debate may be found in external influences on the accounting model and on the financial data that are produced by this model.

Interpretation of Accounting Information

A third area of external influence is the interpretation of accounting information and financial data.

The Use of Accounting Data

Eldon Hendriksen identifies three schools of thought involving the use of accounting data:

1. Integrity of the accounting system. One school deals with the structural integrity of the accounting system, whereby a series of rules is defined and we proceed from the rules to a finished accounting statement. As an example of this, the income statement starts with revenues, then deducts expenses related to the goods sold. Various operating expenses and extraordinary items are next deducted to finally arrive at net income. The problem of this structural approach is that, although we follow all the rules, no one can place an exact interpretation on the meaning of the figure designated net income. It is in fact a theoretical value obtained by the application of these rules. We can never really know whether the net income is correct by checking our figure; we can only check whether the rules are properly applied to the data. It is, in fact, a hypothetical figure, according to many authors.[2]
2. The semantic or interpretational level. This involves a process by which we attempt to relate the figures which we obtain to an external reality. If we say we have productive facilities worth $1 million in the form of a factory, we should be able to observe the factory and obtain expert opinion as to the reliability of the value placed on this tangible reality. This explains in part a return of interest in the balance sheet in the context of an accurate valuation, or a current value approach, to these accounting attributes. The semantic level which relates numerical values to real tangible attributes can be, in fact, a gateway to interpreting accounting information.
3. The decision-makers' behavior. The step beyond this is to evaluate how financial decision-makers actually behave once they have learned this information. Thus a third area of investigation is to examine the behavior of decision-makers

---

2. Hendriksen states, "Accountants have used these terms so often and for so long that we tend to accept them as having interpretation in the real world. It is difficult to accept the fact that they have no significance outside their limited role in the logic of the accounting structure."

and to provide information which will lead to a behavior consistent with the real economic condition of the entity. He would argue, therefore, that the entity which is in distress should provide signals in its accounting statements which would cause the decision-makers to behave in a proper fashion toward this entity. Obviously, this approach to accounting contains the serious problem of potential manipulation.

The Choice of Statements

A second area dealing with interpretation of accounting data concerns the statements that are actually provided. There are different schools of thought: Some say the three multipurpose statements (the balance sheet, the income statement, and the funds flow statement) should be sufficient for all users; others would suggest that all data should be made available to users or that a series of specialized reports should be issued.

As pointed out earlier, the emphasis has changed over the years. Many years ago the balance sheet was important in determining the borrowing capacity of the enterprise. In other words, the proprietor had assets which were invested in the company. Based on these, a bank could determine what he was worth, and how much it would be willing to risk in loans. Later, concern with risk and return were uppermost in the minds of investors, and the income statement became important for the evaluation of risk, future prospects, and earning power. The funds flow statement in combination with the balance sheet grew in importance when enterprise liquidity and the ability to repay debt on a short-term basis became uppermost in people's minds. But the choice of statements is not merely a technical question. Ross Watts would argue that, in fact, the protection of the public accountant and of the economic interests of the corporation are fundamental issues for standard-setters when the information to be included in accounting statements is in question.

The Impact of Social Values

The interpretation of accounting data is also influenced by social values. The problem of how information is interpreted is not only a technical question of the attributes chosen, the numerical measures used, or the profession's approach to the question of presentation, but is also based on a broader issue which is captured by the meaning versus accountability debate. By "meaning," we denote the informational content which a user is able to deduce from the numerical signals, the degree to which he can classify healthy companies and separate them from unhealthy or failing companies, the degree to which he can identify a good year from a bad year; in other words, the discriminating power of the financial analysts in determining the underlying reality which is the economic condition of an enterprise. This dimension, called the meaning problem (that a reality exists which can be measured, quantified, reported, and analyzed), deals with accuracy in representation and reliability.

The Ethical Responsibility

Another dimension of essential importance to accounting involves the ethical responsibility of the professional accountant and the managers of an enterprise. The question of what should be reported has many facets. Even though the managers and accountants may be in a position to give extensive information about the underlying economic realities of the enterprise, there are certain constraints to this freedom. One is the cost of producing the information. Another is the problem of competitors. If too much information is provided, a competitor may use it to the detriment of the enterprise and thus hurt the very investors whom management is seeking to inform. Also, the problem of comprehension requires a certain capacity for summarizing in such a way as to give an overview without losing significant detail that is important.

On the other side of the accountability issue is the question of the level and degree to which the managers and accountants are responsible for not leading users into error, that is for protecting them from false decisions and false signals. The expertise of the users and the simplicity, the complexity, or the accuracy of the information provided, play a role in the judgment about what should be presented from the standpoint of accountability. The ethical question is summarized by William Beaver under the concept of "moral hazard" as a situation in which the manager must not be able to withhold information from the financial analyst or the stockholder which would enable him to profit at their expense. In each of these areas a great degree of judgment is required.

On the accountability side of the issue, we are forced by the model to make estimations and then to treat them as exact values, and we do have the exercise of judgment as to what should and should not be presented in order to protect all commercial parties. On the meaning side of the issue, we have the question of what is significant, what can aid in analysis and influence interpretation. To better understand why meaning and accountability are treated today as opposing concepts, we turn now to a more detailed evaluation of the historical influences on the development of accounting theory.

HISTORICAL INFLUENCES AFFECTING
THE DEVELOPMENT OF ACCOUNTING THEORY

There were three major watersheds in the development of accounting theory in the last 500 years.

Pacioli's Double Entry System

The first watershed, at the time of the Italian Renaissance, was the birth of Pacioli's double entry system of bookkeeping. During this period, which saw the "rebirth" of arts and science in Europe, there was a fundamental ideological change taking place in the world-view of Pacioli and his contemporaries. There was a growing emphasis on nature, which can be seen in the rapid and marked changes in art, literature, and science. The Byzantine emphasis on spirituality began to be balanced by a view of nature as important in its own right. This ideological dualism has been called "the nature and grace problem," and it is the central theme in much of the innovation of the period.

It is in the context of a growing emphasis on the importance of nature that Pacioli published a double entry system of bookkeeping. For the first time in 1,000 years of history, the concern with everyday financial matters became something important and appropriate for the clergy to be concerned with, rather than being rejected on the grounds of spiritual insignificance. The moral aspect of accounting had always been present in the church and, therefore, to a certain extent in the business community as well. But the moral code "Thou shalt not steal" (which implicitly required record keeping), was a negative or restraining force. It was the growing emphasis on the intrinsic value of physical resources that made the task of developing a system of bookkeeping thinkable within the context of a monastery and that brought acceptance of the system within society at large.

The Age of Reason

This period represents a second great watershed in the development of accounting theory because of the introduction of the "unified field" concept in science. Some people argue that the birth of science and scientific discovery dates from the work of Roger Bacon or Robert Grosseteste, who attacked Aristotelian science. A clear statement of this new freedom emerges from Descartes's sixteenth-century *Discours de la Méthode*. When one reads Descartes's treatise on the scientific method, one is struck not so much by the five steps he sets forth for the discovery of scientific truth as by the view he had of truth and of the world. His view, which became the consensus in the next generation, was that all areas of knowledge could and would be reduced to mathematics. He believed that all areas of science and discovery would eventually be related to one another in a grand system. And he believed that man, using reason, could discover truth.

Rationalism has been the centerpiece of humanism in philosophy and science since then. It has shaped the way in which theory is built in every area of learning, including accounting. There are, however, two stages of rationalistic humanism which must be distinguished in the development of accounting theory. The first stage of development is usually called optimistic rationalism because the scientist, philosopher, artist, etc., believed that truth existed and that it could be discovered through reason. Thus we have Rousseau writing on social issues and emphasizing the natural order and a return to the primitive man. The painter Gauguin, whose work "Whence? What? Whither?" hangs in the Boston Museum, also held Rousseau's views but had lost his optimism by the time he painted his work. Thoreau's *Walden* is a well-known example from North America. The optimistic view was reflected in the presuppositional basis of the French Revolution and the later Russian Revolution. In each instance, actions were based on the belief that man by reason could break the shackles of the past and scientifically build a unified field of knowledge which would be founded on discovered truth.

In retrospect, this epistemological framework is probably responsible in large part for the long and determined adherence of accounting theory to the historical cost principle. The fundamental premise was that only one theory was correct, and that this theory could and would be found through scientific discovery using reason and empirical facts. For scientific development, moral constraint was no longer a key factor, as it was at the time of Pacioli, although it remained important to the users of accounting information.

Philosophical Pessimism

The second stage of rationalism represents the third watershed for accounting theory, which came at the beginning of the twentieth century in the form of philosophical pessimism. Up to this point, there had been an optimistic view of truth and the "unified field" approach to knowledge. No tension existed between the "one best way" in a technical sense and the ethical dimension of accountability. One can see examples in art, literature, and science of the radical change from optimism to pessimism in the early twentieth century. The effect on Western culture in general and on accounting theory in particular began to be felt with full force during the second half of the twentieth century.

The rationalistic methodology is retained in accounting as in scientific research, but the concept of truth held in the pre-twentieth century period of development becomes a function of probabilities, randomness, and accounting "numbers." At the beginning of the 1960s Edwards and Bell reiterated an essential question in their book, *The Theory and Measurement of Business Income:* "What is truth in accounting?" Because the present trends in accounting rule-making derive directly from the epistemological framework through which practitioners and academia view "truth" in accounting, it may be helpful to examine the manner in which the views of the surrounding culture came to change accounting thought.

Three distinct changes in world view contributed to current developments in accounting thought. Man's pessimistic view of truth in the twentieth century led to a gradual erosion of the principles of accounting and, in particular, of the concept of historical cost as a single correct measure of economic change. The origin of this pessimism of modern man is relativism. Early in the twentieth century the concept of relativism became strongly rooted in the intellectual community and later became widespread in Western culture. Two early examples of this thought form are Neil Bohr's quantum theory and Einstein's theory of relativity. Popularization of the relativistic concept also came through existential philosophy, modern art, and the film medium.

The importance of relativistic thought to current trends in accounting theory is unmistakable, and it has created a battle in the area of meaning. Before relativism became widely accepted, intellectuals were trying to find truth which, they believed, existed. Once relativism was introduced and accepted, truth as an absolute ceased to exist, at least in the thought forms of the intellectuals. The problem became one of defining a regional truth by defining a set of conditions under which a set of relations would exist. This kind of thinking leads to fragmentation, as opposed to the concept of a unified field, and false oppositions in the dimensions which guide the development of accounting theory. More importantly, it leads to a loss of meaning. Meaning as a concept becomes relative. Things have meaning in the light of their relation to entities which give them importance. If, as existentialism suggests, an act has meaning only as it authenticates the existence of the individual, we are faced with a destruction of categories and hence destruction of meaning in a generalizable and absolute sense.

The effect of this shift in world view was a dramatic shift in the epistemological referents of accounting methodology. The objects or concepts with which accounting methodology worked had changed with respect to their underlying meaning. The assets and debts being accounted for were the same economic entities as before, but their meaning had changed dramatically. There was no longer an emphasis on the intrinsic value of resources to be administered under moral obligation nor on gathering empirical evidence for scientific discovery. Accounting data became "numbers" to be interpreted by "users" according to their particular needs. From a system built around the moral responsibilities of the managers and owners, modern accounting thought turned into a fragmented relativistic world in which meaning depended on user needs and perceptions.

The concept of "standards" instead of "opinions" in American accounting highlights the point of this shift. Opinions originally manifested the concept that a certain body of theory existed from which a highly respected committee could derive certain applications which would be appropriate in accounting practice. The shift to standards and the political process of deriving a consensus opinion from all interested parties reflected an institutional shift to existentialism in accounting. In effect no one body or person is presumed to be able to state an absolute or true meaning for accounting information because the information is assumed to mean different things to different users. Each user has needs of his own, and a process was established to allow the users to bargain with each other for the information content needed in their interpretations. The underlying values and economic processes are really only secondary to the current trend of accounting theory. The focus is on the meaning which users will attribute to economic facts.

It is not surprising, therefore, that the shift in epistemological referents and the concept of meaning in accounting should require a new and different methodology in the post-Vietnam era. A new presuppositional framework for interpreting accounting information forced the formation of a consensus-type mechanism in the development of accounting standards. Not only had the principle of moral duty in accounting for civil magistrates and for owners of resources been discarded, but the concept of a "unified field" approach to accounting theory was dead. Internal managers and owners involved in decision-making became one of a number of power blocs included under the general rubric of "users of accounting information." Their "needs," along with those of all the other groups, must be weighed in a final consensus.

The methodology of synthesis in accounting is a requirement of the epistemological circle by which current accounting thinking is circumscribed. It is a result of the process of consensus building. In an era in which truth is considered as relativistic, information has meaning only with reference to the "user," and each user alone is presumed to be able to determine what is and is not useful in the light of his own experiences. Once this set of presuppositions is adopted, a central rule-making body has no other means of authenticating its rules (in a democratic society) than by obtaining a consensus among its members and then giving this consensus a stamp of authoritative approval. The rule-making body's constituency is presumed to be willing to follow the rules since they were developed through a process of bargaining and negotiation. The fragility of this approach is apparent. First, it is time-consuming and costly because of the long bargaining process involved. Secondly, it is based on a 50% plus 1 majority at the extreme, and can shift with time. Since there is no unifying theory behind the rule, the majority can change their minds and the process would be repeated. Thirdly, the rules are arbitrary and valid only at one point in time. Thus they can be completely undermined by a major change in the power structure.

The fragile nature and process of standard-setting may be apparent to all, but alternatives in the development of accounting theory are limited. N. Dopuch and S. Sunder, in their analysis of the FASB's "Statements on Objectives," suggest that the only reason the FASB wants a Statement on Objectives is to boost its public standing, and to allow it to buttress its decisions in the area of standard-setting. The problem of finding meaning and purpose in standard-setting beyond the political process of appeasing conflicting interests is not limited to accounting. It affects other areas of business and law as well because the presuppositional framework permeates all of society. The central issue, as pointed out earlier, is the choice between meaning or accountability, because these aspects no longer derive from a common source.

The conclusion with respect to accounting theory is quite simple: consensus alone is not sufficient; objectives represent merely a second stage of the same process; and beyond objectives, there is no ultimate authority save the arbitrary authority of the state, major-user power blocs, or some other power elite.

CONCLUSION

There are three basic avenues for escaping the burden of increasing complexity and discontent with the rule-making process in accounting. These three options are: (1) return to a unified field approach, (2) arbitrary rule-making by a power elite, (3) technological intervention.

The unified field approach is not popular today because of the monolithic philosophical consensus of the surrounding culture. It does, however, have merit as a solution. There are two aspects of accounting which can be segmented using the unified field approach to permit harmony of theory and practice in an increasingly complex world. The first aspect is a level of accounting which we shall call the recording and reporting of historical facts. While modern advances in probabilistic theory permit better estimates, and concepts such as the time value of money press us into inflation or price level accounting, these are refinements of our evaluation of underlying information. A unified theory approach would suggest that there is a place for the recording and reporting of historical facts arising from actual transactions.

The second aspect of a unified field approach would be the elimination of the false opposition between meaning and accountability. Both are part of a unified model. This does not destroy the validity of reports, but reintegrates man and his humanity in the judgment required for estimation and selection of data. Restoring man to a position of responsible and creative action is a first step in eliminating false concepts of what the role of accounting is. The relativistic approach assumes to be correct two premises which are in fact false: (1) that man is a machine and has no creative powers to portray truth, except through a rigid mathematical framework, (2) that it is possible to know the future.

While it is possible to make shrewd guesses about the future, no one has certain knowledge of it. Thus the true responsibility of the accountant ends with a reporting of the events which have their place in history. It is the user's job to make whatever judgment he or she desires about the future. This freedom implies a major change from historical cost principles which really date from the era of optimistic rationalism. While historical facts are the responsibility of the accountant, it is not incumbent on him to use an inaccurate measuring device. Any measuring device which is accurate and true for reporting what has happened is worth examining as long as the values are clear to the reader.

Arbitrary rule-making by a power elite is the second alternative to the current standard-setting process. A power elite could be any one of a number of large user groups. For example, the tax law is a product of a power elite which has developed since World War II. Congress has set rules arbitrarily for the most part. Dopuch and Sunder suggest establishing an accounting court. This, too, would be a form of arbitrary rule-making. The federal government could promulgate rules for other areas of accounting in the same manner as it has done for tax law. Institutions such as the SEC or the Canadian Institute are examples of a potential arbitrary rule-making body.

If arbitrary rule-making is to be effective, it must be performed by a power group which has the ability to enforce its decisions by means of sanctions and penalties. For this reason, one would hope that the current standard-setting approach will not evolve into arbitrary rule-setting by a power elite, but this would appear to be the most logical pattern to expect. One disadvantage of arbitrariness is discrimination in favor of the major-user blocs which are served by the rules promulgated. The rules are based on pragmatic considerations and objectives of control of the power elite. The users at large do not have a significant voice in the decision process. Advantages are the reduced cost and increased effectiveness of the rule-making process.

A third and final alternative to standard-setting by consensus is technological intervention. The reduced cost and rapid increases in capabilities of computer technology have brought about the possibility of a quantum jump in machine-to-machine accounting for businesses of every size. It is reasonable to foresee simplification of the reporting process by reducing human intervention. Rather than a better accounting system based on better theory, this alternative would supply a standard reporting package to every business and would reduce cost and complexity through increased machine involvement in the accounting process. While this alternative is the most probable route in the next decade, it does not solve the underlying meaning versus accountability problem, nor does it enable us to apply properly the human information processing capabilities which allow us to see unity and diversity in the natural order.

REFERENCES

BEAVER, W.H., *Financial Reporting: an Accounting Revolution*, Englewood Cliffs, N.J., Prentice-Hall, 1981, pp. 48-54.

BEDFORD, N., "The Income Concept Complex: Expansion or Decline," in *Asset Valuation*, Robert Sterling, Lawrence, Kansas, Scholars Book Company, 1971.

DOPUCH, N., and SUNDER, S., "FASB's Statements on Objectives and Elements of Financial Accounting: a Review.," *The Accounting Review*, January 1980, pp. 1-21.

EDWARDS, E.O., and BELL, P.W., *The Theory of Measurement of Business Income*, Berkeley, University of California Press, 1961, p. 6.

Financial Accounting Standards Board, "Qualitative Characteristics of Accounting Information," Statement of Financial Accounting Concepts #2, November 1980.

GALBRAITH, J.K., *Economics and the Public Purpose*, Houghton Mifflin Co., 1973, p. 9.

HENDRIKSEN, E.S., *Accounting Theory*, 4th edition, Homewood, Illinois, Richard D. Irvin, 1982, pp. 138-167.

IJIRI, Y., *Theory of Accounting Measurement*, Studies in Accounting Research #10, American Accounting Association, 1975, pp. 35-40.

SCHAEFFER, F.A., *The Rise and Decline of Western Thought and Culture*, Old Tappan, N.J., Fleming H. Revell Company, 1976, p. 55.

STERLING, R., and THOMAS, A.L., *Accounting for a Simplified Firm Owning Depreciable Assets: Seventeen Essays and a Synthesis Based on a Common Case*, Lawrence, Kansas, Scholars Book Company, 1980.

WATTS, R., and ZIMMERMAN, J.L.,"Towards a Positive Theory of Determination of Accounting Standards," *Accounting Review*, January 1978, pp. 112-134.

WATTS, R., "The Demand for and Supply of Accounting Theories: The Market for Excuses," *Accounting Review*, April 1979, pp. 273-305.

Reporting Environments: A New Awareness

TERESA ANDERSON

It is my opinion, and one that I think is shared by many, that the accounting profession is entering a new era of awareness about some very fundamental financial reporting issues. Accounting standards have traditionally been developed by attending to practical matters of everyday concern to the preparers and users of financial information. However, the last ten years have altered that course considerably as accounting theory and concepts have played an increasingly visible role in accounting forums. The reasons for this increased interest in theoretical issues are many; its impact is felt on numerous fronts. The purpose of this paper is not to discuss all of these, but to focus on only one aspect of this issue: how attention to the formidable amount of research that has been accumulating in the financial reporting area has forced the accounting profession to relinquish its support for the traditional model of standard-setting. Further, by doing so, the profession has been able to respond much more effectively to the needs and concerns of the users of financial reports.

The accounting profession has historically embraced the idea that a firm's financial reporting is designed to reflect the underlying economic reality of the firm's transactions and its financial position. This theory views a financial report as a measurement device, and a financial reporting practice is deemed optimal in this scenario if it measures consistently and without error what it purports to measure. The term used often in accounting texts to capture this concept is "representational faithfulness", and it has been defended as a desirable objective of financial reporting by many accounting groups over the years. As a theoretical concept, it has been referred to as the "thermometer theory", and its conceptual validity would be difficult to deny.

Such a theory, taken to the limit, suggests that there is only one measurement technique or reporting practice that is an appropriate reflection of a given transaction or state. The only area for judgment in financial reporting becomes the identification of the state or transaction that has occurred. Financial statements, then, to the extent that they perfectly reflect facts, cease to be disputable.

Why the accounting profession might wish to support this model seems apparent. Since providing information has as its main objective to aid decision-making, it follows that accounting information has economic consequences. Although these consequences may occasionally be Pareto-preferred, at least some decisions are likely to adversely affect at least some economic players. Accountants are reluctant to be viewed as having the ability to effect social welfare transfers. Their position in society is founded on their independence, credibility and neutrality. Hence, it seems logical that when a reporting or measurement practice is recommended by standard-setters, being able to defend it as being "right" in the sense of accurate is preferable to having to defend it as being "fair" in any social welfare sense.

THE END OF ONE RULE FOR ALL

None of the above is new. What is new is the recent willingness of accountants to admit (explicitly or otherwise) that this model has not been useful in attempting to deal with many recent issues of practical concern. As business operations became increasingly complex over the years, so did accounting for these operations. It became much less credible to promote any standard in such complex areas as reporting for changing prices or income taxes as being the "correct" way for all companies to account for these items. Users of financial reports began to express their dissatisfaction with the "one rule for all" approach. One very visible manifestation of this dissatisfaction has crystallized into what has become known as the "big GAAP/little GAAP" debate.

This controversy can be briefly summarized as follows:
1. On the one hand, financial report preparers, notably firms that are small and/or privately-traded, argue that the increased complexity of financial reporting practices (issues of both measurement and disclosure) has led to statements that are not meaningful to the users of these firms' reports, nor cost-efficient.
2. On the other hand, standard-setters have been promoting the economic-reality or thermometer theory. Clearly, if a practice is right, it is right for all firms, and not just a subset of them. Adherence to this concept then would lead to an impasse on this issue.

It seems apparent that once accounting standard-setters showed a willingness to relinquish their support for the thermometer theory, the way was clear for taking steps towards solving the conflict by addressing the most fundamental issue surrounding any discussion of information: usefulness. I see the move away from the traditional view as being inevitable and I see the following as the major contributors to the pressure brought to bear on the profession:
1. the increasing complexity of the topics on the accounting agenda;

2. the increased sophistication of report users due to the information/ communication explosion;

3. a general trend towards consumerism and lobbying activities that encourage users of any commodity to be vocal about their demands and more sceptical about any centralized decision-making on their behalf;

4. the formidable amount of research that was accumulating in the area of behavioral accounting and decision theory that identified the numerous variables that interact with each other in the decision environment. Results that support the hypothesis that the optimal information amount, type, and mode of presentation vary across individuals, decisions to be made, and contexts, obviously pressured the profession to more actively consider user needs.

To be seen as unresponsive to these factors would have seriously damaged the profession's position. Nevertheless, it is improbable that the profession would have been willing to alter its position if research in the accounting field had not also been working to develop alternatives to the traditional standard-setting model. There appear to be at present three views that suggest alternative ways of approaching decisions on standard-setting:[1]

1. The predictive-ability model would suggest that standard-setters ought to select those principles that will allow decision-makers (investors, creditors, etc.) to best predict the decision variables that are of interest to them, that is, their cash flows.

2. The social welfare or economic consequences model would suggest that principles be selected to increase overall social welfare.

3. The agency or stewardship model would suggest that principles be selected to facilitate the negotiating and monitoring of contracts between principals (investors and creditors) and agents (management).

A very visible concrete example of the profession's willingness to accept other models of standard-setting was apparent in the first two Statements of Financial Accounting Concepts (SFAC) issued by the Financial Accounting Standards Board (FASB) in the United States. SFAC #1 (1978) identified the main objective of financial reporting as providing information that is useful to present and potential investors and creditors and other users in making rational investment, credit, and similar decisions. SFAC #2 (1980) developed a hierarchy of desirable qualitative characteristics for accounting information. This statement clearly put usefulness in the context of

---

1. The relative merits of each alternative are not at issue in this paper. The reader is referred to the article by C. Robb and C. Robinson (1983) for background and further discussion on this matter.

a decision-maker's environment and identified cost-benefit analysis as a pervasive constraint on accounting information.

As previously indicated, the big GAAP/little GAAP issue on differential reporting is a logical one to address as an outflow from the conceptual framework. If all those concerned accepted the concepts outlined in SFAC #1 and #2, the topic could not be termed a debate or a conflict, simply a reporting problem to be solved by examining the issues within the context of the Statements. This logical progression of attention has indeed been evidenced, as standard-setting bodies in both Canada and the United States have taken steps to address this issue. Some of these are:

AICPA (USA)
1. *Issued a Discussion Paper:*
The Application of Generally Accepted Accounting Principles to Smaller and/or Closely Held Businesses, March 31, 1975.
2. *Formed the Following Committees:*
a) Committee on Generally Accepted Accounting Principles for Smaller and/or Closely Held Businesses, Charles A. Werner, Chairman, August 1976;
b) Special Committee on Small and Medium Sized Firms, Samuel A. Derieux, Chairman, 1980;
c) Special Committee on Accounting Standards Overload, Stanley J. Scott, Chairman, February 1983.
3. *Formed a Technical Issues Committee:*
In its Division for CPA firms, Private Companies Practice Section, formed a technical issues committee, whose report, the Sunset Review of Accounting Principles, was released in 1982.

FASB (USA)
1. *Set up a Permanent Small Business Advisory Committee (1978):*
To ensure communication of the views and concerns of small businesses to the FASB on all issues. Accordingly, the FASB itself attempted to consider these views in each of its standard-setting activities.
2. *Issued Invitations to Comment:*
a) Financial Statements and Other Means of Financial Reporting, May 1980;
b) *Financial Reporting by Private and Small Public Companies,* November 1981.
3. *Set up a Task Force:*
Financial Reporting by Private Companies, Raslad Abdel-Khalik, 1983.
4. *Took action towards differential disclosure:*
Deliberated and took action towards differential disclosure in the following statements:

\# 21. Suspension of the Reporting of Earnings Per Share and Segment Information by Non-Public Enterprises;
\# 33. Financial Reporting and Changing Prices;
\# 35. Accounting and Reporting by Defined Benefit Pension Plans;
\# 43. Accounting for Compensated Absences.

CICA (Canada)
1. *Issued a Report:*
Considered the issue in its Report of the Special Committee on Standard-Setting, December 1980.
2. *Set up Task Forces:*
a) on Disclosure Differences, August 1982;
b) on Financial Reporting by Small Businesses, May 1984.
3. *Took action towards differential disclosure:*
Deliberated and took action towards differential disclosure in the Section 4510, "Reporting the Effects of Changing Prices."
4. *Devoted a session to this issue:*
At its 1983 Annual Conference.

Provincial CA bodies (Canada)
1. *The Institute of Chartered Accountants of British Columbia:*
Set up a task force on Big GAAP/Little GAAP, which reported in July 1981;
2. *The Institute of Chartered Accountants of Ontario:*
Devoted a session to the topic in its 1983 annual meeting.

The above has been reviewed here as one example of evidence of the new approach to standard-setting that I believe has developed out of awareness of and response to recent developments in accounting theory. It is clear that the accounting profession is on a new track and that on this new route it will need new guidelines to help it chart its course.

THE REPORTING ENVIRONMENT

When differential reporting is discussed, size is the dichotomizing variable most often mentioned. However, it is important to remember that this is only one part of a much broader issue that is often ignored: that is, the difficulty associated with trying to be all things to all people. If a given standard cannot be defended as appropriate for all situations, the question then becomes, obviously, When is it appropriate? This is an extremely difficult question and a potentially politically sensitive one to answer. It is comparable to asking the question: If a standard to be recommended cannot be defended as the one true and fair view, what criteria are standard-setters to use in selecting and imposing standards?

The models developed within the academic literature and discussed in the previous section of this paper might be a place to start, but none would be in disagreement with SFAC #2's suggestion that the overriding choice criterion be usefulness within the cost-benefit constraint. Although some work has been done on measuring the costs of compliance, we are far from having an operational definition of usefulness at an aggregate level and know little about measurable benefits of financial reporting. Obviously, there is a need for research in these areas.

Something is needed to set the stage for discussion of this topic at a more conceptual level than is currently being done. I believe that a fruitful first step towards this end would be the complete characterization of the reporting environment. This environment may be viewed as consisting primarily of elements of the company, its operating environment, and the report users. Each of these elements has characteristics that interact with each other. Most business transactions are between the company and its operating environment. The accounting and reporting process communicates these transactions to report users primarily by means of financial statements. It must be acknowledged that the transaction itself may have features that interact with the major elements. The following figure therefore models these four elements and suggests a partial list of the characteristics of each that have been suggested by prior research as relevant in determining the most useful information to present and the most useful mode of presentation. In the past, GAAP has been promoted as the optimal reporting practice without giving explicit consideration to these diverse factors. Given the recent developments here discussed, it seems to be the time to devote attention to all of these considerations.

I believe that, using the research that has been done on the elements discussed in Figure I as a base, efforts are needed to integrate the findings into generalizations that may be useful as a practical guide to standard-setters. Specifically, in order for academic research to have practical significance in this area, the following questions require attention:

1. Can one reporting procedure for a given transaction be decision-useful in all situations?
2. If not, can the situations in which it is appropriate be clearly defined a priori? (i.e., can rules be developed?)
3. If not, can professional judgment be trusted to detect the appropriate procedure in any transactions/situation setting?
4. What are the differential costs of abiding by a particular standard?
5. What are the differential benefits of abiding by a particular standard?
6. What role does other information play in determining the optimal reporting mode?

Some of the more obvious thoughts that come to mind when these questions are considered are the following. A given piece of

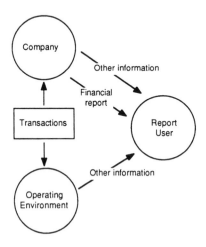

Relevant Characteristics of

Company :	Operating Environment :	Transaction :	Report User :
1. Size			1. Human Information Processing (HIP) Characteristics
2. Objectives (i.e. non-profit)	1. Competitiveness	1. Complexity	
	2. Industry	2. Uniqueness	2. Prior Knowledge
3. Financial Structure (D/E, Public/non-public, etc.)	3. Stability		3. Number
			4. Decision

Figure I — The Reporting Environment

information may have value in the sense of increasing an investor's expected utility. However, if the information is costly to acquire, it may not be worthwhile to do so. Even if its benefit to an individual outweighs its cost, how can needs be aggregated over all investors? Also, presumably, different methods of reporting have different costs. Therefore sources of information other than traditional financial statements must be considered. For example, although it might not be cost-effective to disclose certain data in an audited financial statement, it may be cost-effective to do so by means of a news conference. Alternatively, although the benefits of disclosure may appear to accounting standard-setters to justify costly financial statement disclosure, effectively the same information might already be in the public domain from other sources. These are some simple issues that need to be addressed.

CONCLUSION

In the last few years, the accounting profession has begun to move away from its traditional stance on reporting practices and standard-setting. The firm support it once gave to the "one true and fair answer for all" view has been seriously weakened by its responsiveness to the theoretical and empirical research being performed in the accounting field. This willingness to relinquish a position which has served its needs well is evidence of both the profession's flexibility and the strength of the findings that have undermined the foundations of the traditional accounting model. This break with the past has opened up new vistas for enquiry. New answers to old questions are needed. Decisions on standards will be, if anything, more difficult to make than in the past.

Finding solutions to the problem of determining the optimal reporting practice in a given situation will require, I believe, much more attention to basic research than has been the case in the standard-setting process to date. The demand for such research, some of it along the lines of answering the questions posed in this essay, will continue to grow. The challenge is there for the future.

REFERENCES

American Accounting Association Committee on Concepts and Standards for External Financial Reports, Statement on Accounting Theory and Theory Acceptance, Saratosa, Florida, AAA, 1977.

KAO, R., Accounting Standards Overload: Big GAAP vs Little GAAP, The Accounting Authority of Canada, Vancouver, 1986.

ROBB, C., and ROBINSON, C., "Theories of Standard-Setting: the Simplest is Best," CA magazine, April 1983, pp. 22-29.

La mesure du profit comptable en période de fluctuation des prix

DANIEL ZÉGHAL

La littérature comptable, au cours des vingt-cinq dernières années, a traité abondamment des effets des fluctuations des prix sur les états financiers et, d'une façon particulière, sur la mesure du profit. Il faut noter cependant que ce sont surtout les théoriciens qui se sont intéressés à cette question[1].

Dans la pratique, la comptabilité a très peu progressé dans ce domaine, principalement pour les raisons suivantes :

1. le peu d'intérêt que les utilisateurs d'états financiers ont manifesté à l'égard de ce problème ;
2. les dirigeants d'entreprise estiment que les états financiers traditionnels sont amplement suffisants ;
3. les difficultés et le travail supplémentaires auxquels donne lieu la préparation d'états financiers qui tiennent compte des effets de la fluctuation des prix ;
4. la croyance presque générale que les fluctuations des prix et notamment l'inflation ne sont que des phénomènes passagers.

L'ensemble de ces raisons serait motivé, selon nous, par la multiplicité et la complexité des solutions proposées. L'absence d'une solution pratique au problème dresse un obstacle majeur à sa mise en place.

La multiplicité des solutions et des modèles comptables en période de fluctuation des prix est principalement justifiée, selon la littérature, par les différences d'environnement des entreprises et par les besoins des utilisateurs. Le choix d'un modèle ou d'une approche dépend donc des caractéristiques de l'environnement. D'une manière générale, le comptable fournit l'information selon la plupart des modèles disponibles laissant ainsi le choix d'une solution finale entre les mains de l'utilisateur des états financiers[2].

---

1. Cette littérature porte souvent les appellations de comptabilité d'inflation ou de comptabilité à la valeur actuelle. Le terme « fluctuation des prix, » dans cet article, réfère autant aux fluctuations générales dans une économie qu'aux fluctuations spécifiques à certains biens.

2. Cela se vérifie autant dans la littérature que dans les recommandations professionnelles : aux États-Unis (FASB, 1983, 1979), au Canada (ICCA, 1983, 1981) et au Royaume-Uni (ASC, 1980, ICAEW 1975).

Quelle solution adopter ? Quel modèle choisir ? Quels sont les facteurs qui peuvent déterminer le choix d'une solution et selon quelle logique ? Telles sont les questions auxquelles nous tenterons de répondre. Pour ce faire, nous présenterons les principaux modèles comptables en période de fluctuation des prix et nous discuterons de leur rationalité et de la pertinence de leur utilisation. Nous analyserons ensuite les effets de la fluctuation des prix sur le profit comptable et les fondements conceptuels de la mesure du profit, avant de présenter les modèles de mesure du profit en période de fluctuation des prix.

LA PERTINENCE DU PROFIT COMPTABLE

Les états financiers traditionnels sont préparés en fonction des prix pratiqués au moment de la transaction. Le profit comptable fourni par ces états représente le surplus découlant des opérations auxquelles l'entreprise s'est effectivement livrée ; il constitue une mesure objective des résultats des opérations. Cependant, lors de périodes de fluctuations persistantes de prix, le profit basé sur les coûts d'origine perd de sa pertinence et le besoin de déterminer l'impact des variations de prix sur les résultats de l'entreprise se fait sentir[3].

Le profit comptable est probablement la donnée la plus surveillée, la plus utilisée et, dans bien des cas, la plus controversée. Son calcul demeure d'une importance particulière pour les comptables, les administrateurs, les investisseurs, etc. Pour les comptables, le profit est au centre du processus comptable. La majorité des actions comptables affecte le profit. De plus, tant sur le plan conceptuel que procédural, le profit lie les deux principaux états financiers que sont le bilan et l'état des résultats. Pour l'administrateur, le profit constitue un instrument privilégié pour la prise de décision et pour la mesure de la performance de l'entreprise. Finalement, les investisseurs et les créanciers utilisent principalement le critère de profitabilité dans leur processus décisionnel.

LES FONDEMENTS CONCEPTUELS
DE LA MESURE DU PROFIT

Le lien évident entre le profit comptable et le profit économique constitue pour beaucoup un critère majeur pour juger de la pertinence du profit comptable. Le profit comptable est généralement défini comme étant la différence entre les revenus réalisés, pendant une période, et les coûts correspondants qui ont permis de les

3. Les fluctuations de prix sont de plus en plus une caractéristique commune et dominante des économies industrielles. Elles peuvent être géné-rales, et l'on parle alors d'inflation ; elles peuvent être également ponctuelles (prix des ordinateurs, de l'énergie, etc.)

générer. Selon cette définition, le profit comptable se limite aux recettes d'exploitation ; il ignore toutes les variations dans la valeur de l'actif ou du passif ; il ignore aussi tous les changements dans le pouvoir d'achat de la monnaie et, par conséquent, les gains ou les pertes qui en découlent.

La définition du profit économique la plus souvent adoptée dans la littérature comptable est celle de Hicks (1946). Selon l'auteur, le but du profit est de donner à un agent économique une indication sur le montant maximum qu'il peut consommer, sans pour autant s'appauvrir : « C'est la somme maximale qu'une personne peut dépenser durant une période tout en gardant le même niveau de richesse qu'elle avait en début de période ».

Il ressort de cette définition que la mesure de la richesse est fondamentale pour la détermination du profit. L'interprétation généralement accordée au concept de richesse est celle de la préservation du patrimoine. Les deux principaux concepts de préservation du patrimoine se réfèrent à la préservation du capital financier ou à celle de la capacité physique. Le choix des deux concepts dépend des hypothèses de base qui motivent l'activité de l'entreprise, de l'entrepreneur ou des propriétaires. Ces hypothèses et leurs implications en termes comptables constituent le cadre de la théorie du propriétaire ou la théorie de l'entité.

La théorie du propriétaire et la détermination du profit

Selon la théorie du propriétaire, le patrimoine à préserver est le capital du propriétaire. Ce capital sera représenté, à titre d'exemple, par l'avoir du propriétaire, qui représente les apports en capital et les bénéfices réinvestis. Dans les deux cas, ils sont généralement exprimés en termes de coûts historiques.

En période de fluctuation ponctuelle des prix et dans le cas d'une comptabilité basée sur les coûts courants, l'adoption de cette approche implique la reconnaissance du gain de détention nominal comme faisant partie du profit de la période. En l'absence d'inflation, cette définition du patrimoine en termes monétaires serait adéquate pour préserver le capital, avant la reconnaissance de tout profit.

En période d'inflation toutefois, il sera plus approprié de préserver le capital en termes réels et le propriétaire sera porté à préserver son pouvoir d'achat. Ceci implique que seul le gain de détention net d'inflation serait reconnu comme faisant partie du profit.

La théorie du propriétaire considère le capital du propriétaire dans l'entreprise comme central dans la validation des données financières et de la mesure du profit. La valeur de l'entreprise et l'intérêt du propriétaire devant être préservés, ceci s'effectuera en fonction de l'ensemble des biens et services (changements généraux), plutôt qu'en fonction d'une catégorie particulière d'actifs (changements spécifiques).

La théorie du propriétaire est donc en accord avec le maintien du montant monétaire du capital du propriétaire et, lorsque la monnaie change de valeur, avec le maintien du pouvoir d'achat du capital du propriétaire.

La théorie de l'entité et la détermination du profit

Dans la théorie de l'entité, la préservation de la capacité de production de l'entreprise est l'hypothèse centrale de la préservation du patrimoine. Elle exige que le montant de capital à préserver soit égal au coût actuel des actifs nets de l'entreprise. Ceci implique que le capital — en termes monétaires — en début de période, doit être ajusté pour tenir compte des changements de prix des actifs spécifiques détenus par l'entreprise. De tels ajustements sont nécessaires, toutes les fois que les prix spécifiques changent et indépendamment des changements qui peuvent survenir dans le niveau général des prix.

La théorie de l'entité est totalement liée au concept de coût de remplacement, en raison de l'hypothèse implicite fondamentale de la pérennité de l'entreprise. Ainsi, le coût de remplacement est tout à fait approprié comme base d'évaluation, si l'on considère que l'entreprise doit renouveler ses immobilisations pour continuer ses opérations. L'adhésion à la théorie de l'entité implique donc l'adoption d'une définition du patrimoine qui permet de se préserver contre les variations spécifiques dans les prix des actifs de l'entreprise. Dans le cadre de cette approche, les gains de détention d'actifs sont totalement exclus du calcul du profit et sont généralement additionnés à l'avoir de l'entreprise pour préserver sa capacité de production.

En définitive, la théorie du propriétaire définit le patrimoine à préserver en termes monétaires, alors que la théorie de l'entité le définit en termes d'opérations (capacité physique). La différence majeure entre les deux approches porte sur le fait que la première considère le gain de détention comme profit, alors que la seconde le considère comme réserve nécessaire au maintien de la capacité actuelle de l'entreprise.

LES MODÈLES DE MESURE DU PROFIT EN PÉRIODE DE FLUCTUATION DES PRIX

Comme nous venons de le voir, la détermination du profit nécessite l'adhésion à l'une ou l'autre des deux théories, la théorie du propriétaire ou celle de l'entité.

Lorsque la finalité de l'entreprise et les hypothèses qui régissent ses activités peuvent être formulées dans le cadre de la théorie du propriétaire, le patrimoine à préserver peut être défini en termes de capital financier, exprimé en numéraire, ou en unités de pouvoir d'achat. Dans le cas d'un capital exprimé en numéraire, le profit comprend à la fois le gain de transaction et le gain de détention (modèle I). Lorsque le capital est exprimé en pouvoir d'achat, le profit comprend le gain de transaction, le gain de détention net d'inflation et le gain de pouvoir d'achat (modèle II).

Lorsque le cadre adopté est celui de la théorie de l'entité, le patrimoine à préserver peut être également exprimé en termes monétaires ou en unités de pouvoir d'achat. Dans le premier cas, le profit ne comprend que le gain de transaction (modèle III). Dans le cas où l'unité de mesure est le pouvoir d'achat, le profit comprend le gain de transaction et le gain de pouvoir d'achat (modèle IV)[4].

Illustrons maintenant les concepts et les modèles de profit que nous venons d'exposer à l'aide d'un exemple simple. La compagnie « La poupée magique Inc. » appartient à un seul actionnaire, M. Paul Lajoie. Il s'agit de sa première année d'opération.

Le 1er janvier 1985, M. Lajoie achète au comptant 2 000 poupées au coût de 30 $ l'unité. Le bilan d'ouverture se présente ainsi.

Tableau I   Bilan au 1er janvier 1985 de La Poupée magique inc.

Actif		Passsif	
Encaisse	15 000 $	Avoir du	
Inventaire	60 000 $	propriétaire	75 000 $
	75 000 $		75 000 $

Durant l'exercice de 1985, le niveau général des prix a augmenté de 12 %. Au 31 décembre 1985, M. Lajoie vend au comptant 1 500 poupées au prix de 50 $. Le coût de remplacement d'une unité à cette date est de 35 $. M. Lajoie adopte la politique de retirer, sous forme de dividende, la totalité du profit réalisé.

Déterminons maintenant le profit, selon chacune des quatre options que nous venons de présenter.

4. Signalons que le terme gain peut être remplacé par le terme perte, le cas échéant

Préservation du capital financier en numéraire

Selon cette définition, le profit de la période est calculé, après avoir préservé le capital initial de 75 000 $. Le profit, selon cette approche, s'élève à 32 000 $, soit 22 500 $ de gain de transaction et 10 000 $ de gain de détention. Une fois distribué sous forme de dividende, il restera dans l'entreprise 57 500 $ en encaisse et 17 500 $ en inventaire, soit un total de 75 000 $ représentant le capital monétaire initial préservé.

Tableau II	État des résultats selon le modèle I
Ventes	75 000 $
Coût actuel des marchandises vendues	(52 500 $)
Gain de transactions	22 500 $
Gain de détention* 2 000 (35-30)	10 000 $
Profite de l'exercice	32 500 $

*   gain de détention. . .
** le gain de. . .

Préservation du pouvoir d'achat du capital financier

Selon cette définition, le profit de la période est calculé, après avoir préservé le pouvoir d'achat du capital initial. Le retrait de 23 500 $ sous forme de dividende laisse dans l'entreprise un montant d'encaisse de 66 500 $ et un inventaire d'une valeur de 17 500 $, soit un total de 84 000 $ qui n'est rien d'autre que l'équivalent en pouvoir d'achat du capital initial, soit 75 000 $ x 1,12.

Préservation de la capacité physique

Selon cette définition, la capacité physique initiale de l'entreprise équivaudrait à 2 000 poupées. La distribution de 22 500 $ sous forme de dividende permet de garder en fin de période 67 500 $ dans l'encaisse et 17 500 $ en inventaire, soit un total de 85 000 $. La différence de 52 500 $ entre l'encaisse initiale et l'encaisse finale permet l'acquisition de 1 500 poupées additionnelles au coût actuel unitaire de 35 $, ce qui permet de ramener la capacité physique de l'entreprise à sa situation initiale de 2 000 poupées.

Tableau III État des résultats
selon le modèle II

Ventes	75 000 $
Coût actuel des marchandises vendues	52 500 $
Gain de transaction	22 500 $
Gain de détention net d'inflation:	
2 000 [35-(30 X 1.12)]	2 800
Perte de pouvoir d'achat de l'encaisse:	
$(15 000 X .12)	(1 800)
Profite de l'exercice	23 500 $

Tableau IV État des résultats
selon le modèle III

Ventes	75 000 $
Coût actuel des march. vendues	(52 500)
Gain de transaction et bénéfice de l'exercice	22 500 $

Préservation de la capacité physique et du pouvoir d'achat

Selon cette définition, la capacité physique de l'entreprise (2 000 poupées) et son pouvoir d'achat doivent être préservés avant de calculer le profit. Le retrait de 20 700 $ sous forme de dividende laisse dans l'entreprise une encaisse totale de 69 300 $, dont 52 500 $ permettant de renouveler la capacité physique (1 500 poupées) et 16 800 $ représentant l'équivalent en pouvoir d'achat de l'encaisse initiale. Le patrimoine de l'entreprise (encaisse et inventaire) s'élève, dans ce cas, à 86 800 $.

Récapitulation

Le tableau VI récapitule l'ensemble des résultats obtenus par les quatre modèles. Deux remarques s'imposent :
1. Il existe une relation inverse entre le patrimoine à préserver et le montant de profit : plus le patrimoine à préserver est important, moins il y a de bénéfices à distribuer.

Tableau V État des résultats selon le modèle IV

Ventes	75 000 $
Coût actuel des marchandises vendues	(52 500)
Gain de transaction	22 500 $
Perte de pouvoir d'achat de l'encaisse	(1 800)
Profit de l'exercice	20 700 $

2. La somme du patrimoine et du profit est toujours égale à 107 500 $, quel que soit le modèle sélectionné.

Ces deux résultats s'expliquent par le fait que la valeur de l'entreprise est toujours la même en fin de période et que la différence provient uniquement du niveau de profit de la période et du montant qui doit être préservé pour les périodes futures.

Vers un modèle éclectique

En raison de la multiplicité des modèles existants et du choix possible proposé aux utilisateurs, les comptables se doivent de fournir l'information selon les quatre modèles présentés. Pour simplifier leur tâche, certains auteurs ont suggéré une approche éclectique qui inclurait dans le même état financier l'ensemble de l'information relative aux quatre modèles (Kennedy, 1978).

Le tableau VII reprend notre exemple selon cette approche. Nous remarquons que les différents montants de profit sont reproduits dans cet état unique et que leur calcul n'est pas fondamentalement différent de celui des états séparés.

L'approche éclectique présente l'avantage majeur de synthétiser dans le même état un éventail d'informations disparates, permettant ainsi au comptable d'éviter de trancher parmi les modèles disponibles et de tronquer l'information fournie aux utilisateurs.

CONCLUSION

Le profit comptable est l'une des données les plus importantes fournies par le système comptable. Son calcul est d'une importance capitale pour les comptables, les administrateurs et les utilisateurs d'états financiers. En période de fluctuation des prix, le profit comptable peut être une combinaison de composantes : gain de transaction, gain de détention et gain de pouvoir d'achat.

Tableau VI Récapitulation: modèles de détermination du profit

| Modèle | Patri-moine + profit $ | Patri-moine $ | Profit total $ | Composantes du profit en termes de gain de | | |
				transac-tion $	détention $	pouvoir d'achat $
I	107 500	75 000	32 500	22 500	10 000	S.O.
II	107 500	84 000	23 500	22 500	2 800	(1 800)
III	107 500	85 000	22 500	22 500	S.O.	S.O
IV	107 500	86 800	20 700	22 500	S.O.	(1 800)

S.O.: Sans objet

Tableau VII État éclectique
des revenus et des dépenses

Ventes	75 000 $
Coût actuel des marchandises vendues	(52 000)
Profit de l'entité en termes monétaires	22 500
gain (perte) de pouvoir d'achat	(1 800)
Profit de l'entité en termes réels	20 700 $
gain de détention net d'inflation	2 800
Profit du propriétaire en termes de	23 500 $
pouvoir d'achat	
gain de détention dû à l'inflation	7 200
gain (perte) de pouvoir d'achat (déduit plus haut)	1 800
Profit du propriétaire en numéraire	32 500 $

Il existe un certain nombre de modèles de mesure du profit en période de fluctuation des prix. Nous en avons présenté quatre qui découlent de deux conceptions différentes du patrimoine (patrimoine financier ou patrimoine physique) et de deux unités de mesures (numéraire ou pouvoir d'achat). Finalement, nous avons proposé un état de résultats éclectique permettant de fournir, dans un document unique, l'information présentée par les quatre modèles individuels. Cette approche représente certainement la meilleure façon de simplifier la tâche des comptables, de synthétiser l'information, de la simplifier et de promouvoir son utilisation.

BIBLIOGRAPHIE

Accounting Standards Committee, « Current Cost Accounting », SSAP n° 16, mars 1980.

FASB, « Recognition and Measurement in Financial Statements of Business Enterprises », *Exposure Draft*, décembre 1983.

FASB, « Statement of Financial Accounting Standard No 33 », *Financial Reporting and Changing Prices*, Stanford, Conn., sept. 1979.

GOLDBERG, L., *An Inquiry into the Nature of Accounting*, Evanston, Illinois, American Accounting Association, 1965.

HICKS, J. R., *Value and Capital*, Oxford, Calendar Press, 1946.

HUSBAND, G. R., « The Entity Concept in Accounting », *The Accounting Review*, octobre 1954, 552-563.

ICCA, *L'information au coût actuel*, 1983, 22 p.

ICCA, *L'information financière publiée par les sociétés : évolution future*, 1981, 125 p.

KENNEDY, « Inflation Accounting : Retrospect and Prospect », *Cambridge Economic Policy Review*, n° 4, chap. 7, 1978, 58-64.

The Institute of Chartered Accountants in England and Wales, *The Corporate Report*, 1975.

Finance

L'abandon du modèle de l'utilité espérée

JEAN LEFOLL

La règle de l'utilité espérée est au centre de la théorie des choix en contexte d'incertitude et, de ce fait, le point de départ de nombreux modèles de finance. Lorsque monsieur Tremblay joue au loto, achète une assurance, une maison, ou cherche la meilleure manière de placer son épargne, il se trouve confronté à une situation dont il ne peut définir tous les paramètres, mais qui implique néanmoins de sa part une décision. Est-il possible d'expliquer des décisions aussi variées en recourant à un schéma unique ? De surcroît, ce modèle peut-il être valable pour expliquer les choix de monsieur Gagnon, s'il se trouve devoir prendre le même genre de décision ?

En réalité, tout le monde ne pose pas le problème de cette façon. Certains prennent une attitude normative, en ce sens que, pour eux, la question est de savoir comment un individu devrait prendre ses décisions (et ils définissent ainsi un homme rationnel), plutôt que d'expliquer comment ces décisions sont effectivement prises. Ainsi, parmi les partisans de la règle de l'utilité espérée, les uns y voient une représentation de ce que les individus font réellement en situation d'incertitude. D'autres en font une norme dont il convient de préconiser l'emploi toutes les fois que l'on peut définir un indice propre à représenter les préférences, cet indice permettant notamment de classer par ordre de satisfaction non croissante les différentes utilisations possibles de l'épargne[1].

Dans tous les cas, cependant, la règle de l'utilité espérée est une sorte de dogme sur lequel s'appuie la théorie des choix en situation d'incertitude et qui constitue le cœur de la finance moderne ou de l'économie de l'incertain. On peut facilement dire que monsieur Tremblay n'aime pas le risque, mais mesurer son aversion pour le risque nécessite le recours à un modèle de comportement, actuellement le modèle de l'utilité espérée. Sans mesure précise de l'aversion pour le risque, comment justifier ce qui semble correspondre au bon sens ? Si monsieur Tremblay n'aime pas le risque, il n'acceptera de placer son épargne que s'il est rémunéré pour le risque pris, d'où une prime de risque que doit payer toute entreprise à

---

1. Marschak (1979) n'hésite pas à suggérer la formation de décideurs rationnels se conformant à la règle de l'utilité espérée.

ceux qui financent ses activités et qui accroît le coût de son financement. À partir du risque et du modèle de l'utilité espérée, la
théorie financière propose ainsi toute une gamme de règles de
conduite pour l'épargnant, les institutions financières et les entreprises, tente d'expliquer le fonctionnement des marchés financiers,
mais préconise aussi des outils d'analyse des situations réelles,
d'intervention et de réglementation. S'attaquer à la règle de l'utilité
espérée peut donc, à juste titre, apparaître comme une entreprise
hautement subversive.

LA RÈGLE DE L'UTILITÉ ESPÉRÉE

Supposons que monsieur Tremblay veuille placer 1 000 $ dans
des actions lui donnant, selon ses estimations, un taux de rendement
annuel de 25 % avec une probabilité de 0,3, de 30 % avec une
probabilité de 0,4, et de 35 % avec une probabilité de 0,3 (on parle
alors de distribution des taux de rendement des actions), selon que
la situation économique est morose, que la reprise s'installe ou
qu'elle est particulièrement prononcée. Les probabilités de 0,3, 0,4
et 0,3 constituent une mesure de vraisemblance associée à chacune
des conjonctures envisagées. Ce qu'il recevra, en achetant des actions maintenant et en les revendant dans un an, dépendra donc de
la conjoncture économique qui prévaudra durant l'année à venir et
que monsieur Tremblay ne peut connaître avec certitude aujour-
d'hui. Il lui est également possible de faire un dépôt à terme auprès
de sa banque lui donnant un taux de rendement fixé, par exemple,
à 10 %. Il peut donc décider :
1. soit de placer les 1 000 $ à 10 % ;
2. soit d'acheter pour 1 000 $ d'actions lui rapportant en moyenne
   30 % (0,30(25 %) + 0,4(30 %) + 0,3(35 %) = 30 %) ;
3. soit de répartir ces 1 000 $ entre le dépôt à terme et les
   actions.
Dans tous les cas, il choisit un portefeuille, et la règle de l'utilité
espérée se propose de dire comment il va (ou devrait si la règle est
normative) choisir ce portefeuille.

Selon la règle de l'utilité espérée, monsieur Tremblay va pouvoir
associer une certaine satisfaction à chaque portefeuille accessible
avec ses 1 000 $, et le portefeuille retenu sera celui qui, en moyenne,
promet la satisfaction la plus élevée. Si, par exemple, le portefeuille
choisi comprend 500 $ d'actions et 500 $ de dépôt à terme, les
montants futurs auxquels il peut s'attendre avec ce portefeuille,
dans chacune des éventualités possibles, sont les suivants (en $) :
Dépôt à terme (500 $) :
[probabilité : 1,0, rendement : 10 %] 500 x 1,10 = 550

Actions (500 $) :
[probabilité : 0,3, rendement : 25 %] 500 x 1,25 = 625
[probabilité : 0,4, rendement : 30 %] 500 x 1,30 = 650
[probabilité : 0,3, rendement : 35 %] 500 x 1,35 = 675

En effet, 500 $ placés à 10 % rapportent en fin d'année 50 $ d'intérêt, si bien que le montant disponible est de 550 $. Si, par contre, 500 $ sont investis dans l'achat d'actions, la probabilité d'obtenir par exemple 30 % de taux de rendement, soit un montant de 650 $ en fin d'année, est seulement de 0,4. Sachant que la satisfaction associée par exemple à 625 $ est notée S(625), la satisfaction espérée S(Tremblay), procurée par le portefeuille, est donc égale à 1S(550) + 0,3S(625) + 0,4S(650) + 0,3S(675). Suivant la règle de l'utilité espérée, cette moyenne est la plus élevée des utilités espérées que monsieur Tremblay peut obtenir avec ses 1 000 $ d'épargne.

Cette règle, qui paraît simple, suppose en fait que les comportements individuels vérifient certaines propositions, nommées axiomes par les spécialistes.

Axiome de comparaison

Monsieur Tremblay est en mesure de comparer tous les portefeuilles qui lui sont accessibles et de les ranger par ordre de satisfaction non croissante : il peut toujours dire que tout portefeuille (P1) est préféré ou équivalent à tout autre portefeuille (P2).

Axiome de transitivité

Si le portefeuille (P1) est préféré ou équivalent à un portefeuille (P2), lui-même préféré ou équivalent à un portefeuille (P3), on suppose que (P1) est aussi préféré ou équivalent à (P3). Les préférences de monsieur Tremblay sont alors transitives et peuvent être représentées par une fonction S, dite de satisfaction ou d'utilité.

Axiome de substituabilité

Si monsieur Tremblay combine, dans des proportions identiques, un portefeuille (P1) ou un portefeuille (P2) à un même portefeuille (P3), c'est-à-dire substitue une fraction de P(3) à une même fraction de P(1) ou de P(2), l'ordre établi entre (P1) et (P2) n'est pas modifié. On parle alors d'axiome de substituabilité[2].

Axiome de continuité

Monsieur Tremblay peut combiner (P1) et (P3) dans des proportions différentes et former à chaque fois un nouveau portefeuille. Sachant que la satisfaction associée à la détention du portefeuille

---

2. Dans cet article, l'axiome d'indépendance dû à Savage (1954) ou de substituabilité dû à Samuelson (1952) seront considérés comme équivalents. Aussi les termes « indépendance » ou « substituabilité » seront employés indifféremment. En réalité, l'énoncé de ces deux axiomes est quelque peu différent.

(P1) est plus élevée que celle liée à (P3), il peut former un portefeuille pour tout niveau de satisfaction intermédiaire. Le classement ainsi réalisé vérifie l'axiome de continuité. Il existe, par exemple, un portefeuille (P4) donnant la même satisfaction que la combinaison 0,5 (P1) + 0,5 (P3).

Axiome de dominance

Enfin, la satisfaction associée au portefeuille (P5), et égale à celle de la combinaison de 0,8 (P1) + 0,2 (P2), sera supérieure à la satisfaction procurée par le portefeuille (P4) précédent, la part de (P1) étant plus importante dans (P5) que dans (P4). Le classement de monsieur Tremblay obéit à l'axiome de dominance.

Des cinq axiomes précédents sur lesquels la règle de l'utilité espérée est fondée, l'axiome primordial est sans doute l'axiome de substituabilité. Si l'un des axiomes n'est pas accepté (parce que jugé irrationnel ou si les comportements observés ne sont pas compatibles avec lui, par exemple), la règle de l'utilité espérée ne sera plus valide, à moins que cette règle ne soit normative, auquel cas monsieur Tremblay verra ses décisions qualifiées d'irrationnelles lorsqu'elles ne seront pas compatibles avec le modèle de l'utilité espérée. Il est clair qu'un tel jugement est très discutable.

LA RÈGLE DE L'UTILITÉ ESPÉRÉE EN QUESTION

Des études, de plus en plus nombreuses, tendent à montrer que la règle de l'utilité espérée ne saurait expliquer tous les choix en situation d'incertitude[3]. La critique la plus ancienne, à notre connaissance, due à Allais, est centrée sur l'axiome de substituabilité (d'indépendance)[4] et vise à montrer qu'un individu, dont les décisions ne sont pas compatibles avec cet axiome, n'est pas nécessairement irrationnel.

Supposons que monsieur Tremblay soit un homme prudent. De ce fait, il préfère un placement lui assurant demain un paiement certain d'un million de $ (situation A) plutôt qu'un placement lui promettant certes 4,5 millions de $, mais pour lequel il existe une probabilité de 0,1 de tout perdre bien qu'il ait une probabilité de

---

3. La première du genre est celle effectuée par Allais en 1952 et dont une partie de résultats est publiée dans le livre d'Allais et Hagen. On peut se référer également aux études de McCord et de Neufville (1983) ainsi qu'à celles de Krzysztofowicz (1983), bien que ce dernier voit dans ses résultats une confirmation du modèle de l'utilité espérée, alors qu'Allais (1984) y trouve la preuve du contraire.

4. En fait, le fameux paradoxe d'Allais est le contre-exemple donné par Allais (1953) pour infirmer l'axiome d'indépendance de Savage. Puisque le modèle de l'utilité espérée est présenté ici avec l'axiome de substituabilité, la discussion est limitée à cet axiome et suit l'argumentation donnée par Allais (1953).

0,9 de recevoir 5 millions de $ (situation B). Le choix précédent indique qu'il préfère un gain sûr, même s'il est 4,5 fois plus faible que le gain espéré de la stratégie B. Cela peut se comprendre s'il s'agit, par exemple, de s'assurer d'un certain capital pour un départ à la retraite. Supposons, cependant, que monsieur Tremblay se trouve confronté aux situations suivantes.

Une situation (C), caractérisée par la certitude de tout perdre, est possible. Il ne doit plus classer (A) et (B), mais deux situations complexes (D) et (E) formées respectivement de (A) et (C) et de (B) et (C). La probabilité que la situation (C) arrive avec (D) et (E) est de 0,90 dans les deux cas (on applique ici l'axiome de substituabilité). Avec (D), le gain net espéré est de 100 000 $, la probabilité de recevoir 1 million de $ (avec (A) étant de 0,1 et celle de tout perdre (avec (C)) de 0,9. La situation (E) laisse espérer un gain net de 450 000 $, avec une probabilité de 0,09 de recevoir 5 millions de $ et une probabilité de 0,91 de tout perdre. Puisque la probabilité de tout perdre est élevé et voisine avec (D) et (E), monsieur Tremblay sera-t-il irrationnel s'il préfère (E) à (D), soit un gain espéré plus élevé, alors qu'il préférait (A) à (B), soit un gain plus faible mais dénué de tout risque ?

L'explication des décisions de monsieur Tremblay est facile à donner. Les situations (A) et (D) sont totalement différentes du fait de la prise en compte de la stratégie (C). Comme (B) et (E) sont toutes deux caractérisées par une forte probabilité de tout perdre, il n'y a aucune raison pour que l'ordre établi entre (D) et (E) soit le même qu'entre (A) et (B). En fait, chaque situation a des caractéristiques propres et doit être considérée en elle-même. Notons que l'éventualité de tout perdre (ou risque de ruine) constitue évidemment un paramètre essentiel, dès lors qu'il s'agit, pour monsieur Tremblay, de préparer sa retraite.

Si l'on rejette les assertions selon lesquelles toute violation d'un des axiomes du modèle de l'utilité espérée est la marque d'un comportement irrationnel, car est alors rationnel ce qui est conforme aux axiomes de comportement posés (même s'ils sont arbitraires, auquel cas cette conception de la rationalité est très discutable), ou plus fondamentalement parce que ces axiomes représentent ce qu'il y a de crucial dans les décisions prises par les individus en situation d'incertitude (et alors comment expliquer la violation quasi systématique de l'axiome d'indépendance dans les comportements observés ?), les arguments invoqués pour défendre ce modèle semblent assez faibles. Certains défenseurs de la règle de l'utilité espérée font remarquer que les expériences tentées n'impliquaient pas de gains ou de pertes réelles d'argent (conditions expérimentales). Dans ces conditions, il est également difficile de démontrer la validité du modèle de l'utilité espérée à l'aide de ce genre d'expérience. Le droit à l'erreur a aussi été invoqué, puisqu'après analyse de leur choix initial et devant l'évidence que de tels choix n'étaient pas conformes à l'axiome d'indépendance (situation soulignée et expliquée par l'expérimentateur), les individus semblaient réviser leurs décisions en accord avec les enseignements du modèle de l'utilité espérée[5]. Bien sûr, l'expérimentateur joue un rôle essentiel dans la prise de conscience de l'irrationnel d'un comportement. Il est de ce fait possible d'amener des individus, dont les décisions seraient conformes au modèle de l'utilité espérée, à réviser également leurs choix dans le sens opposé.

Les arguments allant à l'encontre du modèle de l'utilité espérée ne se réduisent pas à une critique de l'axiome de substituabilité (d'indépendance). Certains mettent notamment en cause l'axiome de transitivité, et d'autres la stabilité des préférences dans la mesure où monsieur Tremblay, confronté à plusieurs situations identiques, ne prendrait pas toujours la même décision. De même, la notion de probabilité est au centre de nombreuses discussions, ce qui amène certains auteurs à préconiser l'emploi du modèle de l'utilité espérée subjective[6]. Il n'est pas question de passer ici en revue toutes les raisons invoquées en faveur ou à l'encontre du modèle de l'utilité espérée. Par contre, il semble actuellement se dégager un consensus pour rejeter ce modèle et plusieurs approches sont proposées pour le remplacer.

LES CHOIX EN INCERTITUDE
SANS LA RÈGLE DE L'UTILITÉ ESPÉRÉE

Deux catégories de modèles doivent être considérées, selon qu'ils rejettent ou non l'axiome de transitivité. L'absence de transitivité des préférences de monsieur Tremblay implique :
1. l'impossibilité de définir une fonction de satisfaction associée à ses préférences ;
2. l'éventualité qu'il joue contre lui-même[7].
Aussi, l'on se limitera à donner ici les grandes lignes de deux approches fondamentales acceptant l'axiome de transitivité : la théorie d'Allais et la théorie de l'utilité espérée généralisée de Machina.

La théorie d'Allais

Selon Allais, les individus ne vont pas classer des portefeuilles en ne considérant que l'espérance de l'utilité associée à chacun

---

5. Savage en est le plus fameux exemple.
6. Bernard (1974), et Kahneman et Tversky (1979) proposent une formulation qui peut s'inscrire dans cette catégorie de modèle. Allais (1984) montre toutefois que leur formulation se réduit,
en fait, au modèle classique de l'utilité espérée.
7. Ainsi que le souligne Machina (1983), un individu joue contre lui-même si ses préférences ne vérifient pas la dominance stochastique du 1er degré expliquée plus loin dans le texte.

d'eux, mais au contraire à l'aide de toute la distribution des utilités[8]. De ce point de vue, la règle de l'utilité espérée constitue une simplification valable seulement dans certains cas, particulièrement avec des jeux répétés lorsque le risque de ruine (de tout perdre) est négligeable. Un indice de satisfaction existe donc, à l'aide duquel monsieur Tremblay peut classer les portefeuilles qui lui sont accessibles en fonction de la distribution des gains monétaires prévue pour chacun d'eux.

La théorie de Machina

Partant de cette constatation, Machina montre que, dans certaines conditions, monsieur Tremblay va se comporter comme s'il maximisait une utilité espérée, mais d'une nature un peu particulière et appelée utilité locale, qui ne doit pas être confondue avec la fonction d'utilité (ou de satisfaction) de la règle de l'utilité espérée. En fait, cette fonction d'utilité correspond au cas particulier où l'indice de satisfaction locale est indépendant des distributions de gains futurs à comparer, et donc identique pour toutes ces distributions. Par conséquent, si les choix de monsieur Tremblay peuvent être formulés théoriquement en termes d'utilité espérée, pratiquement, il ne s'agit plus d'effectuer des choix comme le supposait le modèle de l'utilité espérée. En effet, monsieur Tremblay est censé tenir compte de toute la distribution des utilités associée aux gains monétaires futurs de chaque portefeuille.

La différence fondamentale entre le modèle d'Allais et celui de Machina réside dans les propriétés de l'indice des préférences. Selon Allais, il existe une fonction d'utilité cardinale représentant les préférences de monsieur Tremblay en contexte de certitude et qui peut être déterminée indépendamment de toute référence à l'incertitude. Plusieurs études récentes ont en effet confirmé qu'un individu est susceptible de déterminer le montant X de $, tel que la différence de satisfaction, lorsque ses gains monétaires augmentent par exemple de 10 000 $ à X, est égale à la différence de satisfaction ressentie pour des gains passant de 5 000 $ à 10 000 $[9]. Cette fonction d'utilité cardinale permet à monsieur Tremblay d'associer à chaque gain possible une utilité cardinale, si bien que chaque portefeuille sera caractérisé par une distribution de gains futurs et une distribution d'utilités cardinales (valeurs psychologiques), ces dernières distributions étant classées en fonction de tous les moments de la distribution, et non pas seulement de l'utilité espérée (moment

---

8. Allais ne réduit pas son analyse à l'espérance et à la variance des utilités mais prend en compte tous les moments de cette distribution.

9. Ces équivalences dépendent de ce que Allais appelle la richesse psychologique de l'individu et, pour des petites sommes, de son encaisse monétaire. À partir d'un certain montant monétaire (niveau de satiété), l'utilité cardinale n'augmente cependant plus.

d'ordre 1). La fonctionnelle[10] représentant les préférences de monsieur Tremblay en situation d'incertitude ne peut être précisée ; elle doit cependant vérifier deux conditions :

1. La première suppose que si la distribution des gains d'un portefeuille (P1) est identique à celle d'un portefeuille (P2), sauf pour une éventualité où le gain avec (P1) est strictement plus grand qu'avec (P2) (la probabilité correspondante étant la même), (P1) sera préféré à (P2) (les préférences de monsieur Tremblay vérifiant le principe de dominance stochastique du premier degré)[11].

2. La deuxième stipule que l'utilité cardinale d'un portefeuille augmente d'un montant donné Y, si l'utilité cardinale de chaque gain monétaire possible augmente de Y (axiome d'isovariation cardinale)[12]. Machina, qui n'accepte pas l'existence d'une fonction d'utilité cardinale ni l'axiome d'isovariation cardinale, préfère imposer des restrictions sur les fonctions d'utilité locale.

Il ne s'agit pas ici de procéder à une analyse exhaustive des modèles d'Allais ou de Machina et de comparer les mérites de chacun d'eux. Dans un cas comme dans l'autre, la remise en cause de la règle de l'utilité espérée conduit nécessairement à s'interroger sur la validité des résultats financiers qui en sont dérivés.

LA THÉORIE FINANCIÈRE
SANS LA RÈGLE DE L'UTILITÉ ESPÉRÉE

Les modèles d'arbitrage ne semblent pas devoir être révisés, à première vue, si la règle de l'utilité espérée est remise en cause. Après tout, la recherche systématique des bénéfices à réaliser sur les marchés financiers n'implique pas que les agents économiques veuillent nécessairement maximiser leur utilité espérée. De ce fait, les éléments de théorie financière recourant au phénomène d'arbitrage pourraient être conservés. Toutefois, après examen, une telle assertion ne peut être avancée sans réserve. En effet, dans ces théories comme pour toute la théorie financière, le concept d'aversion absolue pour le risque est central. Et s'il est facile d'appréhen-

---

10. Chez Allais, cette fonctionnelle transforme la fonction d'utilité cardinale des choix en situation de certitude, pour tenir compte de l'attitude de monsieur Tremblay face au risque. Le terme fonctionnelle est donc ici synonyme de fonction de fonction.

11. Allais (1952, 1979) parle d'axiome de préférences absolues. Il faut noter que tous les portefeuilles accessibles peuvent néanmoins être classés à l'aide de la fonctionnelle représentant ses préférences.

12. Les gains monétaires associés aux différentes éventualités n'augmentent pas d'un même montant. Au contraire, si l'utilité marginale des gains est décroissante, plus les gains sont élevés, plus l'accroissement nécessaire pour obtenir une augmentation cardinale égale à Y doit être important.

der l'idée fort juste qu'un agent n'aimant pas le risque cherchera à s'en protéger ou demandera une compensation pour l'accepter, sa définition opérationnelle est, pour le moment, donnée dans le cadre du modèle de l'utilité espérée. Machina propose sans doute une généralisation du concept à l'aide des utilités locales[13], mais Allais a montré que le concept d'aversion absolue pour le risque, tel qu'habituellement défini, n'avait aucune signification réelle, puisqu'il est sans aucun rapport avec l'aversion pour le risque qu'il prétend mesurer[14].

Tous les modèles d'optimisation et les propriétés dérivées fondées sur la règle de l'utilité espérée doivent donc, de toute évidence, être revus. Heureusement, il semble que la relation risque-rendement espéré, caractéristique du modèle d'équilibre des marchés financiers (MEDAF), puisse être également dérivée à l'aide d'une fonctionnelle d'Allais et d'hypothèses généralement acceptées en théorie financière. Dans ces conditions, il est possible de généraliser tous les résultats obtenus dans le cadre du MEDAF. Cependant, étant donné la place occupée par le modèle de l'utilité espérée en théorie financière et en économie de l'incertain, il est difficile d'appréhender actuellement toutes les implications de l'abandon d'un tel modèle. Le travail à accomplir, tant pour développer éventuellement une nouvelle théorie générale des choix en incertitude que pour en cerner les implications au niveau de la finance et de l'économie, reste considérable et constitue, selon nous, un des pôles majeurs de la recherche future.

---

13. Concept essentiel dans cette tentative de généralisation des outils développés par le modèle de l'utilité espérée lorsque l'axiome d'indépendance n'est plus acceptée.

14. L'indice d'utilité cardinale, qui n'est pas, selon Allais, différent de l'in-dice du modèle de l'utilité espérée (à une transformation linéaire et positive près), à l'aide duquel le coefficient d'aversion absolue pour le risque de Arrow-Pratt est défini, est obtenu à l'aide de questions d'où toute incertitude et donc tout risque sont exclus.

BIBLIOGRAPHIE

ALLAIS, M., « Fondements d'une théorie positive des choix comportant un risque et critique des postulats et axiomes de l'école américaine », *Colloques internationaux du Centre national de la recherche scientifique*, 40, Paris, 1953, 257-332 ; traduction anglaise dans Allais et Hagen, 1979, 27-145.

ALLAIS, M.,« The So-Called Allais Paradox and Rational Decisions Under Uncertainty », dans Allais et Hagen, 1979, 437-681.

ALLAIS, M.,« The Foundations of the Theory of Utility and Risk ; Some Central Points of the Discussions at the Oslo Conference », dans Hagen et Wenstop, 1974, 5-131.

ALLAIS, M., HAGEN, O., *Expected Utility Hypothesis and the Allais Paradox*, Dordrecht, Holland, D. Reidel Publishing, 1979.

ARROW, K., *Essays in the Theory of Risk-Bearing*, Amsterdam, North-Holland, 2e éd., 1974.

BECKER, G., De GROOT, M., MARSCHAK, J., « An Experimental Study of Some Stochastic Model for Wagers », *Behavioral Science*, vol. 8, 1963, 199-202.

BECKER, G., De GROOT, M., MARSCHAK, J., « Probabilities of Choices Among Very Similar Objects: an Experiment to Decide Between Two Models », *Behavioral Science*, vol. 8, 1963, 306-311.

BERNARD, G., « On Utility Functions », *Theory and Decision*, vol. 5, 1974, 205-242.

FAMA, E. F., MILLER, M. H., *The Theory of Finance*, Hisdale, Dryden Press, 1972.

BORCH, K., MOSSIN, J., *Risk and Uncertainty ; Proceedings of a Conference Held by the International Economic Association*, London, MacMillan, 1968.

FISHBURN, P., « Intransitive Indifference on Preference Theory: A Survey », *Operations Research*, vol. 18, 1970, 207-228.

FISHBURN, P., « Subjective Expected Utility: a Review of Normative Theories », *Theory and Decision*, vol. 13, 1981, 139-199.

HAGEN, O., WENSTOP, F., édit., *Progress in Utility and Risk Theory*, Dordecht, Holland, D. Reidel Publishing, 1984.

KAHNEMAN, D., TVERSKY, A., « Prospect Theory: an Analysis of Decision Under Risk », *Econometrica*, vol. 47, 1979, 263-291.

KRZYSZTOFOWICZ, R., « Risk Attitude Hypotheses of Utility Theory », dans Stigum et Wenstop, 1983, 201-216.

MacCRIMMON, K., « Descriptive and Normative Implications of the Decision — Theory Postulates », dans Borch et Mossin, 1968.

MACHINA, M., « Expected Utility Analysis Without the Independence Axiom », *Econometrica*, vol. 50, 1982, 277-323.

MACHINA, M., « Generalized Expected Utility Analysis and the Nature of Observed Violations of the Independence Axiom », dans Stigum et Wenstop, 1983, 263-293.

MARSCHAK, J., *Economic Information, Decision and Prediction*, 3 vol., Dordrecht, Holland, D. Reidel Publishing, 1974.

MARSCHAK, J., « Utilities, Psychological Values, and the Training of Decision Makers », dans Allais et Hagen, 1979, 163-174.

McCORD, M., De NEUFVILLE, R., « Empirical Demonstration That Expected Utility Analysis Is Not Operational », dans Stigum et Wenstop, 1983, 181-189.

MORGENSTERN, O., « Some Reflections on Utility », dans Allais et Hagen, 1979, 175-183.

MOSSIN, J., « Equilibrium in a Capital Asset Market », Econometrica, vol. 34, 1966, 768-783.

PRATT, J., « Risk Aversion in the Small and in the Large », Econometrica, vol. 32, 1964, 122-136.

RAIFFA, H., Decision Analysis: Introductory Lectures on Choice Under Uncertainty, Reading, Mass., Addison-Wesley, 1968.

ROSS, S. A., « The Arbitrage Theory of Capital Asset Pricing », Journal of Economic Theory, vol. 13, 1976, 341-360.

SAVAGE, L., The Foundations of Statistics, New York, John Wiley and Sons, 1954.

SAMUELSON, P. A., « Utility, Preference and Probability », Colloques internationaux du Centre national de la recherche scientifique, 40, Paris, 1953, 29-33.

SLOVIC, P., TVERSKY, A., « Who Accepts Savage's Axiom ? », Behavioral Science, vol. 19, 1974, 368-373.

STIGLITZ, G., édit., Collected Scientific Papers of Paul A. Samuelson, vol. 1, Cambridge, Mass., MIT Press, 1966.

STIGUM, B., WENSTOP, F., Foundations of Utility and Risk Theory with Applications, Dordrecht, Holland, D. Reidel Publishing, 1983.

VON NEUMANN, J., MORGENSTERN, O., Theory of Games and Economic Behavior, Princeton University Press, 1944.

Variabilité des revenus
et politique de dividende

FODIL ADJAOUD

La réticence des firmes à baisser leur niveau de dividendes s'explique essentiellement par la crainte des gestionnaires de ne pas transmettre un signal au marché, de peur d'amener ce dernier à réagir de manière incontrôlée. En d'autres termes, l'annonce du dividende joue le rôle d'un véhicule d'information au même titre que les états financiers ou une conférence de presse. Le marché perçoit cette information comme l'anticipation de la rentabilité future de l'entreprise à partir des informations privilégiées dont disposent les gestionnaires.

Ce phénomène, basé sur l'hypothèse du contenu informationnel des dividendes, fut abondamment testé, notamment par Charest (1980) et Adjaoud (1984). Il ressortait de l'étude d'Adjaoud que 10 % des firmes étudiées (259 au total) n'avaient jamais baissé leur dividende de 1963 à 1981, que 60 % des firmes n'avaient jamais effectué deux baisses consécutives et que 90 % n'en avaient jamais effectué trois consécutives.

Friend et Puckett (1965, p. 611) allaient plus loin et affirmaient : « In what we know about managerial desire to avoid dividend cuts, it certainly seems logical to expect that companies facing greater uncertainty about future profit performance would adopt lower current dividend payout as a means of hedging the risk of being forced to cut their dividend. » Beaver, Kettler et Scholes (1970, p. 616) faisaient la même observation : « [. . .] if firms follow a policy of dividend stabilization [. . .] then firms with greater volatility in earnings will payout a lower percentage of expected earnings. »

En effet, une façon d'éviter de faire varier le niveau de dividende consiste à tenir compte de la variabilité future des revenus d'exploitation et à fixer le niveau de dividende à un seuil plus bas. Ainsi, on pourrait supposer que les firmes dont les revenus d'exploitation fluctuent beaucoup distribuent une plus petite fraction de leurs profits que celles dont les bénéfices sont plus stables. Notre étude empirique s'appliquera à vérifier cette hypothèse, c'est-à-dire à voir s'il existe une corrélation entre la variabilité des revenus d'opérations et le taux de distribution de dividendes des firmes canadiennes.

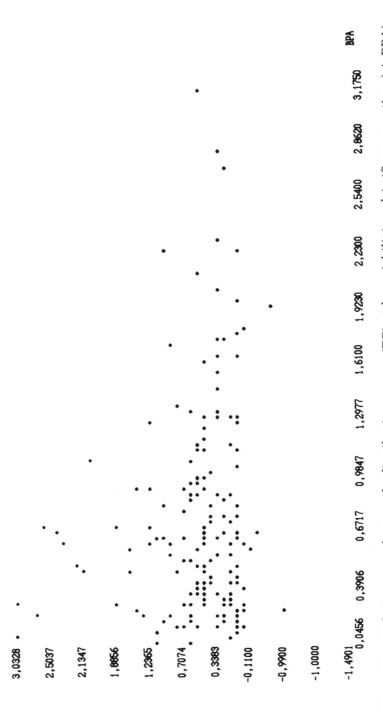

Figure I — Relation entre le taux de distribution moyen (DP) et la variabilité ou bénéfice par action (Δ BPA) — Échantillon global (183 firmes)

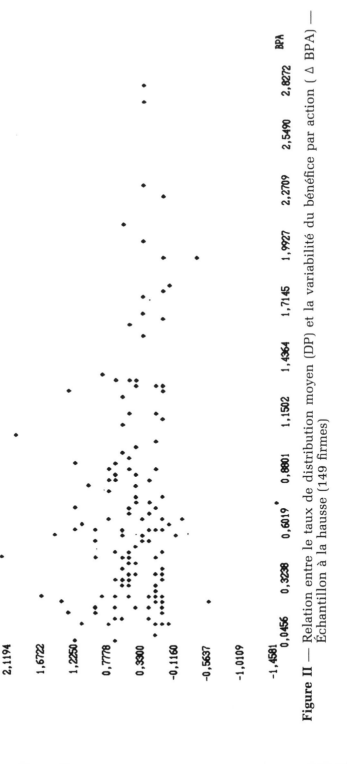

Figure II — Relation entre le taux de distribution moyen (DP) et la variabilité du bénéfice par action (Δ BPA) — Échantillon à la hausse (149 firmes)

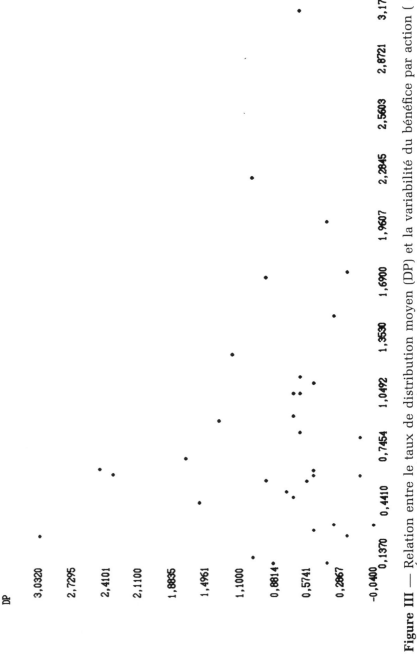

Figure III — Relation entre le taux de distribution moyen (DP) et la variabilité du bénéfice par action (Δ BPA) — Échantillon à la baisse (34 firmes)

Une étude empirique

Notre étude porte sur 183 firmes inscrites à la Bourse de Toronto depuis au moins 5 ans, dont les dividendes ont été modifiés de 2 ¢ minimum (149 à la hausse et 34 à la baisse), sur une période comprise entre 1969 et 1979. Les variables sont exprimées de la manière suivante :

Taux de distribution moyen :

$$DP = \frac{1}{n} \sum_{t=1}^{n} \frac{(\text{dividende par action})_t}{(\text{bénéfice par action})_t}$$

Variabilité du bénéfice par action :

$$\Delta(BPA) = \sqrt{\frac{\sum_{t=1}^{n} (BPA_t - \overline{BPA})^2}{n-1}}$$

Une représentation graphique nous donne une idée préliminaire de la relation existant entre le taux de distribution de dividendes et la variabilité du bénéfice par action. Le message qui se dégage des figures I, II et III est que le taux de distribution en dividende (DP) et la variabilité du bénéfice par action $\Delta(BPA)$ sont négativement corrélés ; plus $\Delta(BPA)$ est élevé, plus DP est faible. Cela signifie que les firmes adoptent un taux de distribution de dividendes d'autant plus faible que la variabilité de leurs revenus est élevée. Cette constatation graphique est confirmée par l'analyse algébrique.

Échantillons	Coefficients de corrélation
Global	-0,1245
À la hausse	-0,1562
À la baisse	-0,1281

Figure IV - Coefficients de corrélation entre (DP) et ($\Delta(BPA)$)

L'analyse algébrique nous apporte cependant une information supplémentaire grâce aux valeurs du coefficient de corrélation. Les entreprises ayant effectué des hausses de dividendes affichent un coefficient de corrélation supérieur (-0,1562) à celles ayant effectué des baisses (-0,1281). Afin de valider le niveau de signification de

ces différences, nous avons testé le modèle de régression suivant :
DP = constante + $\beta 1$ (Δ (BPA)) + terme résiduel.

Échantillons	t de $\beta 1$	F	Coefficients de corrélation
Global	-1,69	2,85	0,02
À la hausse	-1,92	3,68	0,03
À la baisse	-0,73	0,53	0,02

Figure V - Résultats du modèle de régression

Contrastes entre firmes

Sur la base des valeurs de t et de F, il semble que la relation entre DP et Δ (BPA) ne soit négative et significative que pour les échantillons « global » et « à la hausse ». Dans l'échantillon « à la baisse », la relation n'est pas significative à 95 %. Ces résultats confirment que le taux de distribution de dividendes est inversement relié à la variabilité des bénéfices, mais surtout que la relation n'est significative que dans le cas des hausses de dividendes. Cela signifie que les firmes ayant effectué des augmentations de dividendes ont affiché un taux de distribution de dividendes moyen plus bas (0,53) que celles qui ont effectué des baisses de dividendes (0,84). Par ailleurs, nous constatons que les premières accusent une stabilité plus grande de leurs bénéfices par rapport aux dernières. En définitive, nous pouvons conclure que les firmes qui n'ont pas adapté leur taux de distribution de dividendes en fonction de la variabilité de leurs revenus ont plus de chance de recourir à la baisse du dividende (cas de l'échantillon « à la baisse ») que les autres (cas de l'échantillon « à la hausse »).

Échantillons	Taux de distribution moyen DP	Variabilité des bénéfices par action BPA
À la hausse	0,53	0,73
À la baisse	0,84	0,89

Figure VI - Comparaison des résultats pour les deux échantillons

Les résultats précédents complètent ceux donnés par deux autres études antérieures. Gagnon et Papillon (1984) ont constaté en effet que les firmes de petite taille distribuent plus de dividendes que les grandes, c'est-à-dire que le taux de distribution de dividendes est négativement corrélé à la taille de l'entreprise. Adjaoud (1984) a révélé par ailleurs que les baisses de dividendes sont pratiquées principalement par les petites entreprises. Les résultats obtenus ici nous permettent de compléter ces conclusions antérieures et d'avancer que les firmes de petite taille, malgré une plus grande fluctuation de leurs revenus d'exploitation, distribuent un pourcentage plus grand de leurs revenus, ce qui les pousse à recourir davantage à la baisse de dividende, suscitant ainsi une réaction négative du marché.

Il paraîtrait logique que ces petites entreprises versent un taux plus faible de dividende et ce pour deux raisons majeures : d'une part, elles sont relativement plus endettées que les grandes et par conséquent elles devraient essayer de s'autofinancer davantage (Gagnon et Papillon) ; d'autre part, elles affichent des taux de rendement plus instables et la variation à la baisse de leur taux de dividende transmet de mauvaises nouvelles à l'investisseur. Pourquoi les petites entreprises continuent-elles alors à distribuer plus de dividendes que les entreprises plus importantes ? Le font-elles sciemment ou par ignorance ? On ne peut apporter de réponse a priori ; il s'agit d'un axe de recherche à développer si l'on veut mieux cerner cette question tant controversée qu'est la politique de dividende.

BIBLIOGRAPHIE

ADJAOUD, F., « The Information Content of Dividends : A Canadian Test, » *Canadian Journal of Administration Sciences*, décembre 1984, vol. 1, (2), pp. 338-351.

ADJAOUD, F., « La réticence des firmes à baisser le dividende : le cas canadien », *Finance* (à venir en décembre 1986).

BEAVER, W.H., KETTLER, P., SCHOLES, M., « The Association Between Market-Determined and Accounting-Determined Risk Measures, » *The Accounting Review*, octobre 1970, 654-682.

CHAREST, G., « Returns to Dividend Changing Stocks on the Toronto Stock Exchange », *Journal of Business Administration* (UBC), 12(1), automne 1980, 1-18.

FRIEND, I., BUCKETT, M., « Dividends and Stock Prices, » *The American Economic Review*, septembre 1964, 656-682.

GAGNON, J.M., PAPILLON, B., « Risque financier, taux de rendement des entreprises canadiennes et interventions de l'État », étude préparée pour le Conseil économique du Canada, 1984.

Marketing

Du potlach au macro-marketing :
évolution du concept de marketing

GEORGES M. HÉNAULT

Ν
ew York, Chicago, Los Angeles, Montréal,
Toronto, vendredi soir, même scénario. Les foules de consommateurs se ruent dans les supermarchés et centres commerciaux. Mu-
sique d'ambiance, mise en scène efficace sous les néons des magasins, couleurs chatoyantes et emplacement stratégique des emballages,
tout est prêt pour le conditionnement des acheteurs potentiels. On
raconte même que certains psychologues ont poussé leurs études si
loin qu'ils peuvent tester les réactions des cobayes de la consommation en observant l'intensité du clignement des yeux face à des
emballages nouveaux. Des psychanalystes arrivent, paraît-il, à violer
l'inconscient de ces foules solitaires. C'est la raison pour laquelle
d'ailleurs on arrive à vendre si bien les brosses à dents électriques
et autres produits inutiles. Le marketing, en un mot, synthétise ces
manipulations de l'inconscient. Phénomène nord-américain récent
(depuis la guerre de Corée), le système capitaliste semble avoir
trouvé dans cet ensemble de techniques en partie subliminales le
moyen de mieux séduire les acheteurs vélléitaires occidentaux.

Ce tableau manichéen, à peine exagéré, des « mercurophobes »
tels, en guise d'exemple, Marcuse et Packard, correspond à l'image
que nombre d'intellectuels se font du marketing. Or la réalité nous
apparaît tout autre. C'est pourquoi notre objectif consiste en une
analyse de l'évolution de ces notions par le biais d'une tentative de
démystification de ces a priori. Nous essaierons, ensuite, de cir-
conscrire le concept de marketing à partir des sophismes et paradoxes dont il est l'objet, puisqu'il a de tout temps attiré les opprobres
de l'élite bien pensante, pour enfin en souligner l'importance
contemporaine dans la mesure où il permet de mieux servir les
causes sociales, de rendre le service public plus efficace et accessible
ainsi que de répondre aux changements socio-économiques fréquents des entreprises qui semblent redécouvrir son utilité. Il s'impose en effet comme étant la nouvelle priorité organisationnelle.

UNE APPROCHE HISTORIQUE

Avant, cependant, d'aborder ainsi ces trois parties, il nous semble opportun de proposer d'ores et déjà une définition globale de ce en quoi peut consister le marketing afin de mieux saisir son évolution historique et les tendances prospectives. Le marketing est un ensemble d'attitudes et de techniques par lequel l'organisation privée, publique, parapublique ou à but nonlucratif cherche à anticiper les besoins de ses clients (consommateurs de biens, services ou causes sociales) pour mettre en marché des produits ou programmes qui leur procurent une satisfaction optimale à court et moyen terme sans aliéner pour autant le mieux-être sociétal à long terme.

L'historique s'impose d'autant plus que l'essence même du marketing pousse les décideurs à envisager le long terme, la prospective. Ces derniers oublient alors les richesses que procurent les leçons des interventions passées. Le gestionnaire moderne souffre de myopie historique.

Le potlach

Pour Alderson et Kotler, la transaction est l'échange de valeurs entre deux parties. Cette transaction entre acheteur et vendeur, entre producteur et consommateur, consiste en l'aboutissement d'un processus de transformation qui part de la conception du produit jusqu'à sa mise en marché. L'échange devient alors l'élément qui sous-tend le marketing. Quant à Bagozzi, il va plus loin lorsqu'il cherche à placer ce concept dans une démarche systémique. Le système de l'échange consiste en un ensemble d'acteurs sociaux en interaction dont la dynamique est influencée par des variables endogènes et exogènes. Il applique son modèle à la diade client-vendeur. Même si Bagozzi n'a pas pu identifier l'ampleur de l'impact de ces variables sur le processus de l'échange, il a su démontrer son importance fondamentale dans le rôle croissant du marketing.

Les balbutiements de l'échange survivent encore dans les mœurs de tribus dites « primitives »[1]. La coutume la plus connue est celle du potlach autrefois pratiquée sur la côte nord-ouest de l'Alaska[2]. Il s'agit d'un processus en deux étapes : le don et le contre-don qui se déroulent souvent lors d'événements spéciaux tels que mariage ou décès ou ayant lieu lors de phénomènes saisonniers (solstice,

---

1. Primitif est pris ici dans le sens de Guidieri (6) qui précise que « notre siècle a entrepris la réévaluation du primitif... [car] l'archaïque est non seulement l'anté-occidental mais aussi l'anti-occidental ».
2. Le potlach symbolise le plus l'origine anthropologique de l'échange.

Il n'en est pas le seul exemple. On retrouve en effet des échanges similaires sous des vocables différents. On parle, entre autres, de Taonga en pays maori ou de Kula aux îles Trobiand.

pleine lune, etc.). Ces échanges s'opèrent en marchandises de consommation courante qui ont une valeur symbolique à connotation quasi magique.

Le potlach peut être vu comme « un véritable tournoi de largesses » dont le vaincu, celui qui a donné le moins, devient le débiteur du vainqueur et ne règle sa dette qu'en renonçant à certaines de ses prérogatives. Après Davy et Malinowski, Mauss le définit comme étant « des échanges multiples et simultanés, certains désignés comme antagonistes [...] Allant jusqu'au gaspillage [...] essentiellement usuraire et somptuaire [...] pour assurer [...] une hiérarchie ».

Il ressort de ces définitions que le potlach donne à l'échange trois dimensions essentielles à nos yeux : c'est un processus à la limite du métaphysique ; il implique une dialectique du pouvoir ; il s'organise, à l'origine, autour de biens non essentiels et préfigure la notion de crédit.

D'après Braudel, « la genèse du capitalisme est strictement liée à l'échange ». La monnaie ayant été inventée pour le besoin du commerce, écrira Aristote, il est apparu une nouvelle manière d'acquérir. Changeurs et banquiers installent leurs comptoirs sur le marché (les trapézistes, ainsi était leur nom puisqu'ils utilisaient une table à quatre pieds, tetra-peza). Des opérations de change, on glisse aux opérations de banque. La création des villes permet l'éclosion de la spécialisation des tâches. Le commerce procède de l'artisanat. Le marché devient un centre naturel de la vie sociale. « On y entre autant pour acheter que pour discuter ». Au XVe siècle, foires et marchés réaniment et font tourner les échanges. Le XVIe siècle voit l'apogée des foires qui représentent une formule de transition à l'usage d'une époque et correspond à la sortie de la grande noirceur médiévale autarcique et miséreuse. La foire justifie son étymologie, la fête (feria). « Au-dessus des marchés, des boutiques, du colportage se situent [...] une puissante superstructure des échanges », pour reprendre la formule de Braudel. Les bourses et les banques prennent ainsi une place grandissante. Les foires sont créatrices de crédit par le jeu des compensations (utilisation des lettres de change). Les contrats de société où plusieurs marchands s'associent pour financer une expédition, les hanses germaniques (plus corporatistes) font penser aux consortia contemporains d'entreprises allant à la conquête des marchés mondiaux. Ces initiatives activent aussi le crédit.

Les trapézistes

Pour que le système global évolutif que l'on vient d'aborder puisse fonctionner, il est essentiel que « quelle que soit la forme de l'entente et de collaboration marchande, elle exige la fidélité, la confiance personnelle, l'exactitude, le respect de la parole donnée. D'où une sorte de morale marchande assez stricte ». Malgré tout, le commerce reste banni en tant qu'activité « improductive ». C'est une des raisons pour lesquelles les étrangers en prennent la direction ce qui, par réflexe ethnocentrique, renforce le dédain voire le mépris à l'égard des marchands. La bible elle-même dénonce, à plusieurs reprises, l'usage des poids et mesures trafiqués : « Vous ne commettrez pas d'injustice dans les mesures. Vous aurez des balances justes, des poids justes, un setier juste », affirme le Lévitique. « Car Yahvé a en abomination quiconque pratique la fraude ». Platon, qui incidemment fut marchand d'huile, éprouvait un profond mépris pour ceux qui s'engageaient dans les tâches d'échange, de distribution par opposition à ceux qui étaient « productifs » (tels les agriculteurs, les artistes ou les fabricants). C'est pourquoi Platon suggérait que ces activités soient confiées à des étrangers (les métèques[3]). Aristote, disciple de Platon, se montra encore plus virulent que son maître lorsqu'il affirma que l'agriculture est noble car elle n'enlève rien aux hommes à l'instar du commerce de détail.

Les Romains exprimèrent un dédain certain pour le commerce. Cicéron n'affirma-t-il pas à son fils « que le commerce est vil si on achète pour revendre aussitôt car on ne peut gagner qu'à force de mentir. Il ne peut rien y avoir de noble dans une boutique. S'il y a, par contre, beaucoup d'étendue, s'il distribue dans tous les lieux avec bonne foi [...] il n'y a pas de mal à en dire ». Cicéron reconnaît ainsi le bien fondé de l'utilité de lieu que le marketing est censé gérer comme une de ses fonctions essentielles. Dans la pratique, Rome abandonne très souvent le commerce de détail aux esclaves et le commerce international aux étrangers.

Les philosophes grecs et les avocats romains tiennent donc en égale mésestime les activités marchandes. Les prêtres de l'âge féodal n'échappent pas à la règle. Saint Augustin, par exemple, prêche qu'il faut savoir se limiter à demander à la terre de quoi vivre et éviter de tomber dans le piège de la tentation de la richesse (par le commerce notamment). Quant au crédit et aux prêts à intérêt, les trapézistes grecs, les argentarii romains aussi bien que les banquiers médiévaux vont les utiliser en dépit des condamnations éthiques et religieuses dont ils ont été l'objet. La philosophie tomiste s'inspire des principes aristotéliciens qui mentionnent que l'intérêt, c'est de l'argent fils de l'argent. La pensée scolastique a cependant ouvert une brèche dans ses interdits. L'intérêt devient licite quand il y a, pour le prêteur, un risque ou un manque à gagner. L'Église autorise également les prêts au Prince ou à l'État. Le rejet socio-culturel des activités mercuriales et bancaires s'explique, notamment, par le fait que crédit et commerce sont associés à étranger, idées nouvelles,

---

3. Du grec « metoikos », celui qui a changé de résidence, celui qui vient de l'extérieur. À Athènes, il lui est d'ailleurs interdit de posséder un bien foncier. Il détient des capitaux et arme les navires.

changement. Ils sont menaçants. C'est pourquoi leurs activités sont sous surveillance gouvernementale constante.

On ne peut, en effet, saisir l'évolution des activités de marketing dans toute sa dimension si on ne prend pas en considération les faits suivants : d'abord l'État contrôle les échanges et ensuite il est lui-même un marchand (pratiquant, ce que nous appellerons plus tard, le macro-marketing). L'État romain contrôle les marchés publics et possède les silos et les magasins (qui pouvaient accumuler jusqu'à dix mois de stocks). Cette emprise étatique a un coût. Cicéron en écrivant à son ami Atticus semble en être pleinement conscient lorsqu'il précise : « Tu ne comprendras rien au problème des distributions si tu oublies que cela ne peut se faire sans impôts ». De fait, force est de constater que « toutes les civilisations reposant sur la consommation des céréales ont laissé des preuves documentées de l'intervention de l'État dans le commerce des grains, tout au moins pendant les périodes où il y avait un risque de pénurie dans les villes ».

Ces contraintes bureaucratiques pesant sur les activités d'échange se maintiennent pendant la période du mercantilisme[4], tout en manifestant une attitude beaucoup plus positive à l'égard des marchés et des marchands. Le commerce n'est plus une activité inférieure. Il devient dans les faits l'un des fondements de l'État. Richelieu, qui se soucie assez peu des problèmes économiques, n'aura pas d'autres préoccupations, et il affirme qu'il faut « donner prix au traffic et rang aux marchands ». Retour du pendule avec les physiocrates qui s'inscrivent en faux contre les pratiques mercantilistes. La terre (et l'agriculture), disait Quesnay, est la seule cause ; le commerce, qu'un effet. Ce dernier ne produit rien. Il ne peut être utile qu'en transmettant des produits agricoles aux consommateurs. On retrouve cependant les utilités de lieu et peut-être aussi de possession (besoin d'acquisition du produit) chères au marketing. Puis arrive la première révolution industrielle, les débuts de la division du travail stimulant la spécialisation. Adam Smith est un des premiers à insister sur le fait que l'objectif de la production, c'est la vente. L'État semble perdre de son influence relative quant à son intervention sur les marchés. L'entreprise privée assume un rôle clé dans le contrôle et la dynamisation des échanges commerciaux. On entre dans la période du libéralisme économique, de 1850 à 1914, pendant laquelle le volume du commerce mondial tripla.

---

4. Nous n'entrons pas dans le dédale des controverses et paradoxes du mercantilisme qui semble avoir été une quasi-doctrine édictée au XIXe siècle pour expliquer l'évolution des faits économiques et commerciaux des deux siècles précédents.

MYTHES ET PARADOXES DU MARKETING

Le taylorisme et ses applications chez Ford symbolisent l'entrée dans l'ère de la production de masse. La qualité et le prix sont alors les points essentiels d'un programme de marketing. Puis, pendant l'entre-deux-guerres, la nécessité de vendre cette offre accrue s'impose. On développe alors les réseaux de distribution de masse. Après la Deuxième Guerre mondiale et celle de Corée surtout, l'Amérique du Nord se retrouve dans ce que les sociologues appellent la société de consommation. L'apparition de la télévision accélère l'importance des communications de masse. Les principaux outils de la direction commerciale que sont le produit (et sa qualité), le prix, la distribution et la promotion ne suffisent pas à influencer l'entreprise dans la définition d'une démarche proprement marketing. Levitt, dans un article désormais célèbre, démontre que les organisations sont dans l'ensemble préoccupées plus par la production que par les besoins du marché. Elles souffrent de myopie en marketing. Elles cherchent à davantage adapter la demande à leurs produits qu'à adapter leurs produits à la demande. L'utilisation des outils précités se dynamise lorsque Borden les place au sein de l'environnement multidimensionnel que sont les forces incontrôlables (politique, économique, socio-culturelle, technologique, etc.). On parle alors de marketing mix ou de composé de marketing.

L'entreprise (américaine surtout) s'internationalise. La conjoncture économique s'avère particulièrement favorable jusqu'au premier choc pétrolier. Ces succès indéniables contribuent à mystifier l'influence quasi démoniaque du marketing. Les groupes de pression, symbolisés par Ralph Nader, poussent les gouvernements à légiférer. L'opinion publique, ou tout au moins son sous-ensemble élitiste, se fait plus pressante. On assiste à une résurgence et à un renforcement de la mercurophobie. Cherchons donc à en comprendre les raisons, en situant le débat au niveau socio-culturel, afin de combattre certains mythes, d'une part, et en analysant le paradoxe du marketing victime de sa propre myopie technicienne, d'autre part.

Mercurophobie et culture de la consommation

Les mercurophobes fondent, pour l'essentiel, leur argumentation sur deux sophismes : celui de la création des besoins et de la rationalité violée par le conditionnement commercial. La publicité télévisée (de fait la partie la plus visible de l'iceberg nommé marketing) crée les besoins (superflus, est-il nécessaire de le préciser ?) des consommateurs ou spectateurs anesthésiés. Or, dans la société occidentale, les besoins primaires sont satisfaits (manger, boire, se loger, se vêtir). Cet ensemble de besoins est inhérent à la nature humaine. Le marketing ne les a donc pas créés. C'est là une évidence banale. Ce terme fait aussi allusion aux dimensions psychologiques (sécurité, accomplissement, etc.) et psycho-culturelles (le travail, la concurrence, la consommation d'alcool et de tabac) de nos attitudes et comportements. Dans cette catégorie propre à la dynamique sociale, il semble possible d'affirmer qu'elle est le fruit de l'interaction de nombreux facteurs. Nous pensons, entre autres, à l'impact de la technologie qui se manifeste par la création de nouveaux produits et au jeu des forces sociales dont l'influence sur le consommateur est omniprésente.

N'oublions pas que l'acheteur est un animal social. Socrate l'avait bien observé lorsqu'il dit à Xanthipe : « Tu ne sors pas pour voir mais pour être vu ». Ce qui explique partiellement le deuxième mythe que l'on se propose d'aborder. Le deuxième mythe, celui de la rationalité, provient de l'effort des micro-économistes, universalistes dans leur approche, de schématiser le consommateur en un homo œconomicus. Il se propage sous l'influence des bienveillants consommateuristes qui cherchent à imposer aux autres un comportement logique, utile et rationnel. Les psychologues ne s'accordent ni entre eux ni avec leurs collègues économistes à ce propos. Nous nous contentons donc de mettre de l'avant deux écoles de pensée qui, en dépit des apparences, se rejoignent sur le fait que les individus ne sont pas rationnels. Nous pensons à l'approche freudienne qui prône l'irrationnel inconscient (motivations inconscientes fondées sur la libido forçant l'individu à un comportement substitut socialement accepté [...] par le biais de la consommation d'automobiles de sport ou encore de cigares ou de cigarettes) et à l'école de la gestalt qui prêche le non-rationnel conscient. (Autrement dit, on sait fort bien que l'on se procure tel type de voiture afin de mieux s'imposer aux membres de nos divers groupes d'appartenance). Ce mythe de la rationalité est d'autant plus important à combattre, en marketing, que l'entreprise est condamnée à la conquête des marchés internationaux où cette notion revêt des connotations culturelles fort différenciées à travers le monde.

La technicité du marketing à effets de boomerang

Les outils d'analyse des marchés et des comportements se raffinent ; les stratégies des entreprises utilisent de plus en plus l'approche du marketing, c'est-à-dire qu'elles cherchent à satisfaire davantage les désirs des clients. On devrait s'attendre donc à une diminution des critiques à l'égard des techniques marchandes. Il n'en est rien. Levitt souligne ce paradoxe en constatant le nombre croissant de plaintes qui semble augmenter en fonction directe d'une volonté plus systématique de mieux servir le client. Cela s'explique, entre autres raisons, par un ennui que les consommateurs éprouvent face à la saturation des messages publicitaires, dont un petit nombre seulement est censé les rejoindre, les intéresser et enfin les motiver à l'achat.

De fait, il nous semble qu'une technicité de plus en plus élaborée accroît la myopie du marketing et crée des dysfonctions paradoxales.

La recherche en marketing s'est aiguisée, sous l'influence de l'informatique, à un point tel que l'utilisation par les concurrents d'une industrie des mêmes techniques sur les mêmes marchés conduit à l'apparition de produits quasi similaires dont la ressemblance est frappante. En paraphrasant quelque peu Crozier, on peut déduire de l'informatisation de la recherche en marketing qu'elle contribue au renforcement de la myopie marchande. En effet, la mise en place des ordinateurs a renforcé l'importance du contrôle à court terme, au détriment d'une gestion centrée sur une perspective à moyen et long terme. L'analyse des résultats de plus en plus fréquents concentre l'attention des preneurs de décision sur des solutions à des problèmes urgents et pas nécessairement importants. Il nous semble également opportun de préciser que le raffinement des techniques de recherche accroît la quantité d'informations disponibles et fait ainsi mieux prendre conscience des nombreux risques à courir. Une connaissance plus élaborée paralyse l'action. Les preneurs de décision se confinent dans un conservatisme que les contrôles informatiques renforcent.

Les politiques de produit et celles de promotion peuvent se révéler en contradiction alors qu'elles devraient contribuer à une meilleure synergie du système de marketing. Ainsi, le souci impérieux de « positionner » le produit sur un segment précis impose une promotion sur des médias qui dépassent largement, par une audience multidimensionnelle, l'auditoire visé. En d'autres termes, la structure des médias impose une politique de segmentation plus grossière et moins précise que ce que la recherche en marketing suggère. Si un produit peut être adapté sans trop de difficultés à un sous-ensemble précis du marché, sa promotion doit passer par les Fourches Caudines de la programmation des médias.

La publicité de masse deviendrait-elle une variable incontrôlable alors que tous les auteurs ayant défini le composé de marketing la percevaient comme une variable contrôlable ?

LA LÉGITIMATION DU MARKETING

Le marketing s'ennoblit. Il voit ses principes servir des causes telles la Croix-Rouge ou l'UNICEF. Il devient marketing social. Il dépasse les frontières micro-économiques de l'entreprise pour aider les gouvernements à mieux « saisir » les besoins de la population. On parle alors de macro-marketing. Cette légitimation du marketing a donc été le fruit de l'élargissement des applications de son concept. Paradoxalement, cette période (1975-1985) correspond à la récession pendant laquelle les fonctions de contrôle et de finance ont dominé les préoccupations des gestionnaires du secteur privé, et ce, au détriment des activités de marketing reléguées ainsi au deuxième plan. C'est pourquoi on assiste à une résurgence de son importance stratégique, qui se justifie d'autant plus que l'on redécouvre les vertus du troc.

Le marketing social, ou l'obtention des lettres de noblesse en se mettant au service des causes sociales

Kotler fut un des pionniers dans la démystification du marketing perçu comme un outil dont l'unique mission est de créer et maintenir la demande d'un produit. Il a démontré que le niveau de cette demande peut être inférieur, égal ou supérieur aux objectifs souhaités. C'est ainsi qu'il énumère quatre états où ce niveau est inférieur : la demande négative, l'absence de demande, la demande latente, et la demande défaillante. Deux autres états sont jugés satisfaisants : la demande en dent de scie et celle qui est soutenue. Enfin deux états constituent une surdemande : la demande débordante puis la nocive. À chaque état de la demande correspond une tâche spécifique du marketing. Quand la demande est négative, on essaie de la détromper ; quand elle est absente, on cherche à la créer ; quand elle est débordante, on tente de la réduire. De ce schéma, on voit poindre l'exemple de l'utilité du marketing dans la gestion des hôpitaux dont l'offre ne suffit plus à l'afflux de patients. Il faut donc chercher à réduire la demande par un marketing de dissuasion. Ce dernier peut prendre la forme, en guise d'illustration, d'une campagne de sensibilisation à la médecine préventive que tout un chacun peut entreprendre chez soi.

Bref, la porte au développement du marketing social est ouverte. Kotler, encore lui, en propose une définition intéressante. Il s'agit de la mise en marché et de la gestion de « programmes cherchant à accroître l'acceptabilité, auprès d'un groupe-cible, d'une idée ou pratique sociale. Il utilise les concepts de segmentation, recherche sur le consommateur, communication [...] et la théorie de l'échange, afin de maximiser la réponse du groupe-cible ». Les exemples de l'utilisation du marketing social aux causes dites nobles abondent : les fédéralistes mondiaux qui proposent un gouvernement supranational, les différents groupes religieux qui utilisent la publicité et les programmes télévisés pour propager leur foi ; les groupes bénévoles qui s'occupent des délaissés, etc.

Il semble opportun de préciser qu'il y a quelques différences entre le marketing social et celui de l'entreprise privée. Tout d'abord, le gestionnaire commercial cherche à identifier les besoins et désirs d'un marché-cible alors que le responsable d'une cause sociale tente de changer les attitudes et comportements des groupes visés. Ensuite, l'objectif est, dans un cas, d'optimiser l'utilisation des ressources et, dans l'autre, de servir les intérêts de la société. Enfin, le secteur privé met en marché des produits ou des services. Le marketing social « commercialise » des idées et des causes sociales.

Le macro-marketing : l'État au service de ses administrés

« Le macro-marketing est un processus socio-économique qui dirige le flux de biens et services d'une économie [en allant] des producteurs aux consommateurs de façon à harmoniser les capacités hétérogènes de l'offre à celles de la demande, tout en servant les objectifs de la société à court et long terme ». L'accent est placé, dès lors, en comparaison implicite avec le micro-marketing des entreprises privées, sur le système dans son ensemble et sur la façon dont il opère de par l'interdépendance des producteurs et des consommateurs. On peut affirmer, en d'autres termes, que le macro-marketing se préoccupe de l'efficacité avec laquelle une société utilise ses ressources rares et de la justice sociale dans l'allocation de ses biens et services à court, moyen et long terme ; il va sans dire que le tout est fonction des objectifs poursuivis. Cette approche peut donc être utilisée, en principe, indépendamment du système politique en place.

La démarche du macro-marketing (marketing gouvernemental ou public sont, à nos yeux, des termes équivalents) se concentre sur l'analyse du système des relations entre l'administration et son public. Pour Laufer et Burlaud, les composantes de cet ensemble reposent sur l'information du public, l'étude du public (qui se justifie d'autant plus que les canaux traditionnels du système politique semblent défaillants), la distribution du service public et la définition d'une politique cohérente qui procède de la logique globale de l'analyse de système. L'apport de l'approche marketing est alors double : prise en compte des moyens du service public (étude des besoins de la population, communication, le cas échéant la politique de prix, etc.) ainsi que l'identification des facteurs d'environnement. La démarche du macro-marketing se différencie de celle du secteur privé par les distinctions à opérer entre marché et public, par l'existence d'un sous-système politique et d'un mode de financement spécifique. Il s'agit, dans ce dernier cas, d'un système de paiement indirect puisque ce service est, en général, offert gratuitement aux contribuables, quoique financé par leurs impôts. La politique de prix devient alors complexe.

Le micro-marketing, nouvelle priorité de l'entreprise en période de résurgence du troc au niveau mondial

L'état du marketing actuel, dont la dynamique stratégique a été reléguée au deuxième plan au profit de la direction des finances, doit reprendre d'autant plus le dessus dans la conduite des affaires que les marchés nationaux stagnent. Les marchés internationaux, quant à eux, changent structurellement. Le troc y fait une réapparition autant paradoxale qu'impressionnante. On estime qu'il s'accapare dans les années quatre-vingt quelque 20 à 30 % du volume du commerce mondial[5]. Les marchés intérieurs subissent de surcroît

---

5. En juillet 1982, *Business Week* (28) l'évaluait à 25-30 %. En mai 1983, l'Association canadienne des exportations (29) l'estimait à 25 %. En mars 1984, le Département du commerce des États-Unis (30) prédisait qu'en l'an 2000, ce pourcentage atteindrait 50 %.

de profonds changements structurels. Les comportements démographiques et culturels nord-américains vont se caractériser vers la fin de la décennie par un vieillissement de la population, une diminution relative de l'importance de la famille (57 % des ménages seront composés d'une ou deux personnes en 1988 aux États-Unis en comparaison de 47 % en 1970) et l'éclatement du marché de masse en sous-groupes nombreux aux modes de vie différents. Les technologies nouvelles fournissent aux identités culturelles l'occasion de renaître, aux différences personnelles la possibilité de s'affirmer. Aux États-Unis, encore et toujours, pas moins de 4 000 réseaux de télévision par câble reflètent la mosaïque ethnique et religieuse du pays, la diversité des motivations des abonnés, depuis la formation permanente jusqu'aux jeux ou films spécialisés.

Face à cette tendance dichotomisée des marchés de consommation qui, d'une part, s'internationalisent et, d'autre part, se régionalisent (au sens de sous-ensemble du marché national et non de regroupement supranational), la fonction marketing va retrouver sa place prépondérante qui lui est dévolue au sein du processus stratégique de l'entreprise. Quelles en sont les spécificités prévisibles ?

Sur le plan national, les marchés se différencient de plus en plus. Cela implique au moins deux types de changement. Tout d'abord, un positionnement plus précis s'impose afin de freiner la prolifération des marques et emballages et les tendances de microsegmentation non rentables ; la différenciation des produits devient un atout stratégique à dominer. Deuxièmement, afin de mieux coller à la réalité mouvante de ces marchés éclatés, une nécessaire décentralisation des fonctions du marketing s'impose. C'est dans cet esprit que la firme américaine Campbell vient de passer de 4 à 50 divisions afin justement de pouvoir faire face à l'évolution des modes de vie des consommateurs de demain.

Sur le plan international, la résurgence du troc entraîne une conception plus complexe des échanges mondiaux. La fixation du prix se fait alors en fonction de critères modifiés pour refléter les risques différenciés ainsi encourus. Le produit dont on « hérite » dans le cas de troc « pur » (du jambon yougoslave contre des boeings en guise d'exemple véridique) possède des caractéristiques de qualité, d'emballage plus difficilement contrôlables.

CONCLUSION

Fer de lance de la stratégie des organisations, le marketing a de tout temps existé. Même s'il apparaît comme un mal aimé dans l'histoire des civilisations, ses détracteurs lui reconnaissent les fonctions d'utilité de temps (entreposage), de lieu (distribution), de possession (prix et promotion) et d'aspect (conditionnement et emballage du produit). Le marketing, une attitude ainsi qu'un ensemble de techniques, est central à l'échange qui revêt des valeurs anthropologico-économiques. Il doit donc s'adapter aux spécificités culturelles des marchés. Il s'avère un outil indispensable à tous les types d'organisations, indépendamment de leur environnement politique, afin de mieux harmoniser l'offre et la demande. Il est censé fournir un cadre analytique de réflexion et d'action, par lequel l'entreprise conçoit ses biens et services en fonction des attentes des marchés nationaux et internationaux à moyen et long terme.

Cependant, il n'est pas une panacée. Il ne peut être cet outil « scientifique » à visée manipulatrice qui crée des besoins. Il est paradoxalement desservi par une recherche de plus en plus élaborée qui fournit un trop plein d'informations dont l'analyse paralyse et devient une fin en soi ; ce qui nuit à la prise de risque. Il permet une approche rigoureuse, systématique et systémique. Qu'il s'agisse donc de micro ou macro-marketing aussi bien que de marketing social, nous avons là une philosophie d'action dont les résultats, soumis aux impondérables des nombreuses variables incontrôlables, sont fonction de la qualité et de l'éthique de ses utilisateurs [...] à l'instar de la langue d'Ésope.

BIBLIOGRAPHIE

ALDERSON, W., Dynamic Marketing Behavior, Homewood, Ill., Irwin, 1965.

ASUNDI, R., « Marketing as Exchange », Developments in Marketing Science, J. Rogers, édit., vol. 6, 1983, 252-258.

BAGOZZI, R., « Marketing as an Organized Behavioral System of Exchange », Journal of Marketing, vol. 38, décembre 1974, 77-81.

BAGOZZI, R., « Marketing as Exchange », Journal of Marketing, vol. 39, octobre 1975, 32-39.

BIHL-WILLETTE, L. , Une histoire du mouvement consommateur, mille ans de lutte, Paris, Aubier, 1984, 16.

BORDEN, N., « The Concept of the Marketing Mix », Journal of Advertising Research, vol. 2, (2), juin 1964, 2-7.

BRAUDEL, F., Civilisation matérielle, économie et capitalisme, XVe-XVIIIe siècle : Les jeux de l'échange, tome 2, Paris, A. Colin, 1979, 12.

« New Restrictions on World Trade », Business Week, 19 juillet 1982, 118-122.

« Marketing : The New Priority ; A Splintered Mass Market Forces Companies to Target their Products », Business Week, n° 2817, nov. 21, 1983, 96-106.

« Marketing, The New Priority », Business Week, n°. 2817, nov. 21, 1983.

Export Marketing : The Case of Countertrade, Canadian Export Associations, 1983.

CHEBAT, J. C., HÉNAULT, G., Stratégie du marketing : modèles et concepts, Montréal, Presses de l'Université du Québec, 1977, 262 p.

COOPER, R., « Why Countertrade ? », Across the Board, mars 1984, 36-41.

CROZIER, M., Le Mal américain, Paris, Fayard, 1980.

FARCY (de) H., Commerce agricole et développement, Paris, S.P.E.S., 1966, 70.

GUIDIERI, R., L'Abondance des pauvres : six aperçus critiques sur l'anthropologie, Paris, Le Seuil, 1984, 12.

KOTLER, P., « A Generic Concept of Marketing », Journal of Marketing, vol. 36, avril 1972, 46-54.

KOTLER, P., « Marketing et contre-marketing », Le management, juin-juillet 1974, 42-47.

KOTLER, P., Marketing for Non Profit Organizations, Englewood Cliffs, N.J., Prentice-Hall, 1975, 283.

LAUFER, R., BURLAUD, A., Le management public, Paris, Dalloz, 1980, 106-107.

LEVITT, T., Marketing Myopia, Harvard Business Review, juillet-août 1960, 45-56.

LEVITT, T., The Marketing Imagination, New York, The Free Press, 1983, chapitre VIII.

MAUSS, M., « Essai sur le don. Forme et raison de l'échange dans les sociétés archaïques (1923-1924) », Sociologie en anthropologie, Paris, P.U.F., 1950, 152-153.

McCARTHY, SHAPIRO, S., Basic Marketing, 2e édition canadienne, Homewood, Ill., Irwin, 1980, 8-9.

SCARDIGLI, V., La Consommation, culture du quotidien, Paris, Presses Universitaires de France, 1983.

SEDILLOT, R., *Histoire des marchands et des marchés*, Paris, Fayard 1964, 13.

SPITZ, P., « The Public Granary : An Historical Basis for State Intervention », *Ceres*, nov.-déc. 1979, 17.

Social Marketing in Canadian Context

SADRUDIN A. AHMED

In recent years, the role of marketing has expanded beyond the sphere of commercial profit-making organizations. Social marketing (the marketing of social causes) as a distinct application area for public and nonprofit marketing has been known in the United States for well over a decade, but here in Canada, it is a more recent development. However, groups such as health organizations, energy departments, social service agencies, and cultural organizations have begun to apply social marketing to such causes as family planning, energy conservation, improvement of fitness levels, antismoking campaigns, prevention of drug and alcohol abuse, prevention of venereal disease, and promotion of safer driving. While there is still room for improvement, examples do now exist which demonstrate a high level of skill and professionalism in developing and executing nonbusiness marketing programs in Canada.

A number of prominent American academic journals such as the *Harvard Business Review*, the *Journal of Marketing*, and the *Journal of Consumer Research* have given increasing prominence to articles dealing with issues related to social marketing and the contribution made by these articles has been reviewed by Kotler, Zaltman, Fox, Bloom, Novelli, and Shapiro. The reviews provide a conceptual and anecdotal background to the domain of social marketing in general. By using the insights drawn from these extensive reviews of the literature and by examining some of the successes and frustrations encountered in executing social marketing programs here in Canada, this article will demonstrate that these marketing techniques can profitably be applied to the promotion of social causes in this country. Furthermore, it will be shown that managers of Canadian organizations entrusted with responsibility for social change must understand the social exchange process and must define their social product. Realistic marketing analysis and planning will thus enable these social change agents to improve their operations substantially.

To illustrate the effectiveness and feasibility of social marketing as an approach to social change in Canada, the article will begin with the following two questions: What is social marketing? What situations call for social marketing? It will then deal with the tools and techniques applied by social marketers, namely, market analysis, market segmentation, product policy, pricing, distribution channels, and communications. This discussion will identify some of the problems that arise when the marketing techniques used in selling commercial products are applied in the sphere of social change. In conclusion, strategies for introducing marketing into Canadian social organizations will be discussed.

WHAT IS SOCIAL MARKETING?

Social marketing is conceived of as the application of marketing concepts and techniques to the promotion of various socially beneficial ideas and causes. Synonymous terms might be "social cause marketing," "social idea marketing," or "public issue marketing."

One can best understand social marketing by seeing it in relation to the more common approaches used to promote social causes, namely, the legal, coercive, and persuasive approaches. These can be illustrated with respect to the problem of excessive alcohol consumption in Canada, for example. The legal approach is to pass laws which raise the drinking age. The coercive approach pressures bars to refuse to serve liquor to patrons who are already drunk by threatening nonrenewal of liquor licenses. The persuasive approach can be seen in advertising campaigns which draw attention to the effect of excessive alcohol consumption on physical and social well-being.

The main thrust of social marketing lies in the persuasive approach, although elements of the other approaches may also be included. Many cause groups in Canada, impressed by the effectiveness of private sector advertising campaigns, have used advertising to attempt to change public attitudes and behavior. Canadian advertising campaigns designed to reduce smoking, promote safety in the workplace, encourage the wearing of seat belts, prevent drunks from driving, and encourage conversion to the metric system are but some of the examples of the use of a persuasive approach to bring about social change.

However, social advertising alone is not enough. Unless preceded by careful social planning and programming, it amounts to "a shot in the dark." According to the marketing concept, a Canadian social change agent interested, for example, in reducing cigarette consumption in Canada should begin the planning task with a careful analysis of the smoking public. This smoking public may then be divided into subgroups or segments for each of whom a separate antismoking campaign can be launched. For example, adolescent smokers, adolescent potential smokers, adult light smokers, and adult heavy smokers may be treated as distinct groups. For each of these groups a social marketing program dealing with the product, with pricing, distribution, and communication (including advertising specially designed for them) should be formulated. Social advertising, although very important, would only be a part of the total marketing program.

WHAT SITUATIONS CALL FOR SOCIAL MARKETING?

Although social marketing has the potential to be applied to a wide variety of social problems, it appears to be particularly appropriate in situations where new information about new practices is to be disseminated, when counter-marketing is needed, or when activation is required.

Let us consider the case of metric measurement in Canada. Until recently, most Canadians were accustomed to using only imperial measurements in their daily lives. Most of us grew up using yards, feet, and inches as measures of length. It is not easy to persuade such a society to accept the metre, centimetre, and millimetre as new measures. The strong objections raised by segments of the Canadian population to metric conversion are a good example of resistance to change. Because changes in units of measurement have such a widespread impact on our lives, the federal metric commission could not rely simply on the educational system and media publicity to promote the change. New information had to be transmitted widely and rapidly to the general public through television and other mass media channels. A systematic metric conversion program for the production and distribution of goods had to be drawn up with the private sector to stimulate and reinforce the use of a metric measurement system. This is an example of the use of marketing techniques to promote a new practice.

An illustration of counter-marketing is given by the measures taken to discourage cigarette smoking by Canadians. Federal laws requiring disclosure of the nicotine content of cigarettes, high federal and provincial excise taxes which raise the price of tobacco products, federal, provincial, and municipal regulations restricting the smoking of cigarettes in public places, and antismoking advertisements on television are all examples of such counter-marketing.

Often people know what they should do, but do not act accordingly. For example, people "know" that they should get more exercise, but do nothing about it. In such situations, the task of social marketing is one of activation: moving people from intention to action. Hence the "Participaction" campaign by Health and Welfare Canada applied social marketing to move Canadians from the stage of intention to actual participation in physical exercise programs.

METHODOLOGY

Market Analysis

Social marketing begins with the study of the needs, wants, perceptions, habits, satisfaction levels, and desires of the target public before the social cause marketing program is developed. After the analysis of the target public's needs and desires, a social program, product, or cause is developed and other marketing tools, namely, pricing, distribution, and communications are applied to ensure the successful launching of a new or modified social product.

However, many social organizations in Canada have done little consumer research. This is because to gather primary data on their target consumers, they must ask questions about such sensitive topics as drinking and driving, venereal diseases, and drug and alcohol abuse. Such topics touch the public's deepest fears, anxieties, and values. Therefore, people are more likely to give inaccurate, self-serving, or socially desirable answers to such questions. Furthermore, such social behaviors tend to be extremely complex and usually hinge on more than one or two variables.

Nevertheless, it has been contended that with patience and the creative application of survey research techniques, valuable data can be collected. For example, by collecting survey data on drug and alcohol abuse at regular intervals and supplementing them with limited but innovative research on small, specific groups such as heroin users, the Addiction Research Foundation of Toronto has gained insights into the alcohol and drug culture as it relates to Canadian young people. Similarly, in order to prepare for the eventual reformulation of the welfare assistance program as a Guaranteed Annual Income Programme, the federal and Manitoba governments carried out a social test marketing program in Dauphin, Manitoba. Results of the test market were to be used to modify different aspects of the income assistance product and to design the most appropriate promotional strategy and distribution system for the income supplementation program.

Market Segmentation

The process of dividing up the market into homogeneous segments and then developing unique marketing programs for individual target segments is fundamental to modern marketing. However, the notion of treating certain groups of people differentially or with special attention while perhaps ignoring other groups completely is not consistent with the egalitarian and antidiscriminatory philosophies that pervade many social agencies. The data collection problems alluded to earlier also impede this segmentation.

These difficulties can be overcome. For example, the Saskatchewan Advisory Committee on Venereal Disease Control Programme was able to segment the market in its campaign to curb the increasing spread of sexually transmitted diseases. On the basis of secondary data, the public in Saskatchewan was first divided into the potential and actual carriers of sexually transmitted diseases such as gonorrhea and syphilis. It was further subdivided into male and female segments. Opinion leaders such as doctors, nurses, and teachers were given particular attention. It was then possible to carry out an advertising, promotional, and publicity media campaign directed specifically at each one of these segments throughout an overall marketing mix plan.

MARKETING MIX

Product Policy

Once a social organization has chosen its basic markets and analyzed their needs and preferences, it is ready to enter into a more tactical analysis of the problems of achieving the desired market response. There are a great many marketing tools an organization can use to facilitate the relationship it is seeking with its target markets. These tools make up the marketing mix. The most common classification of these tools is product, price, distribution, and communication. A general social marketer should understand the basics of these tools and be able to combine them in preparing a social marketing plan.

Product policy formulation, the first of these tools, is at the very core of business marketing. It determines the range of products which a company offers. The definition of product is more important in the social environment than in the business environment because it is more elusive than just goods and services. Such intangible products as the creation of greater tolerance towards disadvantaged groups such as mentally and physically handicapped persons or members of visible minority groups are very different from physical products such as competing brands of toothpaste.

The complexity of product policy varies from one social organization to another. Some organizations such as the Canadian University Service Overseas can have a relatively simple product policy because their mission is limited to the recruitment and placement of young Canadians abroad for altruistic missions such as teaching, farming, and rural development. On the other hand, launching of a complex social product such as the prevention of automobile accident fatalities in Canada requires dealing with automobile manufacturers, police forces, politicians, and the general public. Decisions might be made to upgrade automobile passenger safety by such federal government measures as requiring automobile manufacturers to provide inflatable air bags as a standard device in cars to reduce the impact on a passenger during a car accident. Attempts might be made to persuade provinces to vigorously promote safety measures such as the use of safety belts. Product policy decisions also play a role in social resource allocation decisions. For example, should oil self-sufficiency in Canada be brought about through increased energy conservation by the public, through extensive resource development in Canada by the oil companies or a combination of both? It is difficult, and often impossible, to assess the actual benefits of current products; it is even more difficult to assess the potential benefits of prospective products.

The problem of assessing benefits is further aggravated when different groups of clients are involved. Making air bags mandatory on motor vehicles may reduce accident fatality rates but the impact of such a move on the Canadian economy must be considered. Mandatory installation of air bags will make cars more expensive and generally have a negative impact on corporate profits and employment in the automobile industry.

By systematic assessment of a social product policy a social organization is able to avoid pitfalls caused by the ad hoc development of social programs. For example, Health and Welfare Canada treated stimulation of physical fitness as a new product and subjected the social product Participaction to all stages of the product development process, including test marketing. Part of the immense success of Participaction can be attributed to the social marketing approach taken to its launch. The experience gained from a preliminary test marketing of the product in Saskatoon was invaluable for building a national communications and publicity campaign for Participaction.

In devising product policy, social administrators face three main decisions with respect to their product line. Product addition is the challenge of finding and adding new products to the line, as, for example, in the addition of Participaction to the "health improvement" product line. Product addition calls for the following carefully handled stages: idea generation and screening, concept development and testing, social cost-benefit analysis, product development, test marketing, and product introduction. Product modification is the challenge of developing or modifying product attributes. An example of this can be seen in the case of income maintenance for Canada's poor by eventually providing a new, improved, guaranteed annual income product rather than the present welfare payments product. The expectation is of course that through this product modification, Health and Welfare Canada will be able to improve the service to its client public. Finally, product elimination is the task of deciding when a product should be dropped from the line (e.g., dropping the baby bonus from the income maintenance line) because it no longer serves a valuable social purpose, and how the product should be phased out.

Product Pricing

In a profit-motivated organization, pricing is used as a tool to meet the long-term objectives of a firm whether they be survival, growth, or a combination of these two. The price is expressed in terms of the monetary cost charged for the purchase of goods and services provided to a customer. In a social organization pricing is used to meet the objective of providing the maximum social gain for the society. More often than not, the price charged for a social product is nonmonetary in nature and can include the more personal costs of time, effort, love, power, and pride. Alcoholics Anonymous, for example, charges a very high price to its members. It requires new members to make a commitment never to drink again and to make public admission of their problem to other members. Canadian police departments promote crime prevention, for example, by reducing the price in terms of the time and effort expended by a household in protection against burglary. A police officer is made available, free of charge, to provide advice on the steps that can be taken by households to make the home more secure against burglary attempts.

One major problem encountered in making a social pricing decision is how to ensure equity in pricing. Medical insurance premiums are charged to most Canadians whether they wish to participate in such a social insurance program or not. Moreover, the medical insurance premium in a province such as Ontario is not directly tied to income. Thus, the real burden of medical insurance coverage for a low income earner in Ontario is higher than that for a person with higher income. Present debate in Canada on health services price items, such as extra billing by doctors and user fees in hospitals, illustrates this problem of equity in pricing. Although there is no magic solution to this problem, by recognizing the issue, one can try to promote equity in pricing. In Quebec, for example, the cost of medical insurance is tied to income; the rich thus pay a higher insurance premium than the poor.

Distribution Channels

In profit-motivated companies, channels of distribution provide a place to sell the company's product and to disseminate information about it. In the business world, retailers receive profit on the products they sell and therefore are motivated to provide a service to their suppliers and their clients. Unfortunately, Canadian social marketers cannot often provide this profit incentive. For example, the ideal way to encourage fitness among the working Canadian population is to promote exercise programs at the work place. However, not all employers are willing to implement such programs. To get around the difficulties involved in the distribution of social products, new and creative approaches are needed. For example, in order to distribute literature dealing with nutrition, Health and Welfare Canada solicited the support of pharmacists and doctors. The health concerns felt by both these groups were instrumental in making better nutrition information available to the members of the public. In another example, the Canadian Red Cross facilitates blood donorship by providing clinics on the premises of large institutions making it easier for potential donors to give blood.

To design efficient distribution, delivery, or dissemination systems, a social organization must first decide on the level and quality of service to be offered to its target market. Usually it cannot afford to maximize the public's convenience, so it resorts to less expensive solutions. The Canadian Red Cross, for example, cannot provide clinics on the premises of small companies, so, in order to serve these donors, it will often hold clinics in major shopping centers. A social organization's second problem is to decide on the number and location of branches given the location pattern of its clients. For example, where should a province locate its offices to provide welfare assistance to those in need? Its final problem is to decide how much of the services should be provided by the organization and how much contracted out to others. Should a social welfare department provide homemaker services for the elderly itself or should the contract to provide the service be given to another institution?

Communication Program

All social organizations find it necessary to direct communications to their publics. The most commonly used communications instruments are advertising, publicity, and personal contacts. The first step in developing a communications program is to clarify the objectives. What is the target public? What target effects are to be sought? This is followed by the preparation of a budget, selection of the medium of communication (television, newspapers, etc.), and the evaluation of the communication strategy.

Communication programs have been widely used by social marketers to bring about social change. Advertising campaigns urging the public to pay attention to road safety, energy conservation, and cancer and heart checkups are already quite familiar to Canadians. It may, therefore, seem that the application of this marketing tool to the promotion of social causes should not present any special problem.

However, a number of problems are encountered in developing communication programs for social causes. Many members of social organizations feel cheapened by the use of hard sell, fear, or humorous appeals, even though these may be the most appropriate creative strategy for them. Social organizations need to say more to a consumer in a media message than does a private sector marketer. For example, prevention of sexually transmitted diseases requires a more detailed explanation of the product to its client groups than does the selling of soft drinks such as Coca Cola or Pepsi Cola.

In addition, it is often difficult to evaluate the effectiveness of a social advertising campaign. If, after an advertising campaign directed at curbing the incidence of sexually transmitted diseases, the number of reported cases of such diseases rises, what conclusions may be drawn? Was the campaign unsuccessful in curbing the diseases? Or was it successful because a large number of individuals who may not have sought help before are seeking it now?

Canadian social marketers can meet the difficulty of evaluating the effectiveness of social advertising in this case by looking beyond such secondary data as epidemiological statistics dealing with the reported incidence of sexually transmitted diseases. More and more, innovative types of research projects are being carried out by enlightened Canadian social organizations. The use of health care professionals as respondents to gather in-depth information on the effectiveness of advertising campaigns dealing with issues such as sexually transmitted diseases is one example of the innovative use of survey research to collect data indirectly. In order to evaluate the economy, efficiency, and effectiveness of social programs, some social marketers are developing new techniques so that information may be gathered in a sophisticated, innovative, and systematic fashion. As more experience is gained with social marketing programs in Canada, it will become easier to interpret the social statistics in order to evaluate the effectiveness of the marketing approach.

INTRODUCTION OF MARKETING
INTO SOCIAL ORGANIZATIONS

In response to public pressure to operate more economically, effectively, and efficiently, managers of Canadian social organizations have begun to take a greater interest in marketing. To meet public demands for accountability these organizations have already looked at financial management, accounting systems, personnel administration, and the formal planning process. Unfortunately, however, marketing as such, which of all the classic business functions is the last to arrive on the scene, has negative connotations for many of the people working in these public and private organizations. They see marketing as an ensemble of manipulative advertising and selling techniques. However, as this article shows, this is not a valid representation of its true objectives, or of its reality.

In fact, the interesting thing about marketing is that many Canadian social organizations do practise it in some form or another, but without using the term "marketing." Some Canadian colleges and universities have set up programs to attract underprivileged and minority students. Hospitals in most provinces have undertaken demarketing (reducing demand) by encouraging patients to shorten the duration of their stay in hospital. This paper contends that a Canadian social organization can carry out its marketing-related functions more efficiently and effectively by formally recognizing the role of marketing. Of course, many subgroups within these organizations may see marketing as a threat to their autonomy or power. Social marketing may initially be viewed simply as social advertising and promotion rather than as a revolutionary new way to view the organization and its purposes. However, the adoption of the marketing concept by innovative social organizations should lead to others developing and advancing the understanding of the marketing concept.

One recommended method of introducing marketing into a social organization is to appoint a marketing committee of key organizational executives, to hire a marketing consultant to carry out a comprehensive marketing audit on the problems and opportunities facing the organization, and eventually to appoint a director or vice-president of marketing to carry out the organization's marketing functions. This top marketing function must be tailored to the needs of the specific institution. As the new appointee's contribution may be carefully scrutinized by other members of the organization, it will be necessary for the marketing executive to develop a strategy to make marketing visible and useful.

CONCLUSION

The real contribution of marketing thinking is to lead each Canadian social institution to search for a more meaningful position for itself in the larger Canadian society. Adoption of the marketing concept by social organizations will lead to a better understanding of the needs of their different client segments, to a more careful shaping and launching of new social products, to a pruning of weak social products, to more effective methods of delivering social products, to more flexible and appropriate pricing approaches, and to a higher level of public satisfaction. Altogether, marketing offers great potential to social organizations to survive, grow, and strengthen their contributions to the general welfare of the Canadian public. If, instead of taking a selling approach to promoting a social cause, a marketing approach is taken, then, as this paper has shown, the implementation of social programs will become easier and more effective for Canadian social organizations.

REFERENCES

BLOOM, P.N. and NOVELLI, W.D., "Problems and Challenges in Social Marketing," *Journal of Marketing*, Spring 1981, pp. 79-88.

FOX, K. and KOTLER, P., "The Marketing of Social Causes: the First 10 Years," *Journal of Marketing*, Fall 1980, pp. 24-33.

KOTLER, P., "Strategies for Introducing Marketing into Non Profit Organizations," *Journal of Marketing*, January 1979, pp. 37-44.

KOTLER, P. and ZALTMAN, G., "Social Marketing: an Approach to Planned Social Change," *Journal of Marketing*, July 1979, pp. 3-12.

SHAPIRO, B., "Marketing for Non Profit Organizations," *Harvard Business Review*, Sept.-Oct. 1973, pp. 123-132.

Information Systems
Systèmes d'information

Management Science and Management Information Systems: le Mariage

DAVID J. WRIGHT

M anagement Science, MS, and Management Information Systems, MIS, are subjects which are continually evolving. They have always maintained strong links with each other, both in their management orientation and in the fact that MS methods are implemented on MISs. This paper focuses on those developments currently occurring in both disciplines and shows that these developments imply increasingly close links between MS and MIS in the future.

I will set current developments in perspective by analysing historical trends. The quantitative approaches which characterize the majority of MS and MIS applications are then described and contrasted with recent qualitative developments. Finally, the improvement of the interface between the MS model and the MIS user is described as an important development for the rest of the 1980s through the use of Decision Support Systems, DSS, and Visual Interactive Models, VIM.

Figure I shows the various stages in the development of MS and MIS. Just after the Second World War, when MS and MIS were in their infancy, there was very little connection between the two. Management Science was applying analytical methodology to operational problems in industry, much as it had been involved with military operations during the war. Computer development was the province of the electronic engineer. During the 1960s, MS and MIS became more closely linked in the sense that the MS methods being developed were put into the form of computer packages for ease of use, for instance, the NAG Library which is still marketed today. The implementation of these packages, with some tailoring to suit individual user needs, became an accepted part of many businesses during the 1970s. A typical example is the routine use of linear programming in the food processing and oil industries. At the same time, the development of computer operating systems offering very large virtual storage allowed these applications to capture all the relevant practical complexity and detail of the business situation.

MS methods implemented on large MISs have thus become established ways of dealing with complex business situations, the

Year	Management Science	Management Information Systems
1950	**Conception** Operational Applications	**First Generation** Vacuum Tubes Symbolic Languages

Year	Management Science	Management Information Systems
1960	**Development** Research into New Techniques Software Packages	**Second Generation** Transistors FORTRAN, COBOL

Year	Management Science	Management Information Systems
1965		**Third Generation** Integrated Circuits Multiple Access Operating Systems Software Packages

Year	Management Science	Management Information Systems
1970	**Commercial Acceptance** Focus on Data rather than Techniques Established Implementations	**Fourth Generation** Chips, LSI, VLSI Microcomputers, Virtual Storage Data Base Package, Graphics

Year	Management Science	Management Information Systems
1982	**User Orientation** Decision Support Systems Visual Interactive Modelling	**Fifth Generation** Artificial Intelligence Decision Support Systems

Figure I — Evolution of M.S. and M.I.S.

results being presented quantitatively on a VDU terminal or line printer. One of the developments for the 1980s is qualitative models and qualitative ways of presenting results. The other, related, development is the increased user friendliness of the computer implementations of MS via the use of DSS and VIM. Essentially the system should be sufficiently friendly for a manager to use, choosing models, designing his own models, and interacting with their operation without requiring the intervention of an analyst.

QUALITATIVE DEVELOPMENTS SUPPLEMENT A QUANTITATIVE BASE

MS and MIS have always been highly quantitative subjects. Indeed the terms "Management Science" and "Quantitative Methods" are sometimes used interchangeably. Information systems, with their basis in digital calculations, are intrinsically quantitative. It is the management orientation of MS and MIS that has given them their qualitative element. The need to communicate results to managers is leading to qualitative methods of presentation.

The models developed in MS over the past four decades have been quantitative: linear, nonlinear and dynamic programming, simulation, forecasting, networks, decision analysis, stochastic models, queuing models and statistics. Recent developments are qualitative models and qualitative methods of presenting quantitative results.

Qualitative Models

Qualitative methods have recently been developed to model situations that exhibit a specific type of behavior, namely, sudden jumps. Instead of behaving smoothly the system changes discontinuously, and this is called a "catastrophe." Examples of catastrophes are a breakdown of negotiations, a stock market crisis, and a disease epidemic. The term "catastrophe" was first coined by the French mathematician Thom (1975) in his "Catastrophe Theory." This theory classifies all possible ways in which catastrophes can occur and describes the features of a system that is liable to catastrophic behavior. Because this work is relatively unknown, but of great potential, I review it in detail, describing the general theory together with a case study of a management application.

The two types of catastrophe most often found in practice are the "fold" and the "cusp." These are shown in Figures II and III. The fold relates the equilibrium value of a variable, x, that describes the state of the system to a parameter, a, of the system. As an example, x could represent stock market prices and a could represent the traders' confidence. The variable x changes with time and equilibrates to a value determined by the parameter a. This parameter, a, is constant unless changed by some external influence. Thus a affects x but not vice versa. The values of x shown are the

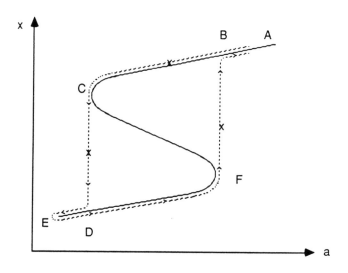

Figure II — The Fold

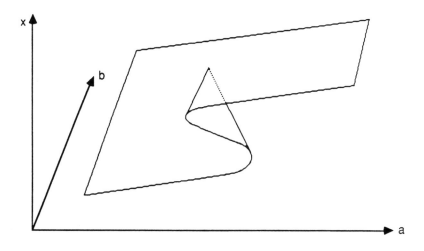

Figure III — The Cusp

equilibrium values. Suppose we start at a point A representing high values of x and a. If a is decreased, x will follow down the curve from A to B to C and then a catastrophic drop in x will occur to D, then continuing to E. If now a is increased, the system will return along a different path EDF, followed by a catastrophe to B, then A. The fact that the paths followed by the system depend on the direction in which a is changed is called "hysteresis." Hysteresis characteristically accompanies catastrophic behavior. The behavior of a system of the cusp type is similar to that of the fold for a fixed value of b. This additional parameter, b, determines the magnitude of the catastrophes and hysteresis as a is changed. As b is increased, the extent of this discontinuous behavior is decreased until it finally disappears altogether, and the system behaves quite smoothly with variations in a.

Thom classified the pattern of catastrophes in systems with three or more parameters. These are not much used in practice, but the important point is that the type of catastrophe is dependent on the number of parameters a, b etc., not on the number of state variables x. Thus, x could represent just a single variable that is equilibrating itself according to the values of the parameters, or a whole set of variables describing different aspects of a complex system. This results in one of the main advantages of catastrophe theory: model simplification. Instead of modelling separately the behavior of a large number of interrelated variables, their qualitative behavior can be captured by a catastrophe theory model which combines them all into one.

In order to apply catastrophe theory two conditions must be met. First, the rate at which x equilibrates must be fast compared to the rate at which a is changed. Secondly, there must be some values of the parameters for which x can take on two different equilibrium values.

I will now turn to a case study in which catastrophe theory was used in natural resource management. This concerns the control of an insect pest, the spruce budworm, in coniferous forest in New Brunswick and was originally described by Holling (1978). Another example of the use of catastrophe theory in natural resource management is given by Peterman (1977), who describes its application to salmon fishery management in the Atnarko River in British Columbia.

Budworm epidemics have occurred at intervals of 30 to 50 years in spruce forest in New Brunswick for the past 200 years. This can be deduced from numbers of eggs left in the tree rings of different ages. The budworms eat the leaves of the trees; an epidemic destroys the trees. Under normal circumstances the budworm population is maintained at a low level by predation by birds. The effect of predation and food supply on budworms is illustrated in Figure IV. If the budworm population is in the region OA, there is a natural tendency for it to increase, since this small number of budworms escapes notice by the birds. If there are more budworms, between A and B, then the predators kill them faster than they can reproduce. For a still larger number, between B and C, there are too many for the birds to control so the insects increase in numbers until they are limited at C by the food supply, i.e., the leaf area. There are therefore two stable equilibrium numbers of budworm, A and C, where the population is stabilized by predation and food supply respectively. O and B represent unstable equilibria in the sense that if the population deviates a little away from these levels, theory dictates that it will continue to deviate further until equilibrating at either A or C. Evidently, the level of the curve depends on the leaf area of the trees, since this is the budworm's food supply. As the forest matures, this leaf area increases, giving a succession of curves as shown in Figure V. The stable equilibrium points form a fold catastrophe when plotted against the tree age (Figure VI).

A young forest, represented by A, can support only a few budworms. As the forest matures it passes through B and C with only a slight increase in the number of budworms until at D a catastrophe occurs, giving a budworm epidemic at H. Before the trees have time to grow to I, they are destroyed by the budworms, which are exhausting their own food supply through G to F where predation takes over, with a catastrophic drop in budworm population to B. By now, however, the trees have been destroyed and the forest must start again from young seedlings. This behavior can be obtained using catastrophe theory from the basic population dynamics curve, Figure IV.

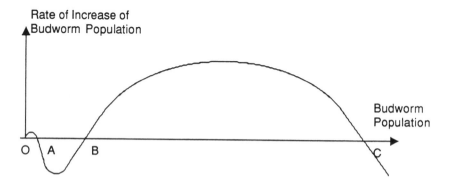

Figure IV — Effect of Bird Predation and Food Supply on Budworm Population

Source: Derived from Holling, 1978.

We note that the two conditions for catastrophe theory apply: first, the trees grow much more slowly than the budworm population equilibrates and, secondly, the intermediate curves, e.g., OCEG in Figure V, show two stable equilibria, C and G. The advantage of model simplification is also clearly demonstrated: the behavior of the whole forest ecosystem with all its complex interrelationships is essentially combined into one variable, budworm population. Catastrophe theory assures us that the qualitative behavior of this variable is reflected in the dynamics of the populations of all other related species, which do not therefore need to be modeled separately.

From Figure VI, we can also obtain qualitative management strategies for the prevention of budworm epidemics. Two strategies are available: (i) harvest the trees, (ii) spray with insecticide. The effect of spraying is to reduce the budworm population, i.e., a displacement to the left in Figure VI. The direction in which a displaced point will equilibrate is shown by the arrows. A displacement to the left of C will simply return to C when the effect of the insecticide wears off, so that spraying cannot prevent an epidemic occurring. Insecticide in large enough quantities can, however, hasten the decline of an epidemic that has already done some damage to the trees. Spraying at G sufficient to reduce the budworm numbers below E will cause a natural further drop to C even after the insecticide has ceased to be effective. The only way to prevent an epidemic of budworms is to harvest the trees before they reach the age represented by D. The forest system then remains in the region ABC.

This case study has shown how a qualitative model of a natural resource system was used to produce qualitative management policies which were implemented in New Brunswick. The advantages of such qualitative models are:

1. a simple model can represent a complex system, since several variables can be combined into one;
2. the descriptive approach facilitates communication between analyst and manager;
3. qualitative management strategies can be analyzed without costly data collection;
4. quantification can be introduced later if required.

Qualitative Information Presentation

Essentially all information system, used in business are digital, i.e., their mode of operation is quantitative. There are two other types of machine: analogue and Fifth Generation (see Figure I). To some extent, analogue computers could be said to operate qualitatively, but their use is restricted to engineering. The Canadarm design was simulated on an analogue machine before being finalized for use in the space shuttle. Moreover, analogue machines are now

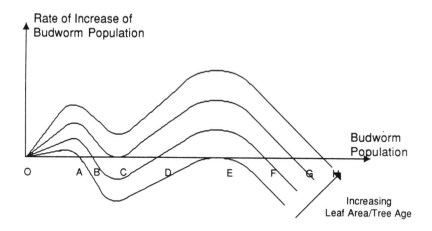

Figure V — Effect of Forest Maturity on Budworm Population (by Rate of Increase of Budworm Population)

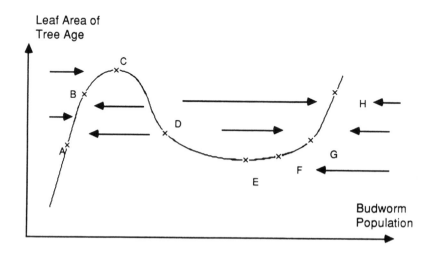

Figure VI — Effect of Forest Maturity on Budworm Population (by Leaf Area of Tree Age)

being replaced by parallel digital processors. The other departure from the traditional digital design of information systems is the Fifth Generation machines, which represent strings of logical relationships such as those used in expert systems for obtaining a medical diagnosis from given symptoms. Again, their main applications are scientific, and Zadeh (1984) has suggested that the business world is too "fuzzy" for their application there.

We therefore concern ourselves only with quantitative, digital information systems. The use of qualitative, i.e., graphical, methods of output is of great importance in business and is discussed next.

Much research has been conducted recently, in both MS and MIS, into the question of methods of data presentation. A recent study by Remus (1984) concerns the choice between quantitative (tabular) displays and qualitative (graphical) displays. Managers undoubtedly prefer qualitative displays, but the relative effectiveness of the two methods in terms of profitability of resulting decisions is less clear cut. Sometimes graphical presentation is more effective and sometimes tabular, depending on the decision "style" of the manager and the type of decision problem. Certainly the market for graphical displays is booming due partly to the plummeting cost of associated hardware. The use of dot-matrix technology in printers enables graphical output to be produced at a much reduced cost compared to that of plotting. This, combined with ink-jet as opposed to impact printing, results in quiet operation that is very acceptable in a manager's office, either as a main-frame terminal or in conjunction with a microcomputer. This significantly increases the interaction that a manager can have with a machine, obviating the necessity for intermediary analysts.

The type of bar charts, graphs, etc. that information systems produce is quite well known. They produce clear descriptions of two or three variables, but their ability to convey information about more than three variables at the same time is very limited. It would take great ingenuity to use a computerized graphics package to match the nineteenth century presentation shown in Figure VII. This graph, prepared by Minard in 1861, describes Napoleon's 1812 march on Moscow. The thickness of the bands represents the size of the army, with shading for advance and black for retreat. Below the map, a graph shows not only the temperature at the corresponding geographical positions, but also selected dates. The whole chart therefore relates six variables: the latitude, longitude, direction of movement and size of the army, the temperature and the date. Figure VII is given in order to emphasize the limited nature of presently available graphics packages. This brings us to the question of recent developments in methods of graphically presenting more than three variables. I will now describe one such method which is little known but of great importance as an innovative method of data description.

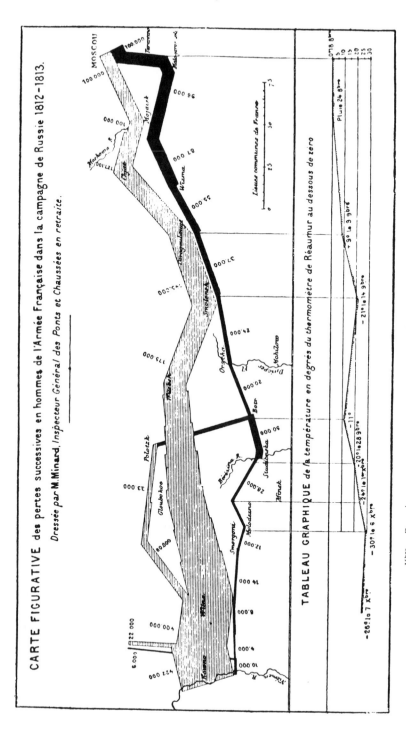

Figure VII — Napoleon's 1812 Moscow Campaign as Depicted by Minard in 1861

It is, of course, very common for an analysis to involve more than three variables, for instance in comparing the socioeconomic status of different communities based on census data covering many descriptive features. Cluster analysis is the appropriate quantitative technique for the classification of communities into groups, for instance, for the application of different socioeconomic government policies. However, it involves the specification of a metric which determines the extent to which a difference in one census variable should counterbalance a difference in another. This involves some judgment and, since the metric must be prescribed before the analysis, it is difficult for the analyst to get a feel for the data.

A qualitative way of describing multivariate data has been given by Chernoff (1973). This involves associating each variable with an element of the human face, e.g., the size of nose, the angle of the eyes, etc. This representation allows many variables to be displayed together in a manner that appeals to the human eye and exploits the very refined ability of the brain to recognize similarities and differences between faces. Analysis based on faces has been applied to (i) mineral analysis of geological data (Chernoff, 1973), (ii) identification of companies from the Dow Jones Transportation Index that move together in terms of percentage return over 25 years (Kleiner and Hartigan, 1981), (iii) association of pollution measures with mortality data in 60 U.S. cities, and (iv) identification of forged bank notes (Flury and Riedwyl, 1981). The results of the latter work are presented in Figure VIII. Based on only six measurements of the notes, e.g., length, width, size of margins, and representing these as eye slant, hair line etc., the forged notes are readily identified. Chernoff faces are particularly useful in identifying (i) groupings of items and (ii) outliers, so that their application in modern business methods such as exception reporting is very direct.

THE MODEL-USER INTERFACE

MISs continually seek to improve their user interface. Often the manager who is the ultimate user of the information produced must go through an analyst in order to describe exactly what he needs. This is also the situation in MS. A manager must go through an intermediate analyst to update the models he wishes to use. This situation has given rise to excessive lead times and several iterations of discussions before the manager gets approximately what he requires. Two recent developments are emerging to tackle these problems, DSS and VIM. These ideas aim to do for the manager what Computer Aided Design and Computer Aided Manufacturing, CAD/ CAM, have done for the engineer. They use the interactive and visual display features of the computer to aid the manager or engineer in his decision making, as opposed to simply producing masses of reports which must subsequently be digested.

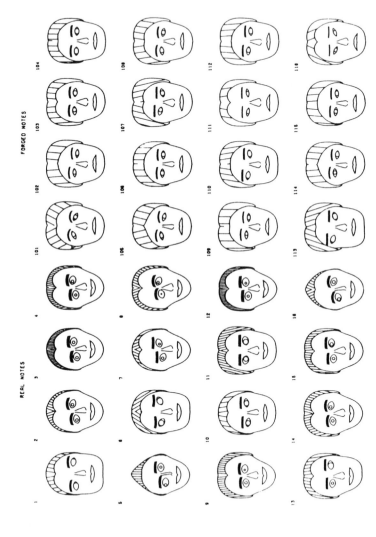

Figure VIII — Chernoff Faces Representing Forged and Real Bank Notes
Source: Flury and Riedwell, 1981.

Decision Support Systems

MISs evolved during the 1970s upon the foundation of Data Base Management Systems, DBMS, to produce relevant information for managers. DSSs give the manager flexibility to analyse the information using a variety of MS models. They therefore provide Model Management Systems as well as Data Base Management Systems. (Sometimes the term DSS is used with no model management at all. In this case it is simply another term for MIS.) These models may be elementary statistical procedures, sophisticated forecasting or optimization models, or models which the user has himself constructed, often based on accounting identities. The essence of such a DSS is to provide the user with a friendly interface to models as well as to information. This development clearly integrates MS and MIS. Both achieve their aims of improved interface with the manager, who becomes less dependent on intermediate analysts. MS achieves flexibility of computer implementation in the sense of user access to a range of models. MIS is able to include providing the user with powerful analytical ability. DSSs of this type are as yet in their infancy, but they provide a direction for development for the latter half of the 1980s which significantly extends the capabilities of currently implemented MIS (Baxter, 1981).

Visual Interactive Modeling

In MS, one of the reasons for several iterations of discussions between manager and analyst is that, after a model has been specified, the results may be unacceptable. The manager is operating in an ill-structured decision environment where it is not possible to specify all the constraints in advance. He/she needs to modify the model results and then rerun the model with the modified results as a constraint. VIM provides this capability via interaction with a graphical display rather than by going via an analyst. A VIM is therefore an example of a DSS with powerful graphics and model interaction capabilities. Bell, Hay, and Liang (1986) describe applications of VIM in workforce scheduling. VIM may be illustrated with an example of production scheduling. Suppose various products must be produced on various machines. Standard MS models are available to derive a schedule that minimizes total production time, for instance. A simplified VIM display of such a schedule is given in Figure IX. Upon looking at a production schedule, the decision-maker may realize, for example, that Job A cannot be processed on Machine 3 during days 7 and 8 due to unavailability of skilled manpower. He may therefore instruct the system to push this operation earlier, say to days 4-6. The system will then reoptimize the allocation of all other jobs to machines and produce a revised schedule. The two important features here are that (i) the schedule is presented graphically, and (ii) the manager can interact

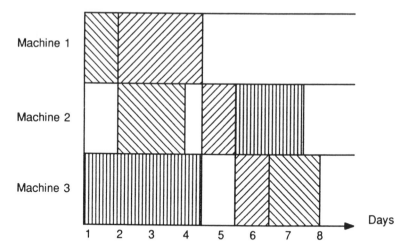

Figure IX — Typical Production Plan for Three Jobs on Three Machines

with the system without recourse to an analyst. The increased user friendliness of MIS, providing such interaction, results in an increased applicability of MS methods at all levels of management.

CONCLUSION

There are many trends and developments taking place in MS and MIS. This paper has highlighted two of these, (i) the use of qualitative as opposed to quantitative approaches and (ii) the improvement of the model-user interface. These two have been selected because they affect both MS and MIS. The paper shows this effect to be one of integrating these two disciplines.

Qualitative models and qualitative means of presenting results are important in MS and MIS as means of facilitating communication with the manager. A practical case study is described of the use of a qualitative model. Examples are also given of qualitative presentations of results which transcend the capability of most currently available software packages, but which exploit the flexibility and low cost of recent hardware developments. Research is in progress in MS and MIS into the types of management situation that benefit from qualitative presentation methods. The interface between an MS model and the manager has traditionally involved an intermediate analyst. The same situation pertains in MIS. In their efforts to achieve more direct interaction between models and their users, both disciplines are coming together in the development of (i) Decision Support Systems which allow the manager access to a range of models by incorporating model management as an extension of the way in which MIS has used data management and (ii) Visual Interactive Modeling, which allows the manager the flexibility of seeing model results displayed graphically, modifying the requirements, and rerunning the model.

The whole issue of qualitative modeling, qualitative presentation methods and identification of the management situations in which they are cost effective is an issue of great importance requiring interdisciplinary research between MS and MIS for many years to come. Likewise, both disciplines are involved with making the user interface more interactive. DSS and VIM approach this issue incorporating elements of MS and MIS. The common management orientation of MS and MIS therefore has the effect of integrating them in the sense that important areas of development can be tackled jointly.

REFERENCES

BAXTER, J.D., "Line Managers Move From MIS to DSS for Decision-Making Help," *Iron Age*, September 1981, pp. 71-73.

BELL, P.C., HAY, G., and LIANG, Y., "A Visual Interactive Decision Support System for Workforce Scheduling," *Information Systems and Operational Research*, 1986, Vol. 24, (2), pp. 134-146.

CHERNOFF, H., "The Use of Faces to Represent Points in k-Dimensional Space Graphically," *Journal of American Statistical Association*, June 1973, Vol. 68, (342), pp. 361-368.

FLURY, B., and RIEDWELL, H., "Graphical Representation of Multivariate Data by Means of Asymmetrical Faces," *Journal of American Statistical Association*, December 1981, Vol. 76, (376), pp. 757-765.

HOLLING, C.S., (ed.), "Adaptive Environmental Assessment and Management," IIASA Series, New York, Wiley, 1978.

KLEINER, B., and HARTIGAN, J.A., "Representing Points in Many Dimensions by Trees and Castles," *Journal of American Statistical Association*, June 1981, Vol. 76, (374), pp. 260-275.

PETERMAN, R.M., "A Simple Mechanism that Causes Collapsing Stability Regions in Exploited Salmonid Populations," *Journal of Fishery Resources in Canada*, 1977, Vol. 34, pp. 1130-1142.

REMUS, W., "An Empirical Investigation of the Impact of Graphical and Tabular Data Presentations on Decision-Making," *Management Science*, May 1984, Vol. 30, (5), pp. 533-542.

THOM, R., *Structural Stability and Morphogenesis*, London, Benjamin, 1975.

ZADEH, L.A., "Coping with the Imprecision of the Real World," *Communications of the ACM*, May 1984, Vol. 27, (4), pp. 304-311.

In Search of Health Informatics: Prospects and Challenges

DENIS H.J. CARO

T he health care system is in the midst of a major technological revolution, the end results of which cannot be predicted with any degree of certainty. The advent and proliferation of microcomputer technology has come upon the field with startling surprise. Add to this the emerging fifth generation and artificial intelligence technologies on the horizon and it is evident that the growth of computer technology is becoming uncontrolled and its potential impact on the dynamics of the health care system is poorly understood at best. As the Science Council of Canada Report (1982) states in its Recommendation 26:

> The new technologies are fostering a revolution in health care. Documentation, diagnosis, pharmacology, treatment, prosthetics and research will be greatly affected. Industry, medical and nursing schools, provincial and federal departments of health, universities, and granting agencies, including private foundations, must be sensitive to the changes in this field and their potential benefits to, in particular, the disabled and those suffering from degenerative diseases.

The introduction and diffusion of computer technology have brought some serious challenges which threaten to erode the fundamental caring functions of the system. There is an urgent need for further research into the new field of health informatics. The primary objective of this paper is to shed some light on the nature of the ethical and policy dilemmas posed by the proliferation of computer technologies and point to some directions in which further research into health informatics is of critical importance.

MEDICAL AND HEALTH INFORMATICS: EVOLVING PARADIGMS

A growing area of investigation that explores the dynamic application of computer technology in the realm of medicine is medical informatics, which Seegmuller defines as the science concerned with the nature, construction, and application of algorithms in medicine. According to Reichertz of Hanover's Medical School Institute for Medical Informatics in the Federal Republic of West Germany, medical informatics is:

> The scientific attempt to map the empirical science of medicine into the formal structure of informatics taking into account the process character of medical practice.

Its fundamental goal is the systematization of medicine: forcing it to become more logical and developing new insights into medical decision-making.

More logical and "systematized" medical decision-making processes can significantly enhance medical education, diagnosis, and treatment outcomes. As an interdisciplinary science, medical informatics encompasses image processing, artificial intelligence, large-scale information systems, database management systems, telecommunications, and all those computer technologies that impact on this medical sphere of human activity. Its underlying paradigm is conceptualized in Figure I, in which medical informatics is viewed as the study of the interfaces of computer technologies on the one hand and medical care processes on the other. It is emphasized that this paradigm is self-limiting in that it not only ignores the wider context in which medical decisions are made, but also propagates a set of values into health care that can undermine one of its most fundamental processes — the caring function. These issues can be examined through a wider paradigm that emphasizes the field of health informatics, which we can define as:

> The systematic study of the synergistic effects of information resources and technology on the systematic provision and delivery of health care processes for the betterment of the human health condition.

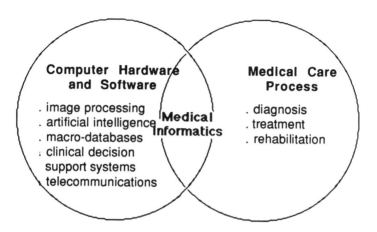

Figure I — The Medical Informatic Paradigm

Informatics and the Technosystem Challenge

Health informatics is an evolution of the medical informatic paradigm that encompasses the dynamics of what can be called the health technosystem, including:

1. information system technologies,
2. health care processes,
3. health care structures,
4. provider behaviors.

These four components are made up of a set of dynamic variables which interact with each other in a highly synergistic fashion, as illustrated in Figure II.

In contrast to the medical informatic paradigm of Figure I, the focus of health informatics is not limited to the essential medical care processes of diagnosis, treatment, and rehabilitation. It also encompasses the processes of prevention, nursing care, pastoral care, and the strategic management of health care resources. Its focus therefore is not only on medical care, but on health care processes. Moreover, the health informatic paradigm inherently acknowledges a larger health care structure within which information system technology interfaces and impacts on health care processes. These include organizational structural variables, policies, procedures, communication flows, management structures, responsibility and accountability structures, norms and values. Technology and medical care processes do not therefore operate within a vacuum, as assumed by medical informatics.

Health informatics also inherently recognizes another key component which is ignored in medical informatics — the behavioral characteristics of the physician and providers of health care. This not only includes the sum total of medical and other professional knowledge and skills, but also the values, norms, and ethical constructs defined by all health professional bodies and organizations.

The structure and dynamics of the health care technosystem are also highly dependent upon the larger environmental variables with which it interacts. If society at large is more open to technological advances through favorable political and economic policies, then the health technosystem itself will become more subject to technologization.

In this highly interactive and interdependent model, changes in any one element can have a significant impact on the other variables. For example, the increasing use of microcomputer technology and the concomitant computer literacy of physicians impacts on the fiscal structure of the hospital, while it also changes the nature of the physician's practice of medicine itself. The advent of nuclear imaging capabilities has dramatically improved our ability to diagnose patients with benign or malignant cancerous tumors, with significant impact on therapeutic outcomes for the patient and on hospital costs. Thus, the emerging and increasingly dominant role

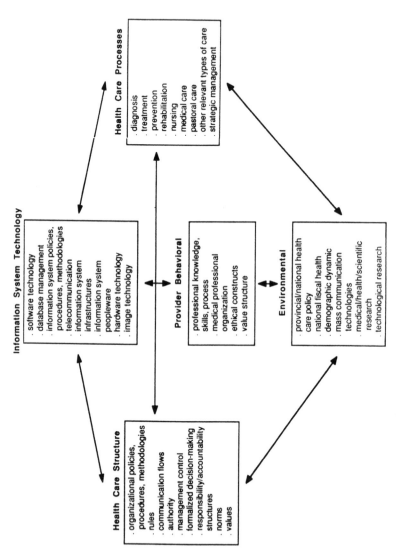

Figure II — The Health Informatic Paradigm

of computer technology on the structure and delivery patterns of health care, or the health technosystem, is very important and forms the object of study of the field of health informatics. This is largely ignored by the medical informatic paradigm, which restricts its view to improving clinical decision-making through the application of computer technology.

Informatics and the Caring Function Challenge

Theobold has made the insightful observation that there is an inherent drive in the introduction of computer technology into an organization. Though computer systems may initially be set up to respond to the need for increased efficiencies, once they become fully operational, a drive emerges towards the total reorganization of the systems and institutions. The end result, warns Boguslaw, is an insistence upon a uniformity of perspective, a standardization of language, and a consensus of values that is characteristic of highly authoritarian social structures. Stimson and Stimson warn that the computer system could become an end in itself and the consequences might not further hospital goals. As technology becomes more sophisticated, the health care system is organized around a dynamic that evolves from and is centered around its own technological requirements and processes. Kisch admonishes us that the use of the computer system under the present model of health care could reinforce the dysfunctions of the system, including its inefficiencies and inequities.

The current state of the art in essence points to the emergence and reinforcement of a medical technostructure in which users/providers and the consumers of health care services become subservient to the constraints and demands of the technology. Rather than systems serving the legitimate needs for information and effectiveness of care, it is the users/providers who must adapt and modify their practices and modalities of care to suit technological requirements.

Nowhere is the thrust towards the technologization of health so evident than in the automation area. Users will rarely question the desirability of systems and spend little time on the issues of economic, technical, operational, and social feasibility of systems. The technological imperative becomes absolute: *Computerization über alles* becomes the slogan of the 1980s.

Battistella affirms that the dominance of patient welfare values is fundamental in hospitals and related facilities, given the uncertainty and complexity surrounding patient care. Until recently productivity and rigid adherence to proper procedures have taken a secondary role to normative values that predominate in health organizations. Healing and the presentation of the subjective aspects of the physician-patient relationship have been more important for accomplishing the task at hand than has the quest for efficiency through the classical management paradigm. This reverence for life and healing is the essence of the patient service ethic.

At the same time, the health care system continues towards an increasing technocratic mode of life, exemplified by its adherence to two basic principles that increasingly direct the efforts and thoughts of everyone working in the system. The first principle is the maxim that something ought to be done because it is technically possible to do it. If it is possible to computerize all our data, then we must do so. The second principle is that of maximal efficiency and productivity. Individuals become purely quantifiable units that must be arranged so as to maximize efficiency and productivity functions, given cost constraints. This is the essence of the technocratic value ethic.

Although the advent of computer technology in the health care system holds enormous potential to upgrade the levels of care, its introduction can embody primarily technocratic ethical constructs which are diametrically opposed to the patient service ones. With greater emphasis on economic efficiency and its ever-accelerating technological imperative, the intelligent and rigorous assessment of the technology itself has fallen by the wayside. Desirability and feasibility studies are either poorly done or even totally ignored in the rush to design, develop, and implement computer systems. The social impact of the technology in the health care sector does not even enter into the assessment equation. The potentially dysfunctional long-term impact of the technology on provider behaviors and medical care processes are discounted as irrelevant. It is assumed and taken as a sine qua non dictum that computerization is an inherent good, as it can only enhance productivity and efficiency. To question this assumption places one in the position of being a heretic. Any calls for wisdom and forbearance through rigorous assessment studies are seen as merely reactionary postures.

This technological imperative with its inherent technocratic value ethic can create untold long-term dangers, including increased conflict, technostress, erosion of the medical care processes, increased social, structural, and clinical iatrogenesis, and a less care-oriented health system. This points to the need for a number of managerial and research strategies to avert a total erosion of the patient service ethic. Without intervening strategies, the critical caring functions of the health care system risk being further eroded to the point where hospitals could become little more than waystations, or garages for the physically or mentally impaired. The patient and physician would interact within an increasingly alienated and impersonal process, and both parties would cease to be truly human entities, but would become mere automatons.

It is precisely here that further research into health informatics must play a critical role. If the patient service ethic is to be fostered and the health technosystem is to retain and perpetuate its caring functions, then a deeper understanding is needed of the elements and interface of information system technology, health care processes, provider behaviors, and health care structures. Health informatics must evolve into the systematic study of the synergistic effects of information system technology interacting with medical care process for the betterment of the human health condition. An optimizing fit between technology and providers can only evolve when the patient service ethic is elevated above the technocratic value constructs. Health informatics as the dynamic study of the interaction of the components of the health technosystem can still reinforce and perpetuate the caring functions of the system with this focus and also take full advantage of technological gains. Only if this is done will the patient and provider interact within a productive and self-actualizing environment. It is only with this focus that medicine and patient care can successfully merge with man as master of technology rather than man as servant of the machine.

PROSPECTS: HEALTH INFORMATION
AND THE FIFTH GENERATION TECHNOLOGY

As yet we know very little about the impact of technology on the delivery and patterns of health practice. This lack of research and knowledge is tantamount to a loss in our ability to effectively manage the technological revolution within the hospital sector. Moreover, there is a risk of the introduction of inappropriate technologies that can adversely impact on the patient service ethic, dehumanizing the levels of care, alienating provider-patient relationships, and ultimately increasing the costs of health care overall.

The technological advances on the horizon, however, hold vast potential for good if properly assessed and systematically introduced. These include developments in clinical decision support systems, ergonomically designed hardware, interactive distributed database systems, patient education courseware, computerized prospective medical profiles, and viewdata systems for surgical consultations, to name just a few. Moreover, recent trends in declining hardware and rising software costs may pave the way for more economically feasible artificial intelligence systems, which are currently in their prototype and experimental stages of development.

Indeed, technological research into artificial intelligence will no doubt be the basis of medical expert systems that simulate the decision-making processes of physicians. With the advent of expert systems, knowledge information processing systems, natural languages processes, robotics, voice and visual recognition systems, automatic programming, and automated systems building, an unbelievable technological panorama will unfold before us. Tomorrow's health services system may see international medical databases for renal transplant patients, further viewdata and courseware development for medical and nursing education, video-satellite surgical consultations, telemetric monitoring of at risk patients, and prospective medical databases.

To understand this technology and its impact, however, health informatics will have to expand its research vista to encompass provider behavior and the structural and organizational components within which the computer technology and medical process interface. The findings of this research must be disseminated and must impact on the strategic policies and management of health care. Without careful research into the dynamics of health technosystems as embraced by health informatics, the full dynamic relationships involved when information system technology is introduced into a medical care setting will not be understood. Without such an expansion of knowledge and wisdom in the use of computer technology, there will be a continuing insidious and deleterious erosion of the patient service ethic. Without the advance of health informatics, the great promise of fifth generation technology may turn into a mirage in which humanized care for the needy population becomes only a shimmering vision on the horizon. The reality risks becoming a hard desert characterized by total erosion of public confidence in medicine, increased clinical and social iatrogenesis, and undiminished health care costs that burden the population disproportionately to health care benefits.

REFERENCES

ANDERSON, J., "Medical Informatics and Medical Education," *Methods of Information in Medicine*, Vol. 21, (1), January 1982.

BATTISTELLA, R.M. and SMITH, D.B., "Toward a Definition of Health Services Management: A Humanist Orientation," *International Journal of Health Services*, Vol. 4, (4), 1974, pp. 701-721.

BOGUSLAW, R., *The New Utopians*, Englewood Cliffs, New Jersey, Prentice-Hall, 1965, p. 186.

BOULDING, K.E., *The Image: Knowledge in Life and Society*, Ann Arbor, 1971.

COVVEY, M.D. and McALISTER, N.H., "Computers in the Practice of Medicine," *Issues in Medical Computing*, Vol. 2, Addison-Wesley Publishing Company, 1980.

DECHERT, C.R., *The Development of Cybernetics: The Social Impact of Cybernetics*, ed. Charles R. Dechert, Notre Dame, University of Notre Dame Press, 1966, pp. 11-37.

FROMM, Erich, *The Revolution of Hope: Toward a Humanized Technology*, Toronto, Bantam Books, 1968.

GOTTINGER, H.W., "Economic Evaluation of Effectiveness in Health Care Delivery," *Methods of Information in Medicine*, Vol. 20, 1981, pp. 101-109.

HALL, H. and ZWEMER, J.D., *Prospective Medicine*, 2nd ed., Indianapolis, Methodist Hospital of Indianapolis, 1979.

KALUZNY, A.D., "Innovation in Health Services: Theoretical Framework and Review of Research," *Health Services Research*, Vol. 9, (2), Summer 1974, pp. 101-120.

KAPLAN, B., " 'Peopleware' and Medical Informatics," *The Journal of the American Medical Association*, Feb. 4, 1983, pp. 574-576.

KINNUCAN, P., "Computers That Think Like Experts," *High Technology*, January 1984, pp. 30-42.

KISCH, A.I., "Adapting Health Manpower to Consumer Needs and Cultural Expectations," *Inquiry*, Vol. 8, (3), 1971, pp. 39-50.

LAZLO, C.A. and VARGAN, L.E., "A Computerized Health Hazard Appraisal System (CHAMP)," *Methods of Information in Medicine*, Vol. 20, 1981, pp. 147-156.

MARSCHAK, J., "Divided Soul-Searching for Multi-Criteria Decisions," in M. Zeleny ed., *Multiple Criteria Decision-Making*, New York, Springer 1976, pp. 1-16.

McKIBBIN, W.L., "Awaiting the Intelligent Computer," *Infosystems*, Vol. 30, August 1983, p. 97.

MEYROWITZ, A.L., "Artificial Intelligence Research: Directions," *Computers and People*, March-April 1983, pp. 12-15.

MISHELEVICH, D.J., "Lessons and Challenges from the Demise of the Department of Medical Computer Science at the University of Texas Health Science Center at Dallas," *Journal of Medical Systems*, Vol. 7, (1), February 1983, pp. 1-9.

PELTU, M., "Artificial Intelligence Key to the Fifth Generation," *Datamation*, January 1982, p. 114.

PERROW, C., "Hospitals in Technology, Structure, and Goals," in Handbook of Organizations, ed. James March, 1965, pp. 910-971.

REICHERTZ, P.L., "Towards Systematization," Methods of Information in Medicine, Vol. 16, 1977, pp. 125-130.

RICHART, R.H., "Evaluation of a Hospital Computer System," Hospital Computer Science, ed. Morris E. Collens, New York, Wiley and Sons, pp. 341-417.

Science Council of Canada, Planning Now for an Information Society: Tomorrow is too Late, Report No. 33, Minister of Supply and Services, March 1982.

SEEGMÜLLER, S., "Discussing Remarks," in Selbmann, H.U., Uberla, K., Greiller, R., eds., Alternative Medizimischer Datenverarbeitung, Heidelberg, Springer, 1976, p. 148.

STIMSON, D.M. and STIMSON, R.H., Operations Research in Hospitals: Diagnosis and Prognosis, Chicago, HRET, 1972, pp. 41-64.

SUBRAMANIAN, M., "Informatics to Improve Medical Care of a Nation," Methods of Information in Medicine, Vol. 21, 1982, pp. 109-113.

TAYLOR, W.J., "The Health Status Report: A Health Surveillance/Assurance Model for Industry," Medical Informatics, Vol. 7, (3), July-Sept. 1982.

THEOBOLD, R., "Cybernetics and Problems of Social Reorganization," in The Social Impact of Cybernetics, Ed. C.R. Dechert, Notre Dame, University of Notre Dame Press, 1966, pp. 36-69.

WHISLER, T. L., Information Technology and Organizational Change, Belmont, Wadsworth Publishing Company, 1970.

YASAKI, E.K., "AI Comes of Age," Datamation, Vol. 26, October 1980, pp. 48-54.

George Abonyi is Associate Professor at the Faculty of Administration in the University of Ottawa. His research is mainly concerned with strategic planning and assessment of development projects.

Fodil Adjaoud est professeur agrégé à la Faculté d'administration de l'Université d'Ottawa. Il se spécialise en stratégie financière et en politique de dividendes.

Sadrudin A. Ahmed is Professor at the Faculty of Administration in the University of Ottawa. His research is mainly concerned with social marketing.

Teresa Anderson is Assistant Professor at the Faculty of Administration in the University of Ottawa. Her research is mainly concerned with accounting and financial statement building.

Pedro Arroja is Assistant Professor at the Faculty of Administration in the University of Ottawa. His research is mainly concerned with economics and public management.

Benoît Bazoge est chargé de cours à la Faculté d'administration de l'Université d'Ottawa et poursuit ses études doctorales en stratégie à l'Université du Québec à Montréal.

Pierre Bergeron est professeur agrégé à la Faculté d'administration de l'Université d'Ottawa. Il se spécialise dans la gestion des PME et leur financement.

A. Louis Calvet is Associate Professor at the Faculty of Administration in the University of Ottawa. His research is mainly concerned with multinationals and foreign direct investment.

Denis H.J. Caro is Assistant Professor at the Faculty of Administration in the University of Ottawa. His research is mainly concerned with management information systems in health services.

André deCarufel is Associate Professor at the Faculty of Administration in the University of Ottawa. His research is mainly concerned with organizational behavior and decision-making psychology.

Alton W.J. Craig is Professor at the Faculty of Administration in the University of Ottawa. His research is mainly concerned with government policy and industrial relations.

Jean-Émile Denis est professeur titulaire à la Faculté d'administration de l'Université d'Ottawa. Il se spécialise dans la gestion internationale des PME.

Georges M. Hénault est professeur titulaire à la Faculté d'administration et directeur de l'Institut de développement international et de coopération à l'Université d'Ottawa. Il se spécialise dans le marketing des pays en voie de développement.

Ronald E. Hoyt is Associate Professor at the Faculty of Administration in the University of Ottawa. His research is mainly concerned with accounting from a philosophical perspective.

Jak Jabes is Associate Professor at the Faculty of Administration in the University of Ottawa. His research is mainly concerned with behavior differences in private and public organizations.

Jean Lamothe est consultant chez Safirmar Inc. à Montréal.

Wilbrod Leclerc is Associate Professor at the Faculty of Administration in the University of Ottawa. His research is mainly concerned with small business management and innovation centers.

Jean Lefoll est professeur agrégé à la Faculté d'administration de l'Université d'Ottawa. Il se spécialise en finance d'entreprise, en gestion de portefeuille et en économie de l'incertain.

Pranlal Manga is Research Professor at the Faculty of Administration in the University of Ottawa. His research is mainly concerned with health economics and biomedical ethics.

Christian Navarre est professeur invité à la Faculté d'administration de l'Université d'Ottawa. Il se spécialise en gestion de projet et en stratégie d'entreprise.

Gilles Paquet is Dean at the Faculty of Administration in the University of Ottawa. His research is mainly concerned with Canadian economic history and public management.

Stylianos Perrakis is Professor at the Faculty of Administration in the University of Ottawa. His research is mainly concerned with economics and finance.

Jean-Louis Schaan is Assistant Professor at the Faculty of Administration in the University of Ottawa. His research is mainly concerned with business policy and project management.

Aremanda Subbarao is Associate Professor at the Faculty of Administration in the University of Ottawa. His research is mainly concerned with human resource management and industrial relations.

John H. Taylor is Associate Professor at the Department of History in Carleton University. His research is mainly concerned with economics and public management.

Rick Van Loon is Professor at the Faculty of Administration in the University of Ottawa. His research is mainly concerned with public policy and public financial management.

David J. Wright is Associate Professor at the Faculty of Administration in the University of Ottawa. His research is mainly concerned with forecasting for decision support.

Daniel Zéghal est professeur agrégé à la Faculté d'administration de l'Université d'Ottawa. Il s'intéresse à tous les domaines de la comptabilité et de la gestion financière.

David Zussman is Associate Professor at the Faculty of Administration in the University of Ottawa. His research is mainly concerned with public opinion regarding management in the public sector.